NATIONALISM
AND THE
POLITICS OF CULTURE
IN QUEBEC

New Directions in Anthropological Writing
History, Poetics, Cultural Criticism

George E. Marcus, Rice University
James Clifford, University of California—Santa Cruz
Editors

Nationalism and the Politics of Culture in Quebec
Richard Handler

Belonging in America: Reading between the Lines
Constance Perin

NATIONALISM
AND THE
POLITICS OF
CULTURE
IN QUEBEC

RICHARD HANDLER

The University of Wisconsin Press

Published 1988

The University of Wisconsin Press
114 North Murray Street
Madison, Wisconsin 53715

The University of Wisconsin Press, Ltd.
1 Gower Street
London WC1E 6HA, England

First printing

Printed in the United States of America

For LC CIP information see the colophon

ISBN 0-299-11510-0 cloth; 0-299-11514-3 paper

For my father's sisters
Gertrude, Esther, Mary, and Talie

CONTENTS

ix   **ACKNOWLEDGMENTS**

CHAPTER ONE

3   **Meditations on *la fête* of November 15**

CHAPTER TWO

30   **Some Salient Features of Québécois Nationalist Ideology**
32   The Individual as a Member of the Nation
39   The Nation as a Collective Individual and a Collection of Individuals
47   The Negative Vision: Pollution and Death
50   Summary: Salient Presuppositions of Nationalist Ideology

CHAPTER THREE

52   **In Search of the Folk Society: Folk Life, Folklore Studies, and the Creation of Tradition**
57   Remembered Changes in Folk Dancing and Family Parties
63   Quebec as a Folk Society
67   In Search of the Folk Society

CHAPTER FOUR

81   **The Founding of the *Ministère des Affaires culturelles***
81   Quebec Cultural Politics before 1960
87   Three Philosophies of National Culture
102   The Founding of the *Ministère des Affaires culturelles*
107   One Culture, Many Contents

CHAPTER FIVE

109   **Holistic Culture, Bureaucratic Fragmentation**
110   Bureaucratic Fragmentation
118   Toward an Anthropological Conception of Québécois Culture

Contents

124   Mutually Exclusive Totalities

129   Can Empty Culture Be Filled?

CHAPTER SIX

140   **"Having a Culture": The Preservation of Quebec's *Patrimoine***

142   Cultural Property Legislation

144   Nationalism, Government Regulation, and the Creation of Cultural Property

152   On Having a Culture

CHAPTER SEVEN

159   **A Normal Society: Majority Language, Minority Cultures**

162   Linguistic Pollution

169   Nationalist Ideology and Language Legislation

175   On Having Minorities

CHAPTER EIGHT

183   **Meditations on Loose Ends: Lament and Dissent, Totality and Appropriation**

199   **REFERENCES**

215   **INDEX**

ACKNOWLEDGMENTS

The present book was written over a period of ten years, and during that time many people aided and encouraged me in ways too numerous and varied to mention. Among those for whose help I am particularly grateful are Samuel Bouchard, James Clifford, Bernard Cohn, Gary Downey, Franci Duitch, Michael Ebner, Denise Gaudreault, Amy Goffman, Earl and Phoebe Handler, Michael Herzfeld, Ira Jacknis, André Jean, Raymonde Jodoin, Michael Lambek, Carmella Lessard, Gordon Lester-Massman, George Marcus, Denis Perron, Dan Rose, Danielle Saint-Laurent, David Schneider, Anthony Scott, Daniel Segal, Michael Silverstein, R. T. Smith, George Stocking, and Bonnie Urciuoli.

Funding and institutional support for research and writing were obtained from a variety of sources. The Danforth Foundation funded much of my graduate work between 1973 and 1978, including my longest periods of field work. The Department of Anthropology at the University of Chicago made it possible for me to obtain a William Rainey Harper Fellowship, granted by the university, which enabled me, during 1978–79, to write my doctoral dissertation (parts of which, revised, are contained in the first three chapters of the present work). Dean Bailey Donnally of Lake Forest College provided funds for summer research in Quebec in 1980. During 1983–84 I was the Quebec Fellow at the University Consortium for Research on North America, a partnership of Brandeis, Harvard, and Tufts Universities, and the Fletcher School of Law and Diplomacy. Michèle de Guire, Helène Gagné, Claude Girard, and Polly Lyman of the Quebec Government Delegation in New England provided invaluable assistance to me during my year at the Consortium. I would particularly like to thank Seyom Brown and Elliot Feldman of the Consortium for their assistance and encouragement. They know the complexities of cultural politics, and the difficulties and rewards of studying it.

NATIONALISM
AND THE
POLITICS OF CULTURE
IN QUEBEC

CHAPTER ONE

Meditations on *la fête* of November 15

*"The simple truth is that we've lost control of
our own borders," Ronald Reagan said, "and no
nation can do that and survive."*
Newsweek, *1984*

Euphoria reigned in the *quartier latin.* The revelers began to arrive in
the middle of the evening as it became apparent that the *indépendantiste* Parti Québécois would win an election victory as stun-
ning as it had been unexpected. By midnight celebrants thronged the
streets, marching to and fro, waving banners, blowing whistles and
horns, singing, greeting friends and embracing strangers. In the bars
and cafés the festive, fraternal spirit was even more intense. In some I
found it impossible to advance from the door to a table, so tightly
packed was the human mass. Only the dancers succeeded in clearing
a bit of space in which to spin themselves round and round in rough
imitation of traditional dances. In others, less crowded, I watched
scenes of pandemonium, televised from Montreal, compared to
which the celebrations in Quebec City seemed calm. Montreal, historic seedbed of French-Canadian nationalist sentiment, exploded on
the evening of November 15, 1976—not only in the Paul Sauvé arena,
where Parti Québécois supporters had massed to await the returns,
but in the streets as well. A reporter for the Montreal newspaper, *Le
Devoir,* described enormous traffic jams which "undid themselves
joyfully without collisions and without the intervention of the police,
who themselves paraded inhabitual smiles." It was, he concluded, *la
fête* (Barbeau 1976:6).

Perhaps the revelry of that night resembled celebrations of past
Quebec elections, in which winners and losers demonstrated the
strength of partisan sentiments that French-Canadian nationalists

3

have never ceased to condemn as divisive for the nation. Yet the evening of November 15 was different. For one thing, many of these celebrants were not partisan supporters—some, in fact, were not old enough to vote. Furthermore, for them the victory of November 15 was not the simple replacement of one political party by another at the level of the provincial government. It was instead a national victory, a victory of the Québécois people in its ongoing struggle for independence and statehood. Their celebration expressed more than mere partisan joy—it marked their belief in the coming of age of a collectivity and their pride in belonging to that collectivity.

Indeed, the celebrations of November 15 could be fairly likened to those states of collective effervescence that Durkheim imagined as central to the social order. Certainly the electricity was there, an electricity that lifts the assembled masses "to an extraordinary degree of exaltation" (Durkheim 1912:247). And certainly for the leaders of the Parti Québécois the victory of November 15 represented a renewal and even a rebirth of the collectivity. "On n'est pas un petit peuple, on est peut-être quelque chose comme un grand peuple"— this was the passionate proclamation of René Lévesque to the cheering throngs in the Paul Sauvé arena.[1] Camille Laurin, soon to become an important minister in the Lévesque cabinet, told the same audience that "we are the government that Quebec has awaited for 250 years. We are going to dance in the streets of Montreal. We are going to dance all over Quebec. We are finally going to make of Quebec the country of which our ancestors dreamed" (Lachance 1976:A8). Following the interpretation of these leaders, then, it would seem that the euphoria of that night was an index of supreme social solidarity, a testimonial to the health of the nation. *La fête* of November 15 was one of those acts by which the collectivity is "periodically made and remade" (Durkheim 1912:470).

Or was it? Even during the weeks of feverish electoral activity that preceded November 15, an outside observer would not infallibly have remarked upon the existence of a political campaign. Had he ignored the mass media and avoided political rallies, he could have lived through those weeks with only the vaguest awareness of the unfolding political campaign, and with no sense at all of the discussion of national identity and destiny that accompanied it. Daily life continued as usual during those weeks and, as is typical of their neighbors the Americans, the Québécois seemed able to live their lives as if nothing out of the ordinary were occurring. Such an

---

1. As reported by Athot (1976:A9): "We are not a little people, we are perhaps something like a great people." To appreciate fully the metamorphosis implied in this assertion, one must remember that the expression *petit peuple* is a standard epithet used by nationalists, especially before the 1960s, to describe the French-Canadian nation (cf. Reid 1974).

observation does not immediately invalidate our evocation of Durkheim, for he himself taught that states of collective effervescence are of necessity transitory and infrequent, the bulk of social life being lived in the sphere of the profane (1912:245ff).

Other facts claim our attention, however. For example, the Parti Québécois received only a bit more than 40 percent of the votes cast among five parties. Of those francophones who did not vote for the Parti Québécois some claimed an allegiance to Canada equal to that which they felt for Quebec; others gave primary loyalty to Quebec but argued that the province ought to remain in the Canadian Confederation; and still others felt no attachment to Canada but nonetheless disagreed with the Parti Québécois vision for the future of Quebec. These Québécois did not participate in *la fête* of November 15, though they were well aware of those who did. Euphoric effervescence might have reigned, but unanimity did not.

Furthermore, it is to say the least ironic that during the campaign *péquiste* (from P. Q., for Parti Québécois) candidates often spoke as if the nation were in imminent danger of disintegration. For there is, in the ideology of the Parti Québécois, something that might be called a "negative vision." This negative vision is a reality not only for the ideologues of the Parti Québécois, but for all Québécois nationalists concerned with *la survivance*—the survival of the French-Canadian or Québécois people. The notion of survival implies struggle in a hostile environment, and, for a small group of French speakers who see themselves as surrounded by a sea of English-speaking North Americans, it is no wonder that Hamlet's question has come to have special relevance. "To be or not to be"—the leading nationalist historian Lionel Groulx asked this on behalf of his people time and time again in the first half of the the twentieth century, and still today this reference to Shakespeare is common in nationalist writing. After the Parti Québécois took power, it would attempt to provide the institutional bases to allow the Québécois nation to answer affirmatively, once and for all, the question of its survival. For example, Bill 101, the controversial language law to be enacted in 1977, would be designed to counter "the cultural and linguistic disintegration of French-speaking Quebeckers" (Quebec 1977:49). And a government paper on cultural development would propose remedies for "our state of advanced deculturalization" (Quebec 1978:155).

This negative vision of the struggle for survival presupposes the positive vision of collective unity and maturity—for how can an entity that does not in the first place exist run the risk of disintegration? The historian Groulx saw the birth as well as the golden age of the French-Canadian people in the past, in Catholic New France, while situating the beginning of its disintegration in his own time. Parti Québécois ideologues and other contemporary nationalists also look back to New France, as well as to the nineteenth century, to find the birth and slow development of the Québécois people. In their view, however, a perfected state of national being depends upon political independence, which leads them to place the golden age in the future. Meanwhile, as for Groulx, the present is marked with the threat of annihilation. In both cases a vision of the integrity of the collectivity coexists with a dark vision of national disintegration.

For the celebrants on the night of November 15, the vision of integrity prevailed. It seemed to them that the people, by electing a Parti Québécois government, had taken the first step towards assuming its destiny as an independent nation-state. The next step would be the referendum.

Nationalism is an ideology about individuated being. It is an ideology concerned with boundedness, continuity, and homogeneity encompassing diversity. It is an ideology in which social reality, conceived in terms of nationhood, is endowed with the reality of natural things.

In principle the individuated being of a nation—its life, its reality—is defined by boundedness, continuity, and homogeneity encompassing diversity. In principle a nation is bounded—that is, precisely delimited—in space and time: in space, by the inviolability of its borders and the exclusive allegiance of its members; in time, by its birth or beginning in history. In principle the national entity is continuous: in time, by virtue of the uninterruptedness of its history; in space, by the integrity of the national territory. In principle national being is defined by a homogeneity which encompasses diversity: however individual members of the nation may differ, they share essential attributes that constitute their national identity; sameness overrides difference.

In principle an individuated actor manifests his life through the exercise of choice, and through the consistent action that follows therefrom. Consistent action is both characteristic and rational: the nation acts in accord with its essence, and according to its needs.

In principle the life of an individuated actor is celebrated through creativity, which is the imposition of one's choices on the physical and social world, and in proprietorship, which is the establishment of permanent bonds between self and the products resulting from creative activity. Nationalism is an ideology of what C. B. Macpherson (1962) called possessive individualism.

It is customary in the literature on nations and ethnic nationalism to distinguish between "nation" and "state." A nation, it is said, is a human group that may or may not control its own state; while a state is a political organization that may or may not correspond to all of one, and only one, nation. It is customary to point out that there are many more nations or potential nations than states; that most nations aspire to statehood yet many have not and will not attain it; and that many states, federal or unitary, encompass more than one nation. It is only slightly less customary to point out that states have created nations perhaps more frequently that nations states; in the classic nation-states of Western Europe state-building bred national identity rather than simply following from it.

It is much less customary to observe that our notions of "nation" and "state" imply similar senses of boundedness, continuity, and homogeneity encompassing diversity. The state is viewed as a rational, instrumental, power-concentrating organization. The nation is imagined to represent less calculating, more sentimental aspects of collective reality. Yet both are, in principle, integrated: well-organized and precisely delimited social organisms. And, in principle, the two coincide.

The nationalist desire for an integrated nation-state can be compared to the overriding concern of social scientists to speak about and privilege integrated social units of whatever level of complexity. *Here I intentionally correlate actors' desires and observers' epistemology.* The presuppositions concerning boundedness that dominate nationalist discourse equally dominate our social-scientific discourse, which takes discrete social entities, such as "societies" and "cultures," as the normal units of analysis, and the "integration" of such units as the normal and healthy state of social life.

Of course, everyone knows that social life is not neatly integrated: the boundaries of nations, states, societies, and cultures are permeable and even vague. Yet to recognize (and then rationalize) "fuzzy boundaries" does not fundamentally question the epistemology of "entitivity" (Cohen 1978) upon which the notion of boundedness depends. In the study of nationalism and ethnicity the characteristic ploy used to get round the fuzzy-boundaries problem is to posit a distinction between objective and subjective groups. A human group, it is argued, can be bounded by attributes or characteristics that each of its members "possesses." This is objective boundedness, though what is objectively shared may be subjective states of mind of the group members—characteristic modes of thought and affect that lead to characteristic actions and social organizations. Objective boundedness means that the group actually exists as a group, and can be shown to exist by an external observer. Subjective boundedness is the sense that group members themselves have of forming a group; that is, national or ethnic self-consciousness. It is customary to point out that an objectively existent group may not be subjectively self-conscious, and that nations and nationalisms become possible only after the emergence of group self-consciousness. It is only slightly less customary to point out that the actors' sense of group integration may be grounded in an illusion and that their perception of sameness may obscure important objective differences among group members. In the face of the continued emergence of evidence of such differences—and of mal- or dis-integration, permeableness, and vagueness of boundaries—many scholars of nationalism and ethnicity have de-emphasized the objective reality of groups and insisted instead on subjective boundedness as the sine qua non of collective existence. Proponents of this position argue that whatever the degree of objective boundedness, it is only the subjective perception (or delusion) of identity that launches a group on its career of collective action. The perception of group identity may even be sufficient to overcome large objective differences and bring a national entity into historical existence.

This appeal to the subjective basis of group unity respects the entitivity assumptions—boundedness, continuity, homogeneity—that both nationalists and social scientists presuppose in their discussions of the reality of nations. The reality that may be denied by a lack of shared objective traits is reestablished by the subjective sharing of a sense of identity, and the nation or ethnic group can again be proclaimed to exist. Once again we find a close congruence between actors' ideologies and observers' theories: the "common will to live together" that nationalists see as the necessary capstone to the list of objective traits which form a national entity becomes "group identity" in the jargon of social scientists.

This book is about the metaphors of boundedness, continuity, and homogeneity that both nationalist ideology and social-scientific discourse presuppose in their understanding of nations as entities. It is an attempt to disentangle social-scientific analysis from what I will call the interpenetration of nationalist and social-scientific discourse.

The persistent refusal to treat seriously the substantive overlap between nationalist ideology and social science theory constitutes one of the greatest obstacles to our understanding of nationalism. It is well known that nationalist ideologies and social-scientific inquiry developed in the same historical context—that of the post-Renaissance European world—and that the two have reacted upon one another from their beginnings; Van Gennep, for example, pointed this out over sixty years ago (1922; cf. Hobsbawm 1983:268–69). The sociological and historical interpenetration of the two is also shown by the many cases in which social scientists, historians, and other intellectuals have played leading roles in nationalist movements. Yet the equally obvious substantive links between nationalist ideology and social-scientific theory have been largely ignored. My response to this situation is to draw out the implications of the following contentions: Most scholarly writing on nationalism is to some extent a rationalization of "native" ideology, while nationalists in turn borrow from these scientistic elaborations of their own more commonsensical notions. It is misleading to present the work of social scientists who study nationalism as the result of neutral observations performed on a discrete body of "actors" or "natives." Our discourse is shaped by theirs as theirs is by ours. This book is an ethnography of two discourses that feed off of each other.

René Lévesque founded the *Mouvement souveraineté-association* in 1967. A year later his party merged with other small *indépendantiste* groups to become the Parti Québécois. The goal of the Parti Québécois was to lead Quebec out of the Canadian Confederation and to establish it as an independent nation. In the provincial elections of 1970 the newly established party won 23% of the vote and seven seats in the Quebec legislature. These elections came during the infamous October Crisis, in which the *Front de libération du Québec* (FLQ) kidnapped two government officials and killed one of them, provoking retaliation from the federal government in the form of martial law. During the elections the federal and provincial Liberals tried to associate the Parti Québécois with the October "terrorists." Under such circumstances *péquistes* saw the results of their first electoral efforts in a positive light. Moreover, they ultimately profited from the FLQ frenzy, for the October Crisis tended to discredit radical and violent solutions to the national question. *Indépendantisme* had become an imaginable option in the 1960s, and many of those who discussed it did so in terms of imperialism, colonialism, and the necessity for a socialist revolution. In the relative calm of the early 1970s the Parti Québécois emerged as the sole viable nationalist alternative, respectably social-democratic and committed to change within the system (Basham 1978:197).

The next chance for the Parti Québécois came in the provincial elections of 1973, in which it won 30 percent of the popular vote, yet captured only 6 of 110 ridings. Despite the fact that almost one-third of the electorate had supported a party whose *raison d'être* was the independence of Quebec, the parliamentary defeat proved particularly difficult for *péquistes* to swallow. They felt that a new strategy was in order, and eventually the party leaders settled on *étapisme* (from *étape*, stage, step) or gradualism, a strategy to lead Quebec to independence one step at a time. The idea that the election of a Parti Québécois government would mean an immediate declaration of independence gave way to the proposition that the accession to power could be followed by a referendum on independence. Thus in the 1976 campaign the Parti Québécois sought to underplay its *indépendantisme* by asking the people simply to vote for a better government than the Liberals could provide. At the same time the party solemnly promised that nothing would be done about independence without prior consultation of the electorate by referendum. Nonetheless, the national question dominated the campaign. The Liberals campaigned under the slogan *"non aux séparatistes."* The *péquistes* spoke indirectly of independence, but tried to present themselves as

9

Meditations on *la fête* of November 15

"the party of the Québécois," the only party that was authentically Québécois and sincerely committed to the best interests of the nation. With the aid of an improbable concatenation of circumstances—an air traffic controllers strike, which piqued Québécois nationalist sentiment, and increasingly obvious mismanagement, even corruption, on the part of the Liberal government—their strategy worked. The Liberals retained only 27 of their 102 seats while the Parti Québécois total rose to 70, touching off the celebrations of November 15 and giving the victors the right to form the next government.

Discussion of the 1976 election did not vanish from the public stage as quickly as post-election news is wont to do. The victory of a secessionist party in a provincial election triggered shock waves throughout Canada, and ripples expanded outward to the United States, Europe, and beyond. Pledged to honesty, reform, and, ultimately, independence, the Parti Québécois government seemed more vocal, visible, and newsworthy than most provincial governments. Nonetheless, the intense discussions that had marked the campaign diminished, though the government's promise to hold a referendum on secession continued to focus the attention of editorialists and experts. But the fever had disappeared from the air, the general excitement of election time had abated and, despite the portentious question that now loomed on the horizon for Quebec, public life settled back into profane routine.

Having made a preliminary fieldtrip to Quebec during the elections, I returned in mid-1977 for eleven months of research. My initial project, which suggested itself to me during the November events, was to construct a cultural account (Schneider 1968) of national identity. Since the public forum established for the elections was now dismantled, I had to search in more deliberate fashion to learn something of the substance and relevance of nationalist ideology. As political events receded into the background I began to look for other contexts in which Québécois expressed their ideas about national identity and culture. Several aspects of Québécois life that seemed relevant turned out to be insignificant with respect to nationalist discussion. The victory of *Les Canadiens* in the 1978 Stanley Cup competition triggered a celebration that outshined even that of November 15. But the alignment of ethnic and partisan elements was different, for French- and English-speaking citizens shared the same joy. True, some Québécois told me that French Canadians suffer discrimination in the National Hockey League, but others pointed out that international hockey tournaments are among the only events that generate displays of pan-Canadian unity. Moreover, North American professional hockey is perhaps the single area in which the integration of Quebec entities into a Canadian and American system is rarely questioned. In the late seventies, local sports fans seemed more concerned with forcing the National Hockey League to admit the Quebec City Nordiques than with attempting to withdraw their province from Confederation. One Quebec City resident told the Task Force on Canadian Unity (Pepin-Robarts Commission) that the federal government could promote national unity by forcing Radio Canada (the French-language branch of the Canadian Broadcasting Corporation) to broadcast games of the local team.

A second area that I explored for nationalist activity was local politics as manifested in the activities of citizens groups. Such groups limit their activites to organizing local residents and pressuring governments with respect to issues directly affecting their neighborhoods. The group I knew best concerned itself with industrial pollution, cooperative housing, and day care in a working class section (Limoilou) of Quebec City. Pragmatic in its use of political contacts, the group played off one level of government against another, using the media to create leverage. The citizens seemed to distrust all levels of government equally, though they suspended judgment with regard to the newly-elected provincial government and were duly impressed when the local Parti Québécois deputy accepted their invitation to attend a group meeting. The deputy presented the group with the national (or provincial, depending on one's point of view) flag, which was displayed thereafter. But members never discussed the national question during meetings, confining their attention to local concerns. I rarely heard even informal talk about nationalist issues, though I found during private interviews that some members strongly favored the independence of Quebec.

Perhaps I was naive to expect political discussion in a nonpolitical context such as hockey, or national debate in the arena of local politics. I gradually learned that direct reference to the national question, continual during an election, could at other times be found only in particular contexts—for example, during parliamentary debates or meetings of patriotic organizations. At the same time I began to realize that the issue of national identity was being played out all around me through the continual "objectification" of what is imagined to be Québécois culture. This first became evident to me at Christmas, when I visited the crafts fairs of Montreal and Quebec City. As marketplaces for handmade, traditional wares, such fairs were similar to those that had once again become popular throughout North America in the 1970s. Yet, as is often the case in Quebec, one found a nationalist variation on a North-American theme: Québécois handicrafts represented a rejection of mass production and the consumer society while at the same time expressing a new infatuation with national culture and identity. They offered what was perceived as a uniquely Québécois alternative to the standardized consumer goods of industrial society. This alternative had become available throughout the year, in the crafts *ateliers* and gift shops of shopping centers and main streets. Nor was this the only manifestation of

11

renewed interest in indigenous traditions. Craft bazaars invariably accompanied the dozens of annual village festivals and carnivals that became so popular during the late 1970s. A bread or shrimp festival, a blueberry or strawberry celebration, a winter carnival or summer fair—each showcased a local product or particularity and, at the same time, aimed to rekindle the warmth of traditional social ties. Parish dances and communal meals were scheduled during festival time, and dances and foods unique to a village or area were chosen to symbolize local, regional—and, through these, national—identity. On all such occasions—at fairs, festivals, feasts, and dances—culture and tradition became objects to be scrutinized, identified, revitalized, and consumed.

Thus in my exploration of nationalist discourse I began to frequent fairs, festivals, and folklore exhibits, observing the reactions of the crowds and asking questions whenever I could. During the 1978 Winter Carnival in Quebec City I witnessed for the first time a staged exhibition of folk dancing. This took place in the Coliseum, home of the Quebec Nordiques hockey club. Several hundred people had come for what had been announced as an old-fashioned square dance, but, as an unexpected preliminary treat, they were to see a folklore *spectacle*. The Coliseum was iceless, its massive scoring cube floating unlit and unattended beneath the rafters, from which a championship pennant hung, equally unnoticed. What commanded the crowd's attention was a canvas backdrop perhaps forty feet square stretched from the rafters to the floor at one end of the rink where a broad stage had been set up.

The stage and its backdrop represented a traditional, if larger than life, farmhouse interior. Plank walls, a grandfather clock, and a stone hearth and chimney had been painted onto the canvas. Several musicians and dancers milled about the base of the fireplace, their heads barely reaching the bottommost blazing log; benches and rocking chairs scattered about the stage were similarly dwarfed by the set. An oval braided rug, large enough to match the painted chimney and clock, covered most of the stage. Perhaps because it was an actual rather than a painted rug it did not seem out of scale with the performers, successfully mediating between set and reality. The audience, willingly suspending disbelief, could imagine itself to be looking into an old-fashioned farmhouse parlor.

Suddenly at the opposite end of the arena a horse-drawn sleigh emerged. A pair of massive farm horses dragged the sleigh and its two fur-bundled passengers across the iceless wooden rink to the stage, where one passenger disembarked, unwrapped his fur coat and joined the family onstage. Then, to the immense delight of the audience, the driver took the sleigh for a couple of gratuitous turns around the arena and exited where he had entered.

That clever touch almost succeeded. The audience had been

transported within the family circle, and we could imagine ourselves there as the dance began. A stocky, gray-bearded fellow took possession of the microphone at center stage, establishing himself as father to the family onstage and as master of ceremonies to the audience. He told tales in quaint accents, sang an ancient folk song unaccompanied, then presented eight young people who took their places for a *danse carrée*. A group of musicians by the clock struck up a lively reel with accordian, guitar, and fiddle, and the four couples bounced and twirled their way through the square dance. Other revelers gathered round to clap an accompaniment, while the audience marveled at the precision with which these youngsters danced "the old dances." As the music ended the circling square collapsed to the middle in a collective embrace, and finally disbanded. The jovial patriarch materialized at the microphone to direct some family banter and introduce the next performer to the audience, who craned their necks and tried vainly to catch each joke.

As the lively, professional *spectacle* progressed, I sensed some bewilderment in the reaction of the crowd. Though the chimney, clock, and rug were large enough for the arena, the performers were difficult to see, and despite the impressive stacks of loudspeakers that flanked either side of the stage, it was not always possible to overhear the remarks of the family revelers. Some spectators whispered to see if their neighbors had caught jokes they themselves had missed. Others began to fidget, unable any longer to suspend disbelief. A glance at the thousands of empty seats, untouched by the familial intimacy of the set, was enough to shatter illusions. When intermission came the audience seemed almost relieved: though people had enjoyed the show, no one knew quite what to make of it.

A folk dance performance may seem a comparatively insignificant event to place at the center of an examination of a "world-historical" force such as nationalism. Indeed, both Québécois nationalists and anthropological colleagues have expressed occasional surprise, if not dismay, at my decision to ground this study of nationalism in an analysis of such phenomena as folklore revivals and, more generally, the politics of culture. Yet my concern here is not merely nationalism, but the relationship between nationalist ideology and social-scientific discourse. With this focus the folkdance *spectacle* becomes a crucial example, for it is a piece of "native" nationalist anthropology, a self-conscious representation or objectification of authentic national culture. James Boon (1982:6) has suggested that "counterparts of anthropologists" who "displace the immediacy of their audience's social lives" exist everywhere (that is, in all "cultures"). It is most certainly the case that anthropologists themselves (and historians, sociologists, demographers, linguists, folklorists, archeologists) play central roles in nationalist politics. The Winter Carnival

folklore performance, as well as an array of cultural events, programs, policies, and regulations to be examined here, are as much
social-scientific as nationalistic, for they are researched—and often
organized and legitimated—by professional social scientists or by
amateur scholars who take the work of the professionals as their
model. And politicians and governments intent on "nation building"
routinely draw on scientific, objectifying analyses of national
culture, either because they believe in them or because they understand the legitimating value of "an appeal to social scientific expertise" (Sullivan 1983:299).

The staged folk dance celebration is an example of what I will
call cultural objectification. I initially took the idea from Bernard
Cohn, who has written of Western-educated intellectuals in India
who "have made [their culture] into a 'thing'" and "can stand back
and look at themselves, their ideas, their symbols and culture and see
it as an entity" (n.d.:5). In my appropriation of a term with a long
pedigree I begin with Cohn because the fundamental notion that I
wish to convey is that of seeing culture as a thing: a natural object or
entity made up of objects and entities ("traits"). As I have argued
elsewhere (1984), according to Western common sense a thing is
taken to be bounded and continuous in space and time, and truly
characterizable in terms of the properties it "bears" (cf. Heidegger
1967:35–54). Westerners believe that a thing, objectively existent in
the real or natural world, presents itself unambiguously to human
subjects who can (at least in the best case, which is, moreover,
routinely attainable) apprehend the thing as it truly is. We believe
that we can know where and when things begin and end, and what
"belongs" to them as part or property—that is, that we can know the
objective facts that distinguish things one from another.

The objectifying vision that dominates modern Western
thought has been a major theme in Marxian sociology, beginning
with Marx's understanding of the roots of alienation in the "fetishism
of commodities": "with commodities [i.e., in a society dominated by
commodity exchange] . . . a definite social relation between men . . .
assumes, in their eyes, the fantastic form of a relation between
things" (1867:83). Lukács (1922) has explicated Marx's vision in mas-
terful fashion, showing how the atomization and rationalization of
capitalist production corresponds to the fragmentation of all social
life and consciousness, including scholarship and science. Weberian
sociology, with its emphasis on the technical efficiency of bureaucracy and the progressive rationalization of the world, approaches the
same aspects of modern society from an only partially different
perspective. In general the "great transformation" from medieval
holism to modern individualism has been a—perhaps *the*—central
concern of Western social theory since at least the time of Burke
(Bellah 1983:377).

Within anthropology, discussion of objectification has recently occurred in the context of the larger epistemological question of how anthropology constitutes its object, a concern not unrelated to the issue of the subjective versus objective boundedness of ethnic groups. Students of ethnicity have had to confront the problems not only of vague or shifting boundaries and of multiple and manipulated collective identities, but of the creation of tradition in the service of ethnic mobilization (Hobsbawm and Ranger 1983; Handler and Linnekin 1984) and the associated issues of genuine and spurious culture (MacCannell 1976). Anthropologists studying ethnic leaders who attempt to recover or maintain an "authentic" culture (routinely drawing on social-science theory to do so) come up against epistemological problems similar to those confronting students of the history of anthropology, particularly the anthropological reduction or "invention" of colonized, non-Western groups as bounded "cultures" (Wagner 1975). Geertz's well known dictum (1973b) that anthropologists "inscribe" their interpretations of their subjects' interpretations of the world denies that anthropological accounts are mere descriptions of fact, and calls attention to the social scientist's role in constructing visions of cultures. Clifford (1983), Marcus and Cushman (1982), and others have begun to explore the rhetorical techniques whereby anthropological writers create the impression that cultures exist as bounded units. These recent developments are not without precedents, which I find in the work of Boasian anthropologists. Sapir's largely misunderstood critique (1917, 1932, 1934, 1939) of social-scientific reification raised issues of central concern today, and Whorf's analysis (1941, 1942) of the grammatical underpinnings of objectification in "Standard Average European" languages remains seminal for the study of Western cultural logic.

These writers and others will contribute to the arguments that follow, but for now I want only to point out that cultural objectification is one contribution of social science to the modern Western world view. Mimicking natural science, social scientists attempt to suspend their subjectivity and occupy a neutral and removed position from which to analyze the social world—which must, then, be understood atomistically, in terms of its bounded elements or parts and the causal interconnections among them. "Nation," "state," "society," "group," "family," and so on—ongoing social relationships which, as Whorf once remarked (1940:215), might in some languages be represented by verbs rather than nouns—are understood in terms of the same presuppositions that underpin our commonsense notion of what a thing is. Like a thing, the nation or ethnic group is taken to be bounded, continuous, and precisely distinguishable from other analogous entities. Moreover, from this perspective, what distinguishes each nation or ethnic group is its culture, which provides the "content" of group identity and individuality. And if culture is pressed into service to distinguish one bounded collectivity from another, it too must be bounded: that is, culture must be analyzable and identifiable, such and such a "trait" belonging to this nation or originating in that region. Dancing folk, for example, can be "recorded," that is, abstracted from an ongoing social milieu; their activity can be redefined as a thing (a dance) which is part of the cultural content unique to a bounded social entity; then, as in the Winter Carnival, the thing (and the people) can be re-presented, in the frame of a theatrical stage, as authentic pieces of national culture. This is cultural objectification as I will use and explicate the concept.

Folkdance exhibitions were not the only occasions for bringing the past to life in Quebec. On the morning of 3 July 1978 the *Compagnie Franche de la Marine,* a relic of the days of New France, marched up a hill in the *quartier latin* and took possession of the statue of Champlain that stands beneath the Château Frontenac overlooking the Saint Lawrence River. A host of dignitaries came out to meet them, among whom were Prime Minister Lévesque, the mayor of Quebec City, the governor of Vermont, and the Minister of Culture and Communications of France. Perhaps a thousand onlookers had gathered to watch the two groups perform. Each of the dignitaries made a brief speech, then laid a wreath at the feet of Champlain. The soldiers marched, maneuvred, and played military music. All the while, scurrying busily among the two groups, photographers went about their business of documenting the occasion. (One would have thought them endowed with the science-fictional power of simultaneous existence in different dimensions, for their presence did not seem to impinge upon the spectators' ability to appreciate the historical recreation.)

This ceremony was only one moment in a great round of patriotic holidays that had been arranged that year. St-Jean-Baptiste day, a traditional religious and patriotic holiday of French Canada, falls on June 24. In 1978 the government passed a law consecrating it as the *fête nationale* of Quebec. The eve of *la Saint-Jean,* as some Québécois call it, also marked the beginning of *la semaine de la patrimoine,* a week-long celebration of Quebec's heritage created by the government in 1976. In 1978 it was to be followed by festivities marking the 370th anniversary of the founding of Quebec City by Samuel de Champlain. These were held on July second and third, after a diplomatic pause for the Canadian national holiday, which falls on the first. Furthermore, the government had invited Americans of French-Canadian descent to return to their roots during the holiday period, and various associations of Franco-Americans had accepted. Among the crowd who watched the soldiers and dignitaries, I met Americans from Louisiana, Massachusetts, and Texas. Some proudly spoke to me and to one another in French, while others sheepishly admitted their inability to do so. For the benefit of these visitors and the general population, the government maintained a genealogical service throughout the holiday period. As a press release explained, "any person who can claim the honor of an ancestor born in Quebec will be able, through this service, to have his direct ascendants traced."

The celebrations of 1978 show that some Québécois take seriously their provincial motto: "Je me souviens"—I remember. Occasionally a disgruntled pessimist will ask just what it is that is to be remembered, but any school child knows that it is history that must be learned and cherished. The historian Groulx described history as spiritual blood—an "incessant transfusion from the soul of the forefathers to the soul of the sons, which maintains a race unchanging in its core" (1924:289). Groulx saw in the era of New France a golden age, a standard of heroism and piety compared to which the world of his contemporaries was sadly deficient. For him the future held promise only as a return to the past. More recent versions of nationalist ideology have assimilated the modern ideal of progress. In this perspective the national society is a perpetually unfinished project to be realized, though its perfection must be based upon the historically conditioned character of the nation. Though the past no longer is imagined as a golden age beyond criticism, it nonetheless is accepted as formative. Present generations have no choice but to build upon a determinative past as they strive to create the future. When, in another outdoor ceremony, the Parti Québécois government resurrected a statue of Maurice Duplessis, the dictatorial prime minister whose death in 1959 had been followed by an attempt to forget him, René Lévesque declared that it was bad business for a society to pretend to erase pieces of its history. With respect to Duplessis, he argued, Québécois must know how to separate the chaff from the grain (*Le Devoir* 1977:1).

History, then, is the lifeblood, conscience, and foundation of the nation, and it is celebrated accordingly. But history serves more pragmatic ends as well. People readily admit that the material legacy of history, adequately conserved and marketed, attracts tourists. They know also that history can be pressed into political service. Thus editorialists criticized the Parti Québécois government for its manipulation of the holidays of 1978. One journalist calmly explained that the 370th anniversary of Quebec City "helped [the government] to compete with the organizers of the Canadian holidays, and thus to have the last word. It was also a question of supporting a public relations campaign by Quebec in the United States; and also, of course, exploiting the nationalist side of this event in the current political context" (Descoteaux 1978:1). Other critics, in the press and in private conversations, were less gentle in their appraisal. They thought that a 370th anniversary was a "ridiculous" pretext for a holiday, one created, as the referendum loomed, for blatantly political ends.

Had I begun this interpretation of Québécois nationalism with an account of its history—or of the history of the nation itself—I would find myself practicing a form of discourse that I intend rather to analyze. Thus I shall question from the outset what almost everyone else who writes on the subject affirms: that "a" nation, grounded in history, exists "in" Quebec. Without yet turning to the vision of Québécois nationalists, let me offer as examples of this affirmation the introductory remarks from sympathetic English-language accounts:

> The people of Quebec . . . have . . . succeeded in retaining, almost unchanged, their language, their religion, their legal and educational systems, and even many of their customs. As a consequence, they constitute a small, homogeneous ethnic group, with a culture, way of life, and set of values quite different in most respects from those prevailing throughout the rest of the continent. (Quinn 1979:xi)

> By North American standards, the most striking feature of French-Canadian society in Quebec is its continuity, its endurance over the centuries in an alien, sometimes hostile, environment. . . . The arguments as to why French Canada survived continue, but there is no denying the fact of survival itself. (McRoberts and Postgate 1980:23)

Much of my concern in what follows will be to explore the naturalistic and objectifying presuppositions that sustain the undeniable existence of a Québécois nation. For example, metaphors of environment and survival liken the French-Canadian nation to a living creature, and national history to a creature's life, as does the following self-consciously feminist analogy that an historian has recently used to convey the consequences of the British Conquest of New France: "Conquest is like rape. The major blow takes only a few minutes, the results . . . can be . . . devastating" (Trofimenkoff 1982:20). For a Québécois reviewer the analogy was decisive; it rescued an even-handed assessment of the Conquest from banality: "A single word and we understand all" (Latouche 1983:25).

My aim here is to call into question such naturalistic—and decisive—images of society and nation. To do this I must question as well the rhetorical ploy of the historical beginning. Though most historians admit the provisionality of all historical tales, the rhetoric of historical narration inevitably objectifies its actors, and the principal actor of a national history is a nation. National historiography

18

thus endows the nation with a reality that it is difficult for readers to question. As de Certeau has put it,

> every story that relates what is happening or what has happened constitutes something real to the extent that it pretends to be the representation of a past reality. It takes on authority by passing itself off as the witness of what is or of what has been. . . . Historiography acquires this power insofar as it presents and interprets the "facts." How can readers resist discourse that tells them what is or what has been? (1983:129–30)

Social-scientific writing often doubly presupposes this authoritative constitution of reality by taking historical scholarship for granted as background, to be used as a prelude to some variety of synchronic sociological analysis. This strategy obliterates any sense of history as story or construct. Relegated to the background, history can be presented in matter-of-fact fashion as what is already known or what needs to be known to understand the present-day problems that one wishes to examine. This procedure is standard for social-scientific and nationalistic accounts of Quebec, especially those focused on the total society (rather than isolated aspects of it) and those addressed to outsiders presumed unacquainted with Quebec (the typical situation for anthropological monographs in which Quebec figures as the exotic other). In sum, to understand the nation's situation one must know "its" story, and Western conventions of storytelling inevitably constitute protagonists as bounded, individuated actors.

Thus to introduce this analysis by presenting a neutral, or even admittedly partisan, historical summary would simply be to call upon "solid facts" to establish the reality of the kind of social entity (in this case, "the" Québécois nation) that conventionally justifies the telling of an anthropological tale. However, to refuse this expected gambit is to risk violating readers' expectations about how they should be situated with respect to an anthropological analysis. Most people want their anthropology (if they want it at all) located in space, in time, and with respect to ethnic or socioeconomic groups. Refusing this, I promise only a coherent narrative, with enough signposts to enable readers to find their way. For those who want more conventional guidance, I suggest putting aside this book and finding Fenwick's (1981) brief summary of Quebec national history. That will fortify them with enough facts and bibliography to situate my unorthodoxies.

Yet what, after all, are we to make of an anthropologist's account, which most natives who think about the same matters would claim to be mistaken? To deny that "a" nation exists "in" Quebec is heretical. Lord Durham, who wrote in 1839 that French Canadians were "a people with no history, and no literature" (Lucas 1912: 2:294–95), is recognized as both the "villain and catalyst" who stimulated the beginnings of French-Canadian historical and literary self-consciousness (Trofimenkoff 1982:81–83). Herzfeld describes a similar episode, at exactly the same time, in the history of Greek nationalism; the German scholar J. P. Fallmerayer's denial of the Greek claim "to descent from the ancient Hellenes" stimulated half-a-century's folklore scholarship in Greece (1982:75–80). Such denials, then, are apparently interpreted as challenges, yet I would judge my work a failure if it did nothing more than stimulate the genre of discourse that it analyzes. My goal is rather to disentangle nationalist discourse and social-scientific theory. In this project the Quebec material serves as my primary example, but more fundamentally as the means to an analysis of the presuppositions of my own scientific world view. Though any number of examples of nationalism and cultural politics could have served in place of the Quebec example, my critique is ultimately directed at a discourse that I share with people in Quebec and throughout the nationalized modern world. To respect the conventions of nationalist and social-scientific historiography would have been to continue an implicit reliance on those presuppositions that most need to be explicitly scrutinized.

Rue Saint-Jean rises from the lower part of the *quartier latin,* passes under the massive walls that enclose the older section of Quebec City, and continues its ascent through the *quartier Saint-Jean-Baptiste.* The street is too narrow for the auto and pedestrian traffic it must bear. Some residents complain that one hears more English than French on "Saint John Street," but francophone Québécois, from the city itself and from elsewhere, make up the majority of visitors who flock there on pleasant evenings. Its shops are intended for tourists rather than residents. There are souvenir shops, expensive jewelry and clothing stores, and arts and crafts boutiques, but only an occasional grocery store.

Some of the crafts boutiques call themselves cooperatives. This collectivist orientation, along with wood-and-brick interiors, hanging plants, and merchandise that is handmade—*fait à la main au Québec,* as the labels proclaim—suggest what was once called the counter-culture. The pottery and jewelry seem no different from that which one can find in most North American cities. The woodworking is more distinctive, though the carven figures have become mundane and predictable in response to touristic demand. But what may strike the outsider as uniquely Québécois is the weaving—the thick, knotted ponchos and gay "catalogne" placemats and rugs. Yet even in this case a stroll along *rue Saint-Jean,* past shop after shop, raises doubts,

for everywhere the ponchos and placemats are similar—mass produced *à la main?*

During the 1980 referendary campaign one of these cooperative
boutiques in the middle of *Saint-Jean-Baptiste* made use of its display
windows to advertise the options of some of its members. A large
Québécois flag served as a backdrop to the sandals, rings and wooden
toys on display. Among the shoes a sign proclaimed that Michel
Gagnon, leatherworker, had decided in favor of the *Oui.* A second
sign, leaning against a wooden rocking horse, announced an identical
decision on the part of the resident carpenter, but whoever had made
the jewelry remained discreet—perhaps one of the "undecideds" who
plagued pollsters throughout the campaign. No other merchant in the
neighborhood had thought it wise to announce his political option.
On the other hand, posters for the *Oui* and *Non* abounded, and if
telephone poles served equally in the cause of both, apartment windows in bohemian *Saint-Jean-Baptiste* heavily favored the *Oui.*

One read frequently of poster skirmishes during the campaign.
Workers from one camp would tear down the posters of the other
side, or cover them with their own. Propagandists fought larger
battles with statistics and public opinion polls, or through the recruit-
ment of public figures to their cause. The *Oui* forces bettered their
adversaries in the use of the latter tactic. Many of the great stars of the
entertainment business declared themselves publicly in favor of the
Oui, as did large numbers of writers, artists and intellectuals. The
media reported all this in great detail and in addition made available
large chunks of space and time for the analyses of experts and the
opinions of the citizenry. As in 1976 Quebec's public forums were
dominated by discussion of the national question. Furthermore, the
general public took part in the debate. A cliché of the referendary
period had it that families were bitterly divided over the question.
"It's unbelievable," a friend told me, "how much people are talking
about this." She added that she was quite sick of the whole business,
and wanted only to vote and be done with it.

Both sides depended on door-to-door canvassing or small neighborhood meetings to get across their point of view. But neither could
dispense entirely with mass rallies, gathering together thousands of
people and reaching an even wider audience through the media. For
the *Non* forces the three rallies that featured Pierre Trudeau drew the
largest crowds and generated the most spirited response. The *Oui*
camp did not resort to large rallies until the end of the campaign, in an
effort to stave off an increasingly likely defeat. These mass gatherings, led by René Lévesque, brought together people dedicated to a
cause. It seemed that for them, the act of gathering together was
enough to generate the kind of euphoric solidarity that marked the
victory celebrations of November 15. That these rallies were, how-

ever, subtly orchestrated, is suggested by the fact that the seemingly spontaneous outbursts of song, applause, and general delirium followed the same pattern in most of the great *Oui* rallies.

One such rally, nine days before the referendum, provided the destination for a motorcade of celebrities who came up to Quebec City from Montreal along the north shore of the Saint Lawrence. This was perhaps the high point of the campaign in Quebec City, with hundreds of people, including myself and friends, being turned away at the doors of the convention hall where René Lévesque, balladeer Gilles Vigneault, and others held forth. I took care to arrive earlier at another rally, held four days later at the Quebec Coliseum. Not wishing to disappoint people a second time, the organizers had arranged an auxilliary hall with closed-circuit television and folding chairs, but their precautions proved unnecessary. Only a few people gathered there, to escape the smoke and heat of the crowd or to see the faces of the orators on the panel of video screens. Inside, in the main hall, six or seven thousand people massed, awaiting René Lévesque and his associates for the *Oui*. Some marched up and down the aisles waving the provincial flag and that of the Patriots of 1837. More Quebec flags hung from the rafters, side-by-side with homemade banners that announced the allegiance of their creators:

**Les employés
Generale electrique
Vanier OUI**

**Contrôleurs
Aériens
Québec
OUI**

**Les OUI
de la rue
Aiguebelle
Vanier OUI**

**Regroupement
des 15–17 ans pour
le OUI**

A young man and woman, standing at either side of the stage, chaired the rally. They began by reciting the prose-poem written by renowned balladeer Félix Leclerc as the inaugural message of the *Oui* campaign. They read it solemnly, as if it were a prayer: "On referendum day, no Liberals, no Unionists, no federalists, no *péquistes,* but six million Québécois, unified like a wall . . . will decide to give themselves Quebec as their country, there to be masters in their own house." After this formal opening, they introduced a succession of speakers, each chosen as representative of a particular constituency. One orator developed an elaborate metaphor in which Quebec and Canada figured as neighboring farmers whose reciprocal goodwill depended on the soundness of the fences that separated them. Another argued that the solidarity of Quebec's anglophone community—nearly unanimous in support of the *Non*—must be matched by a massive *Oui* on the part of francophones. A third spoke of the insults that Ottawa had heaped on Quebec during the campaign. Finally, after the twelfth speaker, René Lévesque came to the podium, to be greeted by seven minutes of delirious applause. When finally able to make himself heard, he launched into a long and fervent rebuttal of the latest pronouncements of Pierre Trudeau.

I saw this scene repeated after the vote, when Lévesque conceded defeat. Many in the audience cried, and there were tears in the eyes of one of my companions as we watched the proceedings on television. Outside, in the streets of *Saint-Jean-Baptiste* and the *quartier latin*, little happened. The television crews stationed there to capture the celebrations they had missed on November 15 could show us nothing but quiet streets. In the studios panels of experts and public figures commented upon the results, some with satisfaction, some with dismay. A representative of the Quebec intellectual community admitted that they had been arrogantly out of touch with the popular mind. Public figures from English Canada spoke of the difficult process of constitutional revision that now lay ahead. Late in the evening Prime Minister Trudeau read a message of reconciliation, first in French, then in English.

For days after the referendum people remarked that the chief of the *Oui* forces had been particularly noble in defeat. This reaction typified the post-referendary mood. The *Non* forces were discreet in their celebration—one would have said that their convincing victory (59.6% to 40.4% with 86% of the electorate voting) brought them little joy. Some among those who had supported the *Oui* expressed bitterness, others bewilderment, still others a surprisingly detached acceptance of defeat. As one acquaintance put it, "with or without a *Oui*, my life goes on."

When I returned to Quebec in 1983 the evident dilution and diminution of nationalist sentiment took me very much by surprise. Friends explained in matter-of-fact fashion that they and others simply were not as nationalistic as they had been a few years before. One couple, for example, told me that they were now considering moving outside Quebec to pursue their musical careers, a move they would not have considered before; another person mentioned that the 1983 celebration of Saint-Jean-Baptiste day had been feeble, adding that I had witnessed extraordinary times in the late 1970s; and still others expressed disgust with the Parti Québécois government for what they saw as futile nationalistic demagoguery. Though the Parti Québécois was convincingly reelected in 1981, the referendum had demonstrated that its deepest aspirations did not correspond to those of the majority (assuming that such aspirations can be measured by a yes-no vote). Even granting that the 40% *Oui* vote represented half the francophone population of the province—since the anglophone vote (about one fifth of Quebec's population is anglophone) went almost entirely to the *Non*—analysts from both sides believed that a third of the *Oui* vote was cast for "strategic" reasons, seeking bargaining power vis-à-vis Ottawa but not independence from Canada (Feldman 1980:18, 22).

These results, and the remarkable shift in public mood, ill accord with a piece of conventional wisdom that I heard time and again, from federalists as well as *indépendantistes:* "All Québécois (or French Canadians) are nationalists." And certainly the referendum belied the Parti Québécois interpretation of the *fête* of November 15 as the birth of a nation. What, then, is the relationship between nationalist ideology and mass belief?

Most analysts believe that the elaboration of nationalist discourse has always been the work of self-consciously patriotic ideologues and visionaries. The Québécois themselves recognize this: their accounts of their own nationalism invariably mention an ideological elite that has played a preponderant role in the formulation and dissemination of national "self-images." These accounts assume the existence of vague sentiments of national identification and allegiance among the general populace, but recognize that the transformation of such sentiments into a more formal, more forceful system of ideas is the work of particular individuals and organizations. For example, Leon Dion distinguishes between the ideologically self-conscious stance of nationalist leaders and "a much more elementary and fundamental state of mind" of the people, which he describes as the defensiveness of a threatened minority. The two are clearly related, ideology being a rationalization of collective sentiment—"the intellectual formulation of the elementary drive for the survival of the collectivity as an original entity." But only in situations of crisis does the public become unambiguously nationalistic. At other times, Dion contends, "variety and even . . . incompatibility of values" is as typical of French Canadians as of any other large group, though nationalists may claim to speak in the name of a homogeneous collectivity (1961:90–93).

It is often argued, by positivists of both Marxist and liberal persuasion, that class is the determining factor in the propagation of nationalist ideology. There is much discussion of which fragment of which class produces which version of nationalist ideology in defense of which interests. Yet such explanations of ideology are inadequate for my purposes on at least four counts. First, as Geertz has argued (1964:201–7), they fail to take ideologies seriously as meaningful formulations, preferring instead to postulate causal links between them and class interests. Such "explanations" often begin with simplistic readings of ideology and proceed to equally simplistic renderings of class interest. Yet the comparative interpretation of nationalist ideology and social-scientific discourse that I propose aims not to reduce ideas to an economic or material infrastructure whose supposedly more primary reality would explain them; but to explicate the two discourses, each in terms of the other, in order to make manifest the arbitrary presuppositions that both share. In other words, even were it possible to explain the genesis and appeal of ideology in terms of social structure, to do so would not tell us what the ideology means. And the problem of meaning, not causality, is my concern here.

Second, the persistence of disputes concerning attempts to identify classes and fragments of classes suggests that "class" itself is not an objective and verifiable reality, but depends instead on analyst's models. In other words, the isolation of one group of people as "a" class depends upon the mode of analysis chosen, and will vary from one model to another. Thus the very notion of class rests on the type of objectifying logic that I question here, for it posits the consistent action and sentiments of a group whose boundedness and homogeneity is established by the terms of the necessarily arbitrary criteria specified in the analyst's model. Class analysts will justify their criteria with reference to the priority of infrastructural to superstructural phenomena, but from the symbolic perspective advocated here, the former are as much cultural as the latter, and no ontological priority can be claimed for either (Sahlins 1976). In sum, to explain actors' concepts of nation in terms of an analytic concept such as class overlooks the fact that both concepts are motivated by the same logic—overlooks, that is, the interpenetration of native and scholarly discourse that most needs to be elucidated.

Third, to explain ideology in terms of interests assumes that the latter can be objectively ascertained. Yet interests are not transparent: the analyst must construct, through interpretation, an account of interests, and there is no guarantee that such an interpretation will match actors' understandings of what their interests are. This indeterminacy of interests gives rise to the notion that actors can be mistaken about their interests; thus, between interests correctly perceived and those that actors misperceive, the class analyst can explain literally any action. Moreover, interests are themselves culturally constructed. As Tocqueville pointed out (1835: 2:7) in comparing the new democratic social order to the aristocratic society it was replacing, "men are no longer bound together by ideas, but by interests." In light of Tocqueville's wider argument I interpret this to mean that interests are neither a pre-cultural nor a rational basis of

25

social integration, but are instead the historically particular form by which people in the "individualistic universe" (L. Dumont 1971, 1977) conceive and construct their relationships. In sum, the *idea* that interests bind individual actors is culturally specific, as are whatever particular interests the actors conceive.

Finally, to associate ideology with class objectifies ideologies themselves as bounded units of discourse. One can speak of, say, petit-bourgeois nationalism and technocratic nationalism as if the two were distinguishable as objectively separated entities. Yet nationalist discourse of whatever school shares features with that of other schools and even other places and times. Discourses (to personify for the moment what is only the product of active speakers and interpreters) converse: ideologues and theorists imitate, borrow, and compare among themselves. One can privilege either the differences or the similarities between two bodies (however delimited) of discourse, but such interpretive choices should not be projected onto the texts themselves as if a particular group of texts existed as an objectively bounded unit. Moreover, when using such reified sets of texts in discussions of class, the reasoning is often circular: a class or fragment of a class is identified by the ideology it produces, just as the ideology is delineated with respect to the class that produced it.

As an alternative strategy to class analysis I offer an interpretive analysis of texts, conversations, and incidents which are unified, for our purposes, only by my experience (and, to the degree that my narrative succeeds, by yours). These are "phenomena having a merely subjective connection," as Boas (1887:642–43) put it—phenomena unified only by "the mind of the observer" (cf. Stocking 1974: 10; Handler 1983:209). Though I shall speak repeatedly of Québécois nationalist ideology, and though most Québécois will know what I intend by that phrase, at least in a rough-and-ready sort of way, I do not pretend that "Québécois nationalist ideology" corresponds to any objectively bounded or isolable entity or body of discourse. As I have explained at some length, to make such a claim would contradict the theoretical argument that I wish to develop—an argument which, if it succeeds, might obviate the necessity for social-scientific accounts to address themselves to bounded social units of whatever kind. This does not mean that nationalist discourse does not exist, but only that the boundaries that I have assigned it, and the reading I have constructed of it, are provisional—as would be, for that matter, any such boundaries or reading.

I began field work in Quebec in 1977 with the intention of constructing a cultural account of Québécois nationalist ideology. Following David Schneider (1968) I sought to explicate the symbols and meanings with which Québécois portray their national identity and allegiance. As research and interpretation progressed I tried to abandon what I came increasingly to see as the reifying implications of Schneider's approach (cf. Maynard 1984) while continuing to work at the type of symbolic (or "cultural" or "interpretive") analysis he advocates. In other words, I no longer claim to be able either to present an account of "the" culture or to demonstrate its integration, but will focus instead on cultural objectification in relation to the interpenetration of discourses—that is, on attempts to construct bounded cultural objects, *a process that paradoxically demonstrates the absence of such objects.* The following chapters are linked neither by a temporally linear narrative nor by their division among a set of topics that would correspond to some real-world entity or social system. Rather, they employ a heterogeneous assortment of narrative techniques, texts, and textualized experiences in order to examine nationalism, culture theory, and cultural objectification . . . "in Quebec."

This narrative heterogeneity reflects the heterogeneity of a research experience adapted to an unbounded social reality. Traditional anthropological projects have focused on preliterate social units of "small scale": village, tribe, or the society of a micro-atoll. In such situations researchers might reasonably (at least within certain epistemological perspectives) privilege observations and accounts they "gathered" themselves, and might also expect to find access to all aspects of a total society. When the perceived complexity of a social arena forces us to abandon this totalizing approach, we find ourselves awash in a sea of data which demands new theoretical concepts in order to partition it. To rescue a bounded object we might narrow our focus to a functionally circumscribed domain, or to a geographical sub-unit considered, with self-conscious recognition and then rationalization of our fictional conceit, as an isolated social entity. In what follows I will try to resist such conceits (I leave it to you to discover those that I have come to rely on). To study the interpenetration of nationalism and social science I have found myself wandering among a disparate assortment of texts, created or discovered through three (roughly speaking) types of research: the field experience itself, library research, and specially arranged interviews with government officials and cultural-affairs activists.

Fifteen months of field work were carried out during three extended visits to Quebec between 1976 and 1980. In the field I employed a number of research techniques. First, I talked with people about the national question, either during formal interviews or informal interactions. In all I conducted over fifty formal interviews, lasting anywhere from one to six hours. Most of these were tape-recorded, though during some I felt that only note taking was appropriate. I interviewed many people engaged in political or folkloristic activities. Friends recommended some of these to me, telling me that I ought to talk to such-and-such a friend or relative who was active in the local Parti Québécois organization, or in a campaign to save historic buildings, or who was simply a person with strong feelings about nationalist issues. I approached others on my own, self-proclaimed nationalists—writers, politicians, citizens who signed patriotic letters-to-the-editor—or people involved in activities and organizations relevant to my interests. I also interviewed friends in formal fashion, though much more important were hours of informal discussion with these people, as well as opportunities to participate with them as they talked with their friends. (Needless to say, nationalist issues occupied only a fraction of the long hours of talk that I shared with Québécois, but it was important to discover the contexts in which nationalist discussion occurred without my prompting.)

Informal discussion shades imperceptibly into what common sense, with its distinction between talk and action, terms incidents and events. I read the newspapers to learn of political rallies, patriotic ceremonies, and folklore celebrations, and attended as many as I could, even traveling from my home base in Quebec City to Montreal and elsewhere if the event warranted it. Often I taped speeches at these events, or, in the case of prominent political figures, wrote afterwards for transcripts of their remarks. In some instances I was able to interview participants on the spot, or to talk with Québécois observers about their reactions to the ceremony or spectacle in progress. And, of course, I wrote my own account of these events, either in the form of field notes or letters to colleagues and friends.

These research activities involved the creation of texts, which will be analyzed—indeed, rewritten—in the pages that follow. But the study of modern ideologies obviously requires extended analyses of texts that the researcher does not himself create. In Quebec, literature on the national question, from the most scholarly to the most propagandistic, is both voluminous and accessible. Major events such as elections and the referendum give rise to masses of printed material discussing nationalist issues from many perspectives, in many genres. Almost every week I spent in Quebec saw the publication of a major statement or study by an important public figure or scholar, and the daily press regularly printed articles, letters, editorials, and advertisements concerning some aspect of nationalist politics or sentiments. I approached this burgeoning literature with a dual strategy, on the one hand choosing material that was making a stir both in the media and among people I knew, on the other hand looking at all sorts of pamphlets, magazines, and books that fortuitously came my way. In the analyses that follow a variety of sources appear, but I have relied especially on (1) the writings of the historian Groulx, whom I take as an exemplar of what I shall hereafter call clerical-conservative nationalism; (2) the writings of René Lévesque and the Parti Québécois, which I take to typify what I shall call contemporary (post-1960) nationalism; and (3) publications of the provincial government. Translations from the French are my own unless otherwise indicated. The historical and sociological relevance of these texts will be sketched as they are brought into play.

Though library research in Quebec City was an integral part of field work, much of the analysis of government documents and secondary sources was carried out at Harvard University, where I held the Quebec Fellowship at the University Consortium for Research on North America in 1983–1984. During this period I was able, thanks to the Quebec Delegation in Boston, to arrange interviews with both government officials and cultural-affairs activists. I made several brief trips to Quebec for the sole purpose of conducting such interviews, which were not part of an ongoing field experience as they were designed to yield specific types of information. In this they differed from the more wide-ranging interviews conducted during field work, when it was often possible to arrange a series of meetings with individuals and so to pursue a variety of topics without the constraint of a mission to accomplish. In the chapters that follow I will indicate, where relevant, the source and type of interview materials that I use.

The next chapter outlines a set of nationalist concepts particularly salient for an understanding of the rest of the book. In chapter 3 I discuss, as an initial example of cultural objectification, the study of Québécois folklore and various attempts to (re)discover a folk society in Quebec. The next four chapters focus on aspects of the politics of culture—that is, on the role that government has played in cultural objectification. Chapter 4 outlines the foundation of a Department of Cultural Affairs within the provincial government in 1961. Chapter 5 compares the holistic approaches favored by theoreticians of cultural development to the fragmentation of the cultural domain that results when bureaucracy attempts to administer it. Chapters 6 and 7 focus on historic preservation and language legislation in order to bring out the interplay of nationalist and social-scientific ideologies in specific areas of cultural policy-making. A concluding chapter completes the theoretical arguments begun here and elaborated in the chapters to follow.

CHAPTER TWO

Some Salient Features of Québécois Nationalist Ideology

We are *Québécois.*

What this means first and foremost . . . is that we are attached to this one corner of the earth where we can be completely ourselves: this Quebec, the only place where we have the unmistakable feeling that "here we can be really at home."

Being ourselves is essentially a matter of keeping and developing a personality that has survived for three and a half centuries.

At the core of this personality is the fact that we speak French. Everything else depends on this one essential element. . . .

We are children of that society, in which the *habitant,* our father or grandfather, was still the key citizen. We are also heirs to that fantastic adventure—that early America that was almost entirely French. We are, even more intimately, heirs to the group obstinacy which has kept alive that portion of French America we call *Québec.*

All these things lie at the core of this personality of ours. Anyone who does not feel it . . . is not—is no longer—one of us.

But *we* know and feel that these are the things that make us what we are. They enable us to recognize each other wherever we may be. This is our own special wavelength on which, despite all interference, we can tune each other in loud and clear, with no one else listening.

This is how we differ from other men and especially from other North Americans, with whom in all other areas we have so much in common. This basic "difference" we cannot surrender. That became impossible a long time ago.

More is involved here than simple intellectual certainty. This is a physical fact. To be unable to live as ourselves, as we should live, in our own language and according to our own ways, would be like living without an arm or a leg—or perhaps a heart.

Unless, of course, we agreed to give in little by little, in a decline which, as in cases of pernicious anaemia, would cause life to slip slowly away from the patient.

Again, in order not to perceive this, one has to be among the *déracinés*, the uprooted and cut-off. (Lévesque 1968:14–15).

Few Québécois would deny René Lévesque's claim that "we are *Québécois*," or, what several people told me, that "all Québécois are nationalists." Yet the results of the referendum, the existence of conservative and progressive nationalisms and of all shades in between, and the characteristic cycle of peaks and valleys in the strength of nationalist sentiment remind us that different people espouse different varieties of nationalism with differing degrees of commitment. The following discussion of some "salient features" of Québécois nationalist ideology must therefore be doubly provisional. First, I do not claim to speak about all varieties of Québécois nationalism, as if I could present an analysis which, isolating the common elements of them all, would represent a body of thought that is bounded in the "real world." Second, I speak of "salient" rather than "fundamental" features to avoid any implications of a "deep structure" whose reality is more "basic" than the reality of other social phenomena. By contrast, salience suggests that the features selected for analysis are pragmatically forceful and suasive, and that they engage active interpreters—myself as well as many of the people I studied. To speak of salient features establishes sociological relevance without grounding that relevance in a bounded ideology or society.

In this chapter I correlate materials drawn from a variety of sources, from ideological formulations to casual conversations, from public statements to remarks gathered during private interviews. I have particularly relied on the works of Lionel Groulx, of René Lévesque and the Parti Québécois, and on formulations that I elicited during interviews in which I asked people to reflect in self-conscious fashion on their national and cultural identity. By knitting together ideas taken from disparate sources I have not meant to suggest that the result corresponds to a seamless cultural whole. But the inclusion of contemporary nationalistic statements side-by-side with "clerical-conservative" formulations, along with the mixture of remarks by professional ideologues with those of ordinary citizens, has made it easier to identify certain similarities and differences among a range of nationalist ideologies. To anticipate, all versions examined in this chapter agree about the existence of a nation which is taken to be bounded, continuous, and at least minimally homogeneous, but there is disagreement and confusion concerning the *content* of national existence. Particularly obvious in this regard is the contrast between traditional and contemporary nationalisms, which, in addition to their differing temporal orientations, differ in the centrality accorded to Catholicism, to ruralism, to political independence, and to other issues. Moreover, both similarities and differences deserve interpretive comment, and I will argue that disputes about content make good sense according to the cultural logic examined here, as does the relative lack of dispute about the primacy of national existence. But it should be kept in mind that lack of dispute concerning the latter issue is only relative; and in Chapter Four we will look at some decidedly anti-nationalistic arguments of Pierre Trudeau, who, as Prime Minister of Canada for almost seventeen years, has been as important as any other political leader to the lives of Québécois, and who has found consistent support among them at the polls.

The Individual as a Member of the Nation

Louis Dumont epitomized the individualistic basis of nationalist ideology when he wrote that the nation "is *in principle* two things at once: a *collection of individuals* and a *collective individual*" (1970:33). Following Dumont, I have interpreted Québécois nationalism by attending to the nation envisioned as an individuated actor and as a collection of individual human actors; and to these I have added a third perspective by examining people's understanding of themselves as members of a nation.

In Quebec I often asked people to explain what it was that made them Québécois, or what criteria they used to determine whether other persons were Québécois, or what were the bases of their attachment to Quebec. Consider some of their answers:

> *What is a Québécois?*
> *Someone who lives in the same spot as I and wants to keep it as much as I do.*
> **Yes, but you once told me that Mr. X (a Montreal-born musician who lives and works in the United States) was a Québécois.**
> *Yes, because he was born in Quebec. But it isn't only that which makes you Québécois. It's a way of life. All peoples*

*have their habits, their customs. All the Québécois—that's
all the people who do the same things during their day, who
have their own food, and so on. It's funny, a Québécois who
eats hot dogs.*

How do you explain your attachment to Quebec?
*You're asking me how I explain the fact that I first saw the
light of day here?! "I first saw the light of day here." These
things aren't rational. Well, they're rational, but it's much
more a question of feeling. You don't just say, "Oh, I'm
going to feel an attachment to this country!" An attachment
is always nonrational.*

What is it that makes a person Québécois?
*Any inhabitant of Quebec is Québécois, if you want the
broad definition. But the Québécois—that more likely would
be the people who have been here a stretch of time.
Certainly in theory any person residing in Quebec is
Québécois. But the popular mentality holds that the
Québécois are those who have been established here for a
long time. And generally, the Québécois speak French and
have a certain way of looking at life. When you talk about
the Québécois you're talking about francophones who are
nationalist and who hold to their heritage, culture, customs,
and traditions. It's more like that, the Québécois.*

Analyzing these responses, we find two attributes that are
thought to make a person Québécois: the relationship of an individual
to a particular locality or territory, and a style of living or "code for
conduct" (Schneider 1968) to which the individual must adhere. This
formulation agrees with that of René Lévesque, expressed in the
passage quoted above. According to Lévesque, to be Québécois is to
be "attached to this one corner of the earth" called Quebec, and to
keep and develop a cultural "personality." Let us examine these two
attributes in turn.

Locality: Attachment to *la terre, la patrie*

The earth, one's native soil, one's fatherland, one's country—attachment to these things is considered by nationalists to be supremely
natural, as is the way of life built on the basis of this attachment.
Consider the notions of land and the national territory found in the
works of Lionel Groulx. The colony of New France, from which
sprang the French-Canadian people, is said to have been planted in
the soil of the New World (1924:104). The soil protected and nourished
the nascent collectivity, providing the material necessities of life and
promoting those moral virtues associated with uncorrupted labor and

33

a pastoral milieu (1917:41; 1919:76–77; 1936:262). But man has also given to the land. The soil has been conquered, developed, "humanized" (1952: 3:97) by the succession of human generations living upon it (1935:140). The people mark the land with their soul and personality (1919:87; 1935:97), and, above all, they love the land.

There is thus a reciprocal relationship between the people and the land, one that Groulx describes as a marriage sealed in sweat and blood (1919:87). The people transform the virgin earth and leave their mark upon it; the earth bears fruit and supports the people and their children. But Groulx also speaks of a relationship of identity between people and land, both of which, he claims, through a long process of mutual adaptation, have come to resemble each other—the land mirrors the features of those who have settled it (1952: 2:175). In either case the relationship of man and land is natural: Groulx speaks of "la patrie naturelle" (1922:104), of the preexistent harmony linking the earth and the French-Canadian race (1918:340; 1924:171). And he adds that people can be bound indissolubly only to the land where they are born and labor (1924:233).

According to Groulx, and to most people with whom I spoke, the attachment of man to his native land is natural. Moreover, this attachment is indissoluble: there is a permanent bond established between people and the place of their birth. One young man, recently returned from several years abroad when I spoke to him, put it this way:

> I don't believe that a person can live away from the country where he was born. Anyway, exile is always a punishment. You could say that we leave our soul or half of our heart there. You could say that our heart is part of the ground, that its roots are in the earth. When we leave we tear out those roots, which seek continually to return to the same soil.

Thus one's native soil is thought to be perpetually attractive. But place of birth determines more than vague longings for the homeland: some interlocutors argued that being born in Quebec creates in the individual an indelible impulse toward *being Québécois*. Québécois ways of living and thinking—Québécois culture, in short—must always be one's original culture. There is no choice in this matter, for, as several people explained, "you don't choose the place where you are born."

To consider national identity in terms of choice—a central element in the individualist world view—is crucial. Birth is a fact of nature which in a sense determines one's national or cultural affiliation, as well as the specific mode of being following from it. An individual's choice has no role to play when it comes to his "original" or "natural" mode of being. As historian Guy Frégault put it, writing of the ancestors of the Québécois: they "didn't choose, as in a European catalogue, the culture, language, conceptions and aspirations that they brought to this virgin continent. It wasn't in their baggage that they brought those things: it was in them. And . . . all that . . . is still in us" (MAC-AR 1964:29).

If Frégault's remark stresses the "French" component of Québécois culture—indelible despite a transatlantic crossing—other remarks suggest that individuals can change not only their place of residence but their nationality. Many people felt that they would never leave Quebec permanently, that they would always remain Québécois—though most thought it worthwhile to experience other ways of life, and some who in 1977 had proclaimed unswerving allegiance to life in Quebec had by 1983 changed their minds. In any case, all admitted that people can choose to leave other countries and come to Quebec, or to leave Quebec and establish themselves permanently elsewhere. In one sense they saw this as a chance for people to improve upon a situation not of their making:

> After you've spent time in several countries, you will have a choice to make. In that case, such a choice would be worthwhile and valid. If you decide to live in another country because the people there correspond more nearly to what you would like to be—well, then you aren't really the same as you were before.

Yet most people could not imagine themselves making such a choice. "My first culture and nationality will always be Québécois, and I hope that I would never want it otherwise." In fact, the decision to change countries, while seen in one sense as a valid exercise in rationality, was at the same time seen as *unnatural* because it would require that one alter naturally given personal attributes. Such a choice would indicate a fundamental change of state: "You aren't really the same as you were before." Most of my interlocutors thought such a change to be practically impossible, for they felt that some aspects of people's original nationality and culture would remain with them no matter where they decided to live.

In sum, choice is subordinate to essence: birth in a particular place determines the kind of person one will naturally become, yet one cannot choose one's place of birth. Even when adults choose to move from one country to another, a naturally given mode of being cannot be completely eradicated. Moreover, any attempt to impose new habits upon oneself is unnatural and, for that reason, destined to fail. As René Lévesque put it, Quebec is "the only place where we have the unmistakable feeling that 'here we can be really at home.'"

Québécois Nationalist Ideology

Code for Conduct

A shared code for conduct was the second element of our series of statements about what makes a person Québécois. The notion of code for conduct suggests norms for behavior, a set of rules that specify what one must do, how one must act and *be,* in order to be Québécois. In general, to be Québécois one must love Quebec and take pride both in Quebec itself and in the fact of one's affiliation with it. More specifically, to be Québécois one must live as other Québécois live, speaking French, respecting Québécois values and traditions, and sharing Québécois history. In brief, to be Québécois one must participate in Québécois culture.

Yet what is the content of this culture? Abbé Groulx would have answered by invoking the Catholic religion and French language and traditions. Addressing himself to French-Canadian students, he once wrote: "Students of Catholic faith and French race. Here, it seems to me, is your definition; it is your originality; you have no other" (1935:188). Today people speak of Québécois rather than French culture, and include Catholicism only as a formative element in national history—if they mention it at all.[1] When asked to specify the elements of Québécois culture, most people immediately mentioned the French language, yet beyond that there was little agreement and even little sense of how to answer the question. Some pessimists claimed that there is no such thing as Québécois culture; as one person, owner of a souvenir shop in Quebec City, put it, "We aren't French, we aren't American, our 'culture' and 'identity' are empty things." And an anthropology professor remarked that notwithstanding all the discussion of Québécois culture, nobody could really say what it was. "Let me know if you find out," she told me.

Some people, however, responded to the question of cultural content by turning to history, giving a general account of the origin and development of Québécois culture. They emphasized the gradual adaptation of the original French settlers to life in the New World and discussed the transformation of French culture under the influence of a new environment. Their accounts posit the initial choice of a handful of colonists from France, and the subsequent consecration of

1. The intellectuals who revolted against Roman Catholicism in the 1950s and 1960s have thus far been reluctant to analyze what is, after all, one of the most remarkable aspects of recent Quebec history: the dramatic collapse of the Church. I suspect that the demise of an institution that had seemed so securely anchored in the lives of French Canadians has to do with the extreme objectification of religion as a symbol of national identity. For French Canada's elites, Roman Catholicism was important less as a theology than as a "trait" of national culture that distinguished them from their "Anglo-Saxon" neighbors. For ordinary parishioners, religion was a discipline to submit to rather than a sacred realm to be entered with unreflexive faith (cf. Rocher 1984:17).

this choice in the crucible of time and nature. The Québécois of today are the "offshoot" of seventeenth-century France, but they are not French. They are not French because their ancestors chose to leave France. Once resettled in the New World, these colonists neither lived in a French manner nor thought of themselves as French. The new style of life, or culture, that developed in North America is seen as an original adaptation to a new environment, or as a unique cultural product resulting from the formative influence of a particular natural region. In either case, the influence of New World geography and climate are seen as crucial, as is the effect of the modified diet of the French in America. In recent years people have stressed the importance of contact with American Indians, and, though they speak of cultural borrowing, there is an underlying sense that the ecologically pure noble savage was yet another "natural" influence. Finally, people speak of the importance of cultural and historical factors—the prolonged contact with "Anglo-American civilization," or the effects of wars and political struggles.

In sum, people describe Québécois culture as the end product of the transformation that an originally European way of life underwent upon contact with a new environment. This transformation began with the choices of those individuals who left France to come to North America. These initial choices were consecrated by time and nature, and a new culture gradually emerged in what is seen as a process of evolutionary adaptation. The final "fixed" product has by now become solidly "anchored in time," as one man told me, and is the basis of the Québécois nation of today.

A second characteristic attempt to counter the inability to specify the content of Québécois culture was to speak of "Latin temperament" and "Latin blood." Québécois culture, whatever it might be, finds expression above all as a certain mentality and way of looking at life, and as a certain social ambiance stemming from this mentality and outlook. People typically summed up the matter by speaking of Québécois *joie de vivre* (a mainstay of travel advertisements) and, above all, of the Latin temperament. The idea of Latin temperament refers to the French tradition which is felt to be central in Québécois culture. But people used this idea interchangeably with another notion: "Latin blood." Québécois warmth and *joie de vivre* result from the Latin blood of the Québécois. There is thus an equation of group temperament and blood—a conceptual interlinkage of spiritual and physical essence.

The idea of Latin blood, evoked so frequently and spontaneously in explanations of Québécois culture, replaces culture with nature, as does the explanation of Québécois culture in terms of a history which is above all envisioned as evolutionary adaptation. Both explanations privilege "the notion that qualitative cultural differences are inborn" (Porter 1975:299), or what I have elsewhere

termed the *naturalization of culture* (Handler and Linnekin 1984:278).
To be Québécois is to act Québécois, and to act Québécois comes
naturally to those who are Québécois. As an illustration of this
somewhat cryptic formulation, consider the example of language. As
we have seen, language—the fact of speaking French—is the one
element of Québécois culture that people invariably specify. Yet they
see language as more than behavior: "your language, that's you," and,
according to the same interlocutor, the Québécois wouldn't be
Québécois if they didn't speak French. Other people told me that in
Quebec people speak French naturally, a theme central to Groulx's
novel *L'Appel de la race,* which discusses the reconversion of an
anglicized French-Canadian family: "French comes back to me like a
language I've already known . . . . I'm a little intuitionist . . . , I have
only to read within myself to learn everything" (1922:124–25). Still
others explicated the notion of "mother tongue" in similarly naturalistic terms. One person projected language back into the womb,
arguing that an unborn infant absorbs the rhythms of what will be its
maternal language from the resonances of the speech of its mother.
Thus the mere fact of birth from a French-speaking mother means
that a person will speak French "naturally." Other interlocutors
looked beyond the parents to the line of ancestors stretching back to
New France. In brief, some people have a vague understanding that
the Latin blood of the Québécois predisposes them to speak French.

As the example of language shows, Québécois behavior is more
than behavior: it is the manifestation of an inner essence that is
physical as well as spiritual, and more natural than cultural in the
anthropological sense of the word. René Lévesque puts it concisely
when he describes the Québécois difference as "a physical fact." And
he adds that "to be unable to live as ourselves, as we should live, in
our own language and according to our own ways, would be like
living without an arm or a leg—or perhaps a heart."

"To live as ourselves"—the phrase suggests a certain irreducible
identity and brings us to the notion of pride. Pride, like Latin blood
and the Latin temperament, is a ubiquitous concept that people use
when questioned about the meaning of being Québécois. "I am a
Québécois and I am proud to be a Québécois. I am proud to go
elsewhere and say 'I am Québécois.' And to save that, to save nothing
more than the fact that I can say 'I am Québécois,' I could do many
things." The same correlation between identity and pride appears in
the opposite view: the person who noted the emptiness of Québécois
culture added that the Québécois, unlike the French or the Americans, have nothing to be proud of (cf. Griffin 1984:164–65). Yet when
questioned more closely people could not break down the concept of
pride. One person explained that as children in school they had
mindlessly repeated that they were proud to be Québécois, but that
he had never thought about what that meant. "We're proud, that's

all," he concluded. Thus the assertion of pride is as irreducible as the individuated existence upon which it is predicated—a parallel nicely expressed in a Parti Québécois pamphlet discussing honest political advertising: "we are proud of what we present to the populace because we try to present ourselves as we are" (Parti Québécois 1971:20).

"As we are," "as ourselves": such expressions evoke what I have called an irreducible identity, and proclaim the existence of an individuated collectivity. To be Québécois one must live in Quebec and live as a Québécois. To live as a Québécois means participating in Québécois culture. In discussing this culture people speak vaguely of traditions, typical ways of behaving, and characteristic modes of conceiving the world; yet specific descriptions of these particularities are the business of the historian, ethnologist, or folklorist. Such academic researches would seem to come after the fact: that is, given the ideological centrality of Québécois culture, it becomes worthwhile to learn about it. But the almost *a priori* belief in the existence of the culture follows inevitably from the belief that a particular human group, the Québécois nation, exists. The existence of the group is in turn predicated upon the existence of a particular culture. To be Québécois is to act Québécois, and to act Québécois comes naturally to those who are Québécois. Québécois culture in and of itself is secondary. What is crucial is that culture symbolizes individuated existence: the assertion of cultural particularity is another way of proclaiming the existence of a unique collectivity.

"We are different because we have a culture," a Quebec City high school student told me.

"We are a nation because we have a culture," a Montreal student told an English-Canadian television audience.

"You [on] can live without formal education; but you don't exist, you leave no trace, if you are without culture," wrote Georges-Emile Lapalme, creator and first head of Quebec's Cultural Affairs Department (1973:226). Or, as his successor, Pierre Laporte, put it, "no one can deny that we have a culture" (MAC-AR 1965:26).

The Nation as a Collective Individual and a Collection of Individuals

Thus far we have examined Québécois nationality as seen from the point of view of the individual human being, explicating the criteria according to which individuals are recognized as members of the Québécois nation. But what are the attributes that characterize the nation itself, both as a collective individual and as a collection of individuals? Two metaphors typical of nationalist discourse suggest

39

answers to this question. First, nationalists liken the nation to a living creature. Second, they speak of it as if it were a biological species. These naturalistic metaphors describe the nation in terms of biological forms and processes characteristic of life in "the state of nature." As we shall see, it is no accident that human individuals encompassed by a collective individual, the nation, should partake of the natural essence of that greater whole to which they belong.

A Collective Individual

> In order to understand French-Canadian history you must understand the French-Canadian soul—the soul that guides, that directs. Since the Conquest the people has lived in the face of adversity. But the French-Canadian soul is patriotic, difficult to crush. That is what lives from generation to generation.

> Your country is like a friend—you have to be around to say hello every now and then; otherwise you become strangers to each other.

> I picture the Québécois people as a tree. Its roots are firmly planted in the soil of the New World, but as it matures it grows heavenward, opening itself to the outside world and reaching for the universal.

In these statements, three Québécois whom I interviewed—a retired veterinarian, a high school student, and a university professor—personified the collectivity or likened it to a nonhuman living thing. Similar metaphors abound in the works of nationalist writers. Lionel Groulx speaks often of the life of the people, of its soul and personality, its struggles, strengths, and weaknesses. He has likened the people to a tree in a storm (1937:238; 1943:79–80) and to a human being: a tenacious peasant (1937:214–15) and a sleeping knight (1922:98). Consider also the following discussion of tradition, in which Groulx depicts the collectivity as a living, striving creature:

> And the word [tradition] evokes the inner thought, the architectural plan according to which a people builds its history even as it lives, creates and evolves, always faithful to the particular impetus of its soul . . . remaining consubstantial with its past, its ancestors, with the genius of its race. (1937:209)

These images of the nation as a living individual—a tree, a friend, a creature with a soul—convey first of all a sense of wholeness and boundedness. They establish the integral, irreducible nature of the collectivity as an existent entity. This is particularly true in the works of Groulx, where historical passages recounting the trials of

ɪadian pioneers end with the emergence of a collective
ɪne creating, evolving people that always remains
ɪs past. Groulx literally describes the genesis of the race,
ɪesult of this divinely directed process is a fixed entity, an
ɪorical personality, the collective individual. In Groulx's work the
individualist metaphor conveys a sense of a perfected, fully-formed
creature which need only remain as it has been in the past. Groulx
uses this rhetorical device to insist, first, on the existence of the nation
and, second, on its existence as a unique and bounded entity.

These metaphors are particularly effective in conveying a sense
of the boundedness of the nation—for what is more complete and self-
contained than a living creature? Furthermore, once the nation is
established as a living individual, it is possible to impute to it various
attributes and actions. The nation can be shown to build, struggle,
and create; it can be said to have a soul, spirit, and personality; it can
be treated as a friend or a parent. Most important, the metaphorical
individual can be discussed in terms of its freedom to choose and its
ability to control its own destiny. During the period of my field work,
individualist metaphors were repeatedly used to convey a sense of the
nation's struggle to assert itself as a completely free individual—that
is, to establish its independence. The Parti Québécois based its referendary campaign on this metaphor and idea, epitomized in the slogan
d'égal à égal—"equal to equal": the Québécois and Canadian nations
must form "a new partnership between equals" in which neither
collective individual surrenders its autonomy or will to the other
(Quebec 1979).

This crucial idea of national will and choice—self-determination, in fact—emerges in slightly different fashion in discussions of
the life stages of the collective individual. Modern indépendantistes
look to the future as well as the past. Like Groulx, they see the present
as a time of great danger, but they also see it as a period of preparation
for the future. For them the French colonial period witnessed the
birth of the nation, the years from the Conquest to the present
marked its slow progress through childhood and adolescence, and
today the nation stands on the brink of adulthood. Within the terms of
this conceit the present relationship of Canada to Quebec can be
envisioned as the outmoded dominance of a parent over a child
recently come of age. The sovereignty of a nation, it is said, is
analogous to the liberty of an adult. When a child grows up his
parents must relinquish control over him. Their concession of authority must be total: the freedom of the young adult cannot be compro-
mised or shared. Similarly, when a nation comes of age it is entitled to
full sovereignty. It is thus nonsense to see the current relationship of
Quebec with Canada as a situation in which sovereignty is shared
between the federal and provincial governments. Sovereignty, like
individual freedom, cannot be shared.

Québécois Nationalist Ideology

Such rhetoric allows nationalists to psychologize history—that is, to discuss the history of the nation as if it were the history of a person. The long years of French-Canadian association with English Canada are seen as years of childhood entailing submission to the authority of another, and the 1950s and 1960s become an adolescence that culminated in the 1970s with the emergence of an adult. Since history can be thus viewed as personal development, it is not surprising that nationalists often make use of the concept of normalcy in their analysis of the present situation. The period of submission, in its very length, is said to be "abnormal"—an unnaturally prolonged childhood. At the same time, the independence of the Québécois collectivity represents a return to normalcy (a return, because it is assumed that the development of New France would have proceeded normally had it not been interrupted by the Conquest). This insistence upon "the normal health of an adult people," as one Parti Québécois tract puts it (1972:7), brings us to the full significance of the idea of collective adulthood. Normal adulthood carries with it the most complete autonomy that an individual, collective or otherwise, can attain. Adulthood means complete self-responsibility: choice and the control of his future course fall solely to the individual who, through mature deliberation, must take stock of his circumstances and decide what is best for him.

This cry for normalcy and adult autonomy is not confined to abstract discussions. For example, the Parti Québécois government argued that the stringency of its proposed language legislation was necessary because the situation in Quebec was not normal. Explaining Bill 101 (see chapter 7) to the public, it argued that "in stating that everyone must know French in a society like Quebec, the government . . . wishes merely to ensure that there is a communal language base similar to that found in all other normal societies" (Quebec 1977:29). Several months later Prime Minister Lévesque described Bill 101 to the *Assemblée nationale* of France as "a law for the defense and promotion of a language which, in a normal context, would never have needed such a prosthesis" (1977:5).

Still more important, provincial politicians often justify their quarrels with the federal government in terms of such concepts as choice, maturity, and responsibility. The Parti Québécois has always based its case against the Canadian Confederation on the right of an adult people "to construct a society responsible for itself" (1972:56). By proclaiming the Québécois nation to be a unique collective individual, utterly distinct from Canada and standing on the threshold of adulthood, *indépendantistes* can argue against the federal government and in favor of the independence of Quebec. Parti Québécois government ministers have complained bitterly of their powerlessness with regard to matters falling under federal jurisdiction: for example, "we will not be the primary agents of our economic development as long as the necessary tools remain in the hands of those for whom Quebec and its government are entities whose will may be scoffed at" (Thellier 1978:13). During my months in Quebec the newspapers reported countless quarrels between the two levels of government, with the Parti Québécois government consistently arguing that federal jurisdiction in the many domains that affect Quebec's well-being reduces the government of Quebec—and the collectivity it represents—to the role of passive dependent. Disputes were especially acrimonious in the domain of foreign affairs—a symbolically crucial arena in which nation-states interact. In questions of immigration and international aid, cooperation and cultural exchange, the provincial government has consistently tried to expand its dealings *as an independent government* with other national governments, while the federal government has tried to counter these efforts and to maintain the exclusiveness or primacy of its jurisdiction. Central to the provincial government's attitude is the idea that an autonomous nation must be free to conduct its own business with other national individuals. As one *indépendantiste* put it, "there are no colonies or provinces represented in the United Nations. It is only when we become independent that we will be able to communicate with other nations" (Bourgault, quoted in Lebel 1978: A12).

A Collection of Individuals

In addition to their use of the collective-individual metaphor, people sometimes speak of the nation as if it were a biological species or type. For example, in his monograph *Les Québécois,* Marcel Rioux set out to describe "l'homo quebecensis"—the "human specimen" found in Quebec (1974:3). And Fernand Dumont has written about the preservation of what he calls "the French-Canadian species":

> For the moment, there is still a French Canadian. He is difficult to isolate and define—slightly more so, no doubt, than the American or the Frenchman. But it is enough to travel in the Beauce or Charlevoix and even in certain sections of our big cities to recognize this singular being, and to feel one's own heart leap in that unmistakable way. Is there point in this curious variety of human fauna continuing to exist? (1974:37, 32)

These examples depict individuals as representative of a type. The type, or species, is the collectivity, the nation. If the nation is a species, then it is a natural entity whose boundaries can be fixed by a scientific description of its qualities. (However "difficult to isolate and define" he may be, the French Canadian is still "a singular being," a recognizable "variety.") The historian Groulx, in his preoccupation with the past, used this metaphor to fix once and for all the collective personality of the French-Canadian group. In one remarkable passage he explains that "God cannot form a race as He does an individual." God creates a human soul in an instant, but "the soul of a race" requires several human generations for its creation. Groulx goes on to describe the divinely orchestrated hardships unleashed against the first generations of French pioneers in America. The result: "soon a new set of traits is fixed, and a human type of superior essence begins to exist" (1919:175–76). The contemporary nationalist vision differs in two respects from this. First, the formative forces acting upon the nascent species are natural and historical, whereas for Groulx, God is the ultimate force, though He works through nature and history. Second, the process of evolution has not yet stopped, and the Québécois type will continue to develop. Nonetheless, contemporary nationalisms, like the clerical-conservative varieties, rely on the notion of a fixed national essence, though they add a developmental dimension not stressed by writers like Groulx. In other words, even when evolution is envisioned as ongoing, it is said to proceed on the basis of what has been fixed, once and for all, in the past.

Like the metaphor of the collective individual, the species metaphor facilitates the attribution of boundedness to the nation. Envisioned as a self-contained actor, the nation is bounded in terms of its autonomous will and unique personality. Envisioned as a species, it is bounded physically by the attributes that distinguish it from all others, and temporally by its endowment with an evolutionary "beginning." Moreover, both the collective individual and the national species have a history: a personal history or life cycle, in the one case, and a natural history of evolution in the other. In the second case, the emphasis on natural history implies adaptation: not only has *homo quebecensis* been formed by the influence of the New World environment; he has undergone in the course of this evolutionary process an adaptation that binds him indissolubly to the niche into which he has settled. Groulx calls this niche "the national milieu" and describes it as the geographical, historical, and cultural forces that have shaped the nation: "it creates a human variety, just as the soil and climate create biological varieties." And like a biological type, the human species can only survive in its environmental niche:

> For a people to change, impair, or revolutionize its national milieu would be the gravest of experiments, a supreme risk. Literally it means pushing back the current of its heredity and trying to forge for itself a new soul. Such an enterprise cannot go on without an upheaval of the innermost being, without infallibly creating a long period of spiritual instability. Melancholy fate of the adult tree violently transplanted in a new soil and condemned to

vegetate there in expectation of the final withering!
(1937:178)

Thus far we have seen that the species metaphor implies a set of attributes similar to those suggested by the metaphor of the collective individual. The collectivity envisioned as a species or as an individual organism has fixed boundaries, describable qualities, and an environment and history which have made it what it is. However, the species metaphor suggests one further "fact" about the nation, a fact of the greatest importance. If the nation is a species, the individuals who compose it are all characterized by the same specific qualities. They are equivalent to one another, and to the generic type. When Fernand Dumont speaks of the French Canadian, he refers at once to a type and to examples of the type—to those individuals encountered in the Beauce or Charlevoix who, in their particularities, exemplify the French-Canadian species. Thus human differentiation occurs first of all at the level of collectivities: human nations are so many varieties of the human race; individual persons are equivalent in their particularities to their type or nation, and belong to the universal race only by virtue of their national particularities. Just as the collective-individual metaphor establishes the nation as one individual among the many who make up humanity, the species metaphor sets up nations as the particularized forms into which humanity is differentiated.

This fundamental equivalence of the human individual and the national species is strikingly described in *L'Appel de la race*. Groulx's novel, controversial in its time, describes the reconversion of a French-Canadian lawyer who, as a result of his marriage to an English Canadian and his English life style in Ottawa, finds himself in danger of losing his French-Canadian nationality. In the following passage the lawyer's priest and spiritual mentor explains why his protégé has felt the need to return to his roots:

> Personality—psychological, moral, the true one—cannot be composite, made up of disparate pieces. Its nature, its law, is unity. Heterogeneous layers may affix and adapt themselves to it for a time. But an inner principle, an incoercible force, pushes a human being to become uniquely itself, just as the same law leads the maple to be nothing other than the maple, the eagle nothing other than the eagle. (1922:110)

Just as an individual maple tree or eagle can become nothing other than a fully formed example of the species, a human individual must become "uniquely itself." But to be "itself" in the context of this novel means to be French Canadian: in other words, the human individual becomes itself only insofar as it represents the generic type.

Recent nationalist rhetoric again implies the equivalence of individual and group. There is an easy transition between "a Québécois," "we the Québécois," and the "Québécois nation." For example, René Lévesque's statement of national identity, quoted at the beginning of this chapter, begins in the plural: "We are *Québécois.*" To be ourselves, he argues, is "a matter of keeping and developing a personality that has survived for three and a half centuries." The metaphor of personality personifies the plural reference—"we" has become a collective individual. And throughout the passage Lévesque implies the equivalence of individual persons and the group by fixing his focus for a phrase upon the single individual, then upon a collection of individuals, and still later upon the collective individual: "We are children of that society. . . ." "All these things lie at the core of this personality of ours. Anyone who does not feel it . . . is not . . . one of us."

Lévesque's "to live as ourselves" and Groulx's "to become uniquely itself" both suggest the naturalization of culture. If the significant particularities of individual human beings are those which define them as members of a given subgroup of the human race; and if this subgroup is itself envisioned as a natural entity, a species "fixed" by a process of evolutionary adaptation; then the particularizing attributes of individual human beings are precisely those which characterize the collectivity as a natural entity. In other words, since each Québécois individual is equivalent to the Québécois species, it is to be expected that those cultural (in the anthropological sense) attributes which define the national species as a natural entity should appear in individual human beings as natural traits. As Groulx and Lévesque proclaim, Québécois have no choice but to be what they naturally are.

We have now come full circle. I began this chapter by explicating individual statements of what makes a person Québécois. They agreed on two criteria: land and culture, or residence in the national territory and common code for conduct. Moreover, culture—like land—was viewed naturalistically, either as a function of birth or of "Latin blood." When we examined representations of the group, we found two dominant metaphors. The metaphor of the collective individual facilitates the attribution of will, choice, and the ability to act to the nation. The metaphor of the national species equates individual and group and suggests as well that all individual members of the group share an essential character. Furthermore, the notion of the national species implies that the distinguishing cultural traits of individual persons are precisely those traits which define the collective species as a natural entity. Finally, both metaphors endow the nation with uniqueness and a continuous life. Like a willing, acting individual, the nation is precisely defined in relation to the world; its boundaries are evident, as are its autonomy and integrity. Like a biological species, the nation is composed of many individuals, each of whom shares certain fundamental (natural) characteristics which bind him to his kind and distinguish him from all who are not of his kind—just as the national type is itself distinguished from all other national types. And both the national species and the supra-individual actor possess a history that has been uninterrupted since the birth of the nation. Thus these conceptions of the nation and its members privilege boundedness, continuity, and homogeneity as central to a healthy national existence. Yet precisely because these metaphors draw the boundaries of national existence so sharply, they invite people to speculate about what is *not* included in national life as well as what is. As I learned during the 1976 elections, the "positive vision" of national affirmation is invariably accompanied by a "negative vision" of assimilation and death.

The Negative Vision: Pollution and Death

From the nationalist point of view—that is, from a point of view that constructs history as a function of bounded national entities—the force and influence of four larger nations have weighed decisively upon French Canada and Quebec: depending upon the era and context, France, Great Britain, English Canada, and the United States have loomed as powers in opposition to which the nation has had to struggle to maintain its identity. These incarnations of "not-Quebec" complement the positive vision of a Québécois nation endowed with definite political, cultural, and historical boundaries. Given this cruel linkage of Quebec and not-Quebec, and the assessment of relative strength that goes with it, it is not surprising that Québécois nationalists fear the political, economic, and cultural pressure that not-Quebec can exert. Concern for this overwhelming influence is a theme so prevalent in nationalist discourse that one can speak without exaggeration of a pervasive fear of pollution and contamination—metaphors frequently used by the nationalists themselves. Thus we find a negative vision of national disintegration and death inevitably accompanying the positive vision of national affirmation. As Mary Douglas has suggested, "pollution is a type of danger which is not likely to occur except where the lines of structure, cosmic or social, are clearly defined" (1966:113). Or, as André J. Belanger has put it, writing of Quebec nationalism of the 1930s, "whoever devotes himself to the defense of order will inevitably attend only to disorder" (1974:58).

As we have seen, Abbé Groulx looks above all to the past in his discussions of the French-Canadian nation. A handful of French colonists, worked upon by New World environment and history, became the French-Canadian nation, an entity whose essential characteristics have been unalterable since the period of their fixation. Indeed, to alter those characteristics would be to change the nation beyond recognition, that is, to destroy it: "and do we not know that peoples begin to die the day they cease to be the same expression of history?" (1917:36). For Groulx, there are several ways in which a people can "cease to be the same"—that is, several sources of corruption and dissolution. Each involves the incorporation of some "unassimilable" element into the fabric of the national being: "it is the same for a people as for any living being: he who introduces into his life an unassimilable element inoculates himself with a source of death" (ibid.:39). Such foreign elements can be material or spiritual, and Groulx warns against the mixture of blood through exogamous marriages as well as the moral evils of Anglo-Saxon individualism and materialism, the virus of American civilization, and foreign ideologies such as communism (1952: 2: 218; 4:200, 216). "For us," he wrote, "what is it to live if it is not in the first place to forbid ourselves the doctrines and works of death?" To do this, he continued, is nothing more than an "elementary measure of moral hygiene" (1935:23).

Yet how, more specifically, does the ingestion of foreign elements lead to disintegration and death? Consider the effects of mixed marriage in Groulx's novel, *L'Appel de la race*. First, the protagonist and his wife are shown to be incompatible because their most profound attitudes, dictated by racial instincts, clash; what is lacking, according to the narrator, are those "perfect spiritual affinities, those identical, connatural ways of thinking and feeling" (1922:128). Second, their children suffer from intellectual "imprecision" (130), a defect that one daughter overcomes by relearning French: "as I refrenchify myself, I think more clearly and discriminate more finely" (125). In the case of the children we have, not the ingestion of foreign elements, but a mixture of two distinct categories that must be inferior to untainted specimens of either. However, from a broader perspective the protagonist's family, which ought to have been completely French-Canadian, is seen to be corrupted—and it is implied that such a family, as a tainted element of the wider society, will in turn pollute the collectivity.

The notion of imprecision is crucial. Children who are both French and English are neither and nothing at all. Similarly, a nation that abandons its natural culture and tries to assimilate ways of acting and thinking incompatible with its "essence" will lose its identity and, ultimately, disappear. There is no place for imprecision, for mixture, for hazily defined boundaries. An individual is either French-Canadian or he is not, and the French-Canadian nation will either survive integrally or it will not survive at all: "there is no longer a place for the 30 or 50 percent French Canadian; only one French Canadian has a chance to survive: the 100 percent French Canadian" (1935:236–37).

In more recent versions of nationalist doctrine we find the same intolerance of imprecision and unwillingness to accept the conjunction of inviolable categories. Contamination by ideologies antagonistic to Catholicism is no longer the major issue it was for Groulx, and the idea of the pollution of the race through intermarriage has lost the biologic significance it once had. On the other hand, mixed marriages are still feared as harbingers of linguistic assimilation. And for modern nationalists, as for their predecessors, the perception of ongoing political, cultural, and linguistic assimilation gives rise to major fears. American culture and the English language are sometimes seen as irresistible in their power to seduce individuals away from their natal traditions and to invade the national territory itself, corrupting the Québécois people against their will. Furthermore, *indépendantistes* believe that continued adherence to the Canadian Confederation constitutes a compromise of the collective self that carries the same implications for annihilation as cultural and linguistic assimilation, and even federalists are not unaware of such dangers. With respect to all these issues, what is feared is a dilution and eventual loss of national identity, a negation of boundaries and distinctions and, in the end, the disappearance of the Québécois nation. The crucial axiom is always the same: an individual, human or collective, cannot be two things at once. To divide one's allegiance, affiliation, or identity is to court disaster.

We saw above that adherence to Confederation is imagined by some to obstruct the exercise of choice and autonomy on the part of the nation. To abdicate, even partially, national responsibilities in political matters leads to the loss of national selfhood, or, at the very least, to the maintenance of the national individual in a situation of permanent childhood or dependence. At the worst, the continued political conjunction of the Québécois and Canadian nations must lead to changes in the essence of the former and perhaps to its total absorption by the latter. As one person explained, "Confederation itself has an identity, and we can't adhere to it without changing our own national character." This reasoning is thought to apply even more inevitably with regard to individual human beings. Several nationalists told me that a person could not feel two patriotic attachments at once; Canadian and Québécois patriotism are mutually exclusive, and individuals will have to choose one or the other. And this is the key assumption that Québécois federalists do not accept: though they agree with the nationalist vision of collective affirmation and maturity and support measures to protect and encourage Québécois culture, they do not conclude that loyalty to Canada contradicts their feelings for Quebec. As people argued during the referendum, "why can't we be both Canadian and Québécois?"

In contrast to the lack of agreement concerning the consequences of the current political arrangement, most nationalists—

indépendantistes as well as federalists—are sensitive to the perceived threat of cultural assimilation. At the center of the negative vision is the assumption that an authentically Québécois culture which existed in the past has come under attack from outside cultural forces. Authentic culture, the culture of the past, is seen as the original product of a distinctive people, conceived and chosen by those who lived it. The evolution of this culture was a natural process, a manifestation of the essence of collective life. In recent times, however, Quebec has become industrialized and urbanized according to patterns designed, financed, and executed from outside; these processes have been accompanied by the rise of mass media. These forces together have led to a breakdown in traditional social and cultural forms, and their partial replacement by a seemingly omnipotent "mass culture" which levels all that stands in its way. Thus from the perspective of the negative vision, the original, authentic culture of the ancestors has been replaced by an imported and standardized culture, and a people who once created its culture now only consumes the culture of others. But creation involves the exercise of choice and the assertion of self—indeed, the projection of self into external forms. By contrast, mere consumption of the other's creations reduces the consumer to passivity and becomes a form of alienation. This is true for individual human beings and, above all, for the collective individual, which will not survive if it lives only upon the products—words, ideas, and values, as well as material goods—of others.

Summary: Salient Presuppositions of Nationalist Ideology

The following chapters explore some of the efforts of cultural-affairs activists to protect Quebec from cultural pollution and to promote national cultural development. In examining cultural policies and the politics of Québécois culture I will elaborate the interpretation of nationalist ideology begun in this chapter. But before continuing, let me summarize what has been provisionally established.

1. Nationalism is an ideology of individuated being. It is thus a variety of Western individualism, the dominant, encompassing ideology of modern societies. A living individual is one, precisely delineated with reference to a spatial and temporal environment. In other words, it is bounded in space, continuous in time, and homogeneous within those spatiotemporal boundaries. Metaphors of the collective individual and national species establish the individuated being of the Québécois nation. The belief that human individuals are

Québécois uniquely and in their "essence" aligns human individuality with the collective individuality of the nation.

2. In modern ideology, individuated being is defined in terms of choice and property. Modern individualism is above all "possessive individualism" (Macpherson 1962; Dumont 1977). Individuals demonstrate their being, their individuality, through choice; choice is the creative manifestation of self, the imposition of self onto the external world. Property is what results from choices—products that exist in the external world yet remain linked through proprietorship to the self that created them. Thus the nation and its members "have" a culture, the existence of which both follows from and proves the existence of the nation itself. To lose one's culture, or to abdicate responsibility for cultural creation and autonomous choice, is to renounce life itself.

However, choice and creativity are not only proof of being, they are, or should be, a function of it as well. People cannot choose their national essence; they cannot choose what they naturally are. Moreover, people's choices and creations should respect, or follow from, this natural identity. Above all, the collective individual must be free to make its own choices and create its own life, for only the nation can know what is most in accord with its character and being.

To be Québécois is to act/choose/create Québécois, and to act/choose/create Québécois comes naturally to those who are Québécois.

3. The content of national being is national "character," "personality," "culture," and "history." Yet in nationalist ideology, these are subordinate to individuated being, which is the primary reality. In other words, the existence of a bounded entity is central, whereas the cultural content within those bounds comes after the fact. The existence of a national entity is a primary assumption of nationalist ideology, rarely questioned; but the content of national being is the subject of continual negotiation and dispute.

4. The national individual has a natural reality; its existence is that of a natural thing. It has an essence that has been fixed by natural processes, and it cannot change this essence without becoming something else, some other thing.

5. National being is perpetually threatened. To define existence in terms of boundedness and autonomy simultaneously defines the rest of reality as "other" and sets up an adversary relationship: the nation either controls its destiny or is controlled by others. Positive visions of national life and affirmation are inevitably complemented by negative visions of pollution and annihilation.

The next chapter sketches aspects of a long tradition of cultural objectification aimed at discovering the "folk" foundations of Quebec national culture. In it we confront the paradox that self-conscious attempts to preserve culture inevitably change it.

51

CHAPTER THREE

In Search of the Folk Society:
Folk Life, Folklore Studies,
and the Creation of Tradition

I spent Christmas 1977 with the Lauriers, a farm family in Beauce county, south of Quebec City. That was my first visit under the auspices of Vacances-Familles, one of several organizations established to foster tourism in rural Quebec. Vacances-Familles recruits families across the province to provide room and board for tourists, particularly for families of modest means who wish to see Quebec. I found Vacances-Familles to be a useful tool for a field worker. It also provides us with an initial example of the institutionalization of cultural objectification. Organizations like Vacances-Familles direct city dwellers to country folk, middle-class white-collar families to small farmers, intellectuals to "natural" Québécois. It caters to those in search of their roots, or to those who want their children to experience country life as they imagine their grandparents had experienced it. At the same time Vacances-Familles inevitably changes the lives of the host families it employs.

During my months in Quebec I stayed with several Vacances-Familles families in the Beauce, the Eastern Townships (or *l'Estrie,* the rural area east and south of Montreal), on the Gaspé Peninsula and in Kamouraska County (upriver from the Gaspé, on the south shore of the Saint Lawrence). In each case I found people whose lives had become the object of a new kind of attention. These families differed in their degree of awareness of their new popularity, and in the degree to which these new interpretations of their life had influenced the way in which they looked at themselves. I consistently came away with an impression of people who still followed certain "traditional" practices unconsciously, but who would soon come to realize that their lives are indeed "folklore."

The Vacances-Familles program can have an important economic impact on its host families. Two families that I visited whose farming operations seemed impoverished, functioning at little more than subsistence level, had come to depend on Vacances-Familles income to make ends comfortably meet. One woman explained that tourism was now her main occupation, and that thanks to Vacances-Familles she no longer had to work with her husband on the farm. Indeed, tourism has become a business for Vacances-Familles families, for both planning and paperwork are necessary. Families not only must meet the standards of the organization as to cleanliness and general suitability; they must be able to accommodate their daily routine to the demands of a new schedule. Several hostesses showed me long lists of guest reservations, explaining that they had to calculate carefully the number of visitors that they could handle at various times. "In one respect it's like a hotel," one woman remarked. "There are no excuses for not having clean sheets." Other families, somewhat better off, participated in Vacances-Familles because they enjoyed having company. But for them too the extra income was a windfall that made luxuries possible or provided a financial cushion for retirement.

During my first Vacances-Familles experiences I was puzzled by the interpersonal dynamics of the situation. Host families treated visitors almost as members of the family, yet also ignored them in an unfamilial way. Family life went on around us, and we were free either to observe or to participate. One visitor claimed that the tradition of large families among French Canadians made it natural for host families to include extras at the table and in their houses. And one hostess, who had desired but not had a large family, said that a houseful of guests was just as good as having a large family. In general we were made to feel neither like mere boarders nor like privileged guests. Some families used the term *vacancier* in introducing us to their neighbors—"these are my *vacanciers.*" I felt that the term conferred quasi-kin status upon us, allowing our inclusion in community activities yet establishing a comfortable distance between local folk and ourselves.

The quasi-kin status granted *vacanciers* suggests the relatively unselfconscious understanding that host families have of their role in touristic encounters. They are certainly aware that tourists interpret their lives as folkloric manifestations of true Québécois culture, yet they did not generally rearrange their routines in order to demonstrate their authenticity or to treat us to the folklore we had come to see. Rather, we were included simply and artlessly as *vacanciers,* as temporary household residents who had the right to participate in local activities were we so inclined. Several families told me of the excitement that some *vacanciers* had shown upon discovering some functional folkloric implement or practice, but they seemed unaffected by it. Rarely did I find people who suddenly felt the need to make an effort to keep up established practices in order to cater to tourists. On the other hand, host families were gradually becoming aware of the value of their folklore. Several people claimed that only recently had they learned from the remarks of *vacanciers* how valuable some of their old furniture might be. Others had begun to see their homemade bread as "natural" and their kitchen gardens as evidence of pastoral purity. Most continued to follow routines in an unreflective manner, but some were beginning to feel that it was important to continue them and to make new efforts to ensure the survival of what might have been in the process of falling by the way.

In rural, Catholic Quebec Christmas Eve is celebrated with a *réveillon,* a supper party that begins after Midnight Mass and continues into the night. Because the Lauriers had had to attend a wedding reception on Christmas Eve, they held their *réveillon* on Christmas night. Most of the children of the family, with their spouses and children, had come home for Christmas and the *réveillon,* some having made lengthy voyages to attend. In addition to these people M. Laurier's parents and siblings attended, as well as their children and families. (The wedding reception of Christmas Eve had been an affair of our hostess's family. As one would expect, the Lauriers calculated their holiday socializing to satisfy a range of overlapping social obligations.)

The revelers began to arrive in mid-evening, and soon filled the small farmhouse. In addition to chatting and renewing old relationships, people played cards and *pichenette* (a table game resembling pool, in which small wooden disks are shot with the finger or with a small stick into net pockets.) The main activities of the evening, however, were dancing and feasting. We had been given to understand that our host and his brother were among the finest dancers in a locality noted for its folk dancing. Once the guests had arrived, our host brought out his harmonica, put on a pair of shoes with taps, and installed himself in a corner of the kitchen. He tried out various bits of reels and *gigues,* accompanying himself by jigging in his seat, as it were, a technique that produces a vigorous, irresistible rhythm. As M. Laurier warmed up, four couples gathered in the kitchen for a *danse carrée* (square dance). Their initial attempt showed them to be rusty, for the square broke down several times until those who best knew the dance took it upon themselves to instruct the others. After this rehearsal the square went on without difficulty, for the dances are repetitive and easily relearned. Mme Laurier then organized another square in order to accommodate those of her *vacanciers,* myself and my wife included, who had expressed a desire to dance a *danse carrée.*

After these squares Mme Laurier sent her youngest son to the basement to fetch a large piece of linoleum, which she placed in the center of the dancing area. As M. Laurier continued to play, several of the younger women began to *gigue* in a tentative fashion. A second pair of shoes with taps was brought out, and M. Laurier's brother put them on. We then gathered round to watch and applaud a real *gigue*. After this the young women soloed each in turn, but seemingly against their will. Those who had already danced forced the shoes, now lined with wool slippers for the smaller female feet, on those whose turn had come. The victim offered half-serious resistance but eventually yielded and performed amid much applause and good cheer. M. Laurier, considered to be the finest dancer, was the last to dance, and while he did his brother played the harmonica and stamped out the rhythm. His performance excited much admiration, but also brought the dancing to an end. He then took up his harmonica and returned to his corner, continuing to play *gigues* with a wistful look, as if he wanted the dancing to go on all night. The abandoned dance floor was now filled by several of the youngest children, who hopped and danced to the music with much glee. One little girl, perhaps seven years old, seemed almost to *gigue* in the true style, balancing with her arms away from her body and displaying complete mastery of the tricky rhythm. Though none of the other adults paid much attention, M. Laurier was willing to play as long as the children danced.[1]

After the dancing of the *gigue* the women enlisted some of the boys to clear a new space for the meal. But at 11:30 Mme Laurier directed everyone's attention to the television, which, to my surprise, was now tuned to the CBC (English-language) channel. As part of a special Christmas edition of the late news, the network was reporting about Christmas tradition in the Beauce, and the featured performers were the Lauriers and their neighbors. Mme Laurier explained that two weeks earlier a television crew from the city had come and they had staged a complete *réveillon,* with dancing and supper, for the cameras. Thus we found ourselves interrupting an ongoing celebration to watch a recorded version, narrated in English, in which that night's celebrants performed dances and festivities which they were in the very act of doing. Everyone gathered round the television, eager to catch glimpses of those they knew. Then it was over as suddenly as it had started, and people quickly forgot about it and resumed the festivities.

This juxtaposition of "live" and recorded folklore suggests a transition between unconscious lifeways and objectified "tradition." The Lauriers have lived all their lives in a quaint rural area said to be characterized by the fact that its "folklore has remained tied to daily life," as one government traveler's guide puts it (MTCP 1978:109). M. Laurier, one of the best dancers in the area, has danced and played

---

1. Doyon (1950:174) has given a similar account of dancing the *gigue* in Beauce County based on observations made in the 1940s. She mentions in particular the individual, competitive nature of the *gigue.*

harmonica all his life. He learned it as he grew up, just as the children at the *réveillon* would learn to jig to the music of M. Laurier. Midnight Mass and the *réveillon* with its square dances, jigs, and late supper are part of a round of Christmas events that the Lauriers have followed for many years. Their kitchen dances are the same dances that I saw staged half-a-dozen times in folklore shows such as that of the hockey rink; "the same" except, of course, that the Lauriers' dances are not normally staged for public audiences.

Yet by the time of my visit the Lauriers had already been asked to re-create their dances and *réveillon* for a television audience, and I saw them interrupt an ongoing ceremony in order to watch the recorded version of it. At the time I felt that they did this with no self-consciousness. The program over, the women had immediately returned to their cooking, the young men to their cards, and M. Laurier to his harmonica. Yet if the Lauriers were able to take their television appearance in stride, the incident nonetheless points to the existence of new interpretations of established routines. The Lauriers are beginning to witness, unknowingly perhaps, the objectification of aspects of their culture. The most glaring example of this was the recorded ceremony within the live one. But beyond that, there was the presence of us *vacanciers*—an anthropologist as well as a Montreal nationalist consciously exploring what he called his "cultural milieu." And, perhaps, there was the beginning of a feeling that the *réveillon* was traditional and, as such, worthy of being preserved. For example, Mme Laurier had requested that Vacances-Familles bill us an additional charge for the *réveillon*. This was ostensibly to cover the cost of an extra meal, but it also indicates an awareness on the part of Mme Laurier of the value of their *réveillon* as a tourist attraction. Furthermore, during the *danses carrées* Mme Laurier made a special effort to recruit couples for the square, though some people expressed a great deal of reluctance to dance.

The process of cultural objectification that has begun to influence the Lauriers' domestic amusements may lead to changes in the significance, as well as in the formal properties, of their dancing and celebrations. The intensity of this influence was perhaps peculiar to the time of my field work, when heightened nationalist concern for traditional culture was magnified by all the techniques of electronic mass media. But cultural objectification has been a part of the life of rural Quebec for much longer than words like "tradition" and "folklore" imply. In the remainder of this chapter I examine, first, some of the changes in forms of entertainment that Québécois interlocutors reconstructed for me, and, second, material suggesting that such changes have a longer history than one might imagine. Ultimately I shall suggest that the attempt to objectify folk dance forms as traditional culture is an important element in a long tradition of change.

Remembered Changes in Folk Dancing and Family Parties

Once I became intrigued by the objectification of folk dancing, I began to question older Québécois, particularly those who had experienced rural life, about the customs of their youth. They explained that "in the old days" dancing took place regularly in the home. One Kamouraska farmer and musician told me that after work on Saturday if people felt the urge to dance, something would have been immediately arranged. Four musicians lived in the neighborhood, including himself and his brother (who played, respectively, guitar and accordion). Music was thus always at hand, and in addition there was always someone to provide the space and refreshments for a party. In those days people made their own liquor, including beer and blueberry wine. This would be served to the revelers, though only the musicians were allowed more than two glasses (they needed it for their work). People danced long into the night and, best of all, "ça coutait pas un sou"—it didn't cost a penny. An elderly woman from Sherbrooke spoke also of dancing in the home, though the details that she gave were different:

> We danced in the evening on Tuesdays, Thursdays, Saturdays, and Sundays. The boys came to visit the girls and court, and we danced right in the home, with our parents sitting there watching. However, in those days dancing was a sin, and we never would have danced on Mondays, Wednesdays, and Fridays. Even so, when we went to confession and the priest asked us if we had committed any sins, we would say "Yes, we've danced." And then he would say, "Well, don't do it any more," and we'd say that we'd try our best. But we always ended up dancing again.[2]

In those bygone days—within the memory of middle-aged and elderly interlocutors at the time of my field work—dancing in the home was a regular, informal event. These same people described, sometimes with a touch of sadness, the changes in family life that have occurred since that time. They spoke of the demise of family solidarity and the rise of individualism, a set of phenomena that the historian Groulx, as well as such sociologists as Miner (1939) and Hughes (1943), had noticed several decades ago. For Groulx this trend

2. In her monograph on the traditional civilization of Ste-Brigitte de Laval, Sister Marie-Ursule (1951:119) mentions that the young men went courting on Sundays and on "les bons soirs" during the week—Tuesdays, Thursdays, and Saturdays. The opposition of the clergy to dancing has been remarked by Gérin (1898:191), Barbeau (1920:87), and Miner (1939:161).

indicated the pernicious influence of "Anglo-Saxon" materialism which, if unchecked, would lead to the destruction of French-Canadian culture (1952; vol. 4, pp. 197–200). Miner likewise cast a cold eye upon such developments, though his disapproval stemmed not from nationalistic sentiment but from his attempt to see Quebec as a "folk society."

My use of such terms as "traditional," "folklore," "custom," and even "established routines" and "change," follows native usage and is not meant to suggest that I too see earlier phases of French-Canadian social history in terms of a timelessness and integrity that have since been disrupted. All evidence indicates that family life has changed greatly during the past hundred years; in this my observations and the opinions of my interlocutors agree with those of Groulx, Hughes, and Miner. Yet, as M. E. Smith has argued (1982), social life never literally repeats itself. All aspects of social life are constantly changing, and rather than presume a baseline of stability in order to study change, social scientists ought to explore those differential conditions under which "natives" (and, I would add, observers) will perceive social reality to be changing or stable. Seen from this perspective, those outmoded practices that people remember should not be taken as the starting point in a process of change—for some of what seems traditional today would have been seen, in traditional times, as new. In other words, in the present-day context certain social forms have been interpreted as traditional and folkloric, and in the analysis that follows I will be concerned with these cultural interpretations of tradition rather than an objectively ascertainable traditionality. In no way do I wish to imply that those social practices which appear traditional or "old" are the last remnants of a timeless folk culture.

All people that I questioned described the same manifestations of change with respect to folk dancing and sociability, as well as correlative changes in family life. First, the spontaneous, informal parties among kin and neighbors gave way to dancing and socializing outside the home. Local dance halls and hotels became the scene of Saturday-night parties. Gatherings intended strictly for members of an extended family were organized on a less spontaneous and more formal basis. My interlocutors invariably remarked that people began to rent halls for family reunions. Second, family life and the quality of kinship ties changed as the urbanization and industrialization of Quebec brought with it a great increase in individual mobility. Young and old agree that today youth has much more independence than children had one or two generations ago. Younger people feel less bound by what they perceive as traditional forms of kinship solidarity—though those who see folklore as crucial to national identity advocate in principle a return to traditional solidarities.

As folk dancing and socializing moved out of the home to public settings, several important changes occurred. In addition to the older squares, quadrilles, and cotillions, people danced waltzes, fox-trots, and other dances of the big-band era. Learning to dance was no longer strictly a matter of unplanned imitation in a family context. The new ballroom dances had to be taught more methodically, and dance instructors appeared. One woman explained that square dances still are learned in the home during childhood, but that in recent years people in her area have had an instructor come once a year to teach other dances.

A more significant change involved the clientele for traditional dancing. According to several Québécois, public dance halls were at first frequented by entire families: "Whole families, kids and all, went to the Saturday-night village dances. Mothers would nurse their babies right there in the dance hall." But by the 1960s only the older generations continued to attend these Saturday-night village dances to enjoy the "old dances." Teen-agers, accustomed to more freedom, became less willing to participate with their parents in community recreation. At the same time their interest shifted from traditional dances to currently popular music and dance forms. One woman told me that it was the generation after her own—those who were between 25 and 35 years in 1978—that gave up traditional dancing. Many people claimed that their children had learned the old dances but then forgot them as they grew up and became interested in contemporary dances. Among some families with whom I visited only younger children accompanied parents to village dances, whereas most teen-agers indulged in disco dancing. In other families even the elder folk have stopped attending local dances. "We used to dance the squares and quadrilles, but we haven't gone for a number of years now. There are still some dance halls in the area, but it just isn't the thing to do anymore." In sum, according to all accounts that I gathered from rural folk or people with rural backgrounds, traditional dancing became increasingly rare during the 1960s and 1970s, and in some places all but disappeared.[3]

As people reflected upon these changes they expressed a sense of loss with respect to the spontaneous family parties that they remembered from their youth. The contrasted the unselfish hospi-

3. The obvious reasons for the emancipation of young people are the rapid postwar expansion of economic opportunity and a money economy and, later, during the 1960s, the educational reorganization that established large consolidated school districts. In his 1949 re-study of St. Denis, Miner had already noticed changes in the quality of intergenerational relationships, which he attributed to the "glow of economic expansion" (1963:268–69). In a re-study of Gérin's St. Justin, Garigue noticed similar changes (1958:35–37). My interlocutors invariably stressed the importance of the demise of the local *école de rang* and the rise of the consolidated school district; children who, from an early age, commuted to school soon grew accustomed to a large dose of independence. For a more recent assessment of changes in family structures and roles, see Caldwell (1976).

tality of the past with the current situation in which entertainment has become a business. They complained that today it is prohibitively expensive to hire musicians, and expressed even greater dismay at the recent practice of hiring public halls for family parties. Some people explained this as the result of family size, arguing that extended families have become too large to gather in a private home. Others suggested that people are no longer willing to do the hard work necessary to host such large gatherings, and that the considerable expense involved presents another obstacle.

Most important, however, in my interlocutors' interpretation of the demise of traditional family gatherings is what they saw as the changing quality of kin ties. Not only are younger people unwilling to do the work connected with large parties; they also see family parties in terms of obligation and constraint. Several of my friends who had left rural homes to study or work in Quebec City expressed this in terms of the notion of choice. For their parents, kin ties imply an "axiom of amity," to use Fortes's lovely phrase (1969). One has obligations towards, and owes allegiance to, *all* who are recognized as kin. Personal preference has no place here. Yet, according to these younger interlocutors, an individual ought to have the right to choose, on the basis of personal compatibility, those of his relatives that he will frequent, just as he should be able to choose not to frequent those he dislikes. This philosophy was seen to be contrary to that of older generations: "My mother doesn't understand why I like Mathieu and detest Luc. She sees that it's so, but says that I ought to love them equally because they're both my cousins." These interlocutors contrasted kinship and friendship on the basis of this element of choice, claiming that in their own kin relationships they tried to appeal to choice, to the personal element, in a way that their parents would never have done. At the same time they claimed to overlook distinctions that their parents applied:

> My parents treat certain relatives, like my Aunt Orpha's child by a previous marriage, as being not on the same level as the others. Or my cousin Pierre—they don't say "Pierre," they say instead "Dorvil's adopted boy." But I find that pejorative. I never say that, I say "Pierre," period. I don't see the need to do that. For me, they are children, period.

In either case the treatment of relatives according to criteria of kinship categorization is to be rejected in favor of treatment appropriate to a particular personal relationship, freely chosen or refused.

These values influence attitudes towards family parties. Some younger Québécois claimed that such parties were anathema to them because they disliked most of the people who attended. Others simply said that parents and, especially, grandparents valued family gatherings more highly than did children. According to one group of three sisters (all university students), the supreme social value for their father (a farmer) is the family. For him traditional social activities such as the *réveillon* belong in a familial setting. It is important to gather together the family at certain times and, for their father, this means all the family. Their distinction between relatives they like and those they dislike is not acceptable to him. However, the sisters pointed out that their father's siblings did not accord family traditions the same importance, and that had their father not acted as an upholder of tradition, many family functions might have been abandoned. They also felt that their attitude differed from both their father's and that of his siblings:

> *Would you say that kin relationships have become*
> *less important to you?*
> *Yes, I'd say so. For us it's more folkloric. We'll get together*
> *during the holiday season for big meals and* veillées
> *[evening parties]. But it's more folkloric. It's practically an*
> *obligation, because at holiday time you* have to *see the*
> *relatives. Though, of course, it's pleasant.*

> *Can you explain your use of "folkloric" and*
> *"obligation" in reference to the same phenomena?*
> *It's both at the same time. Folkloric in the sense that,*
> because *it's traditional we go see grandfather at Christmas.*
> *And it's for that reason that we all get together—because*
> *it's always been done and we're going to continue to do it.*

> *Is it like that for your parents as well?*
> *Oh no! For my parents it's* living. *They visit their brothers*
> *and sisters and parents regularly, and wouldn't think of*
> *doing otherwise.*

Values and interpretations such as these suggest a displacement and self-awareness that I have called cultural objectification. In contrast to their parents, who unquestioningly live certain established practices, these young women, having removed themselves from their natal milieu, now look back at it and interpret it as folkloric and traditional. This is not to say that they are not moved by a sense of loyalty and feelings of love towards their family. Yet their reasons for wishing to continue family customs differ from those of their parents. The young people have objectified those customs as "tradition" and believe that because they are traditional they are to be valued and preserved.

In general, then, we might posit the following sequence in a hypothetical history of popular amusements in rural Quebec. Several decades ago dancing took place in the home, as relatives and neighbors gathered at a moment's notice for an informal dance. There were usually a few musicians in the neighborhood and neither music nor refreshments had to be bought. As the rural society that my interlocutors knew continued to change, particularly after the 1930s, new settings for dancing and socializing appeared, as did new forms of dancing and styles of music. Dances in public halls continued at first as family affairs, but as younger members of the rural family became more independent, old-style dances became more and more an affair of the elders. At the same time, families began to plan large-scale gatherings and reunions on a more formal basis, renting public halls and hiring musicians for the occasion.

This sequence, pieced together from discussions with Québécois in the late 1970s, fits well with material recorded by Marcel Rioux in a Gaspésian village during the early 1950s. As in St. Denis at this time (Miner 1963), post-war economic expansion brought new forms of recreation and leisure to Belle-Anse. According to Rioux (1961:51–52), the villagers passed most of their leisure time gossiping and "doing nothing." Two restaurants, one with a pool table, provided the only "commercialized recreation" in the community, but even these were more familial than commercial in their ambiance, with villagers gathering there as if for a *veillée*. Rioux describes domestic *veillées* as spontaneous affairs: "People find themselves in a home and decide to have some fun; they dance, drink, and enjoy themselves." By contrast, organized gatherings—*veillées invitées*—were a new phenomenon that some villagers failed or refused to distinguish from their spontaneous parties:

> In the past and still today if there is a *veillée* somewhere everyone is invited—or, rather, everyone invites himself. One day I was asked . . . to a *veillée invitée* for the following Saturday night; we were to be only a dozen. A good sixty people came.

This anecdote suggests a transitional moment in the social history of Belle-Anse, when formal social gatherings began to replace spontaneous ones and established boundaries between private and public life began to be redrawn. According to the people I interviewed, this transition has continued in their villages in the same direction, as domestic *veillées* and even public Saturday-night dances have become increasingly rare since the early 1950s. New tastes in music, dance, and entertainment have continued to come into rural communities and, as in the past, residents have responded openly to the novelty, adopting exogenous amusements and abandoning older forms suddenly become unfashionable. Yet, as we shall see, this process of change is not new. *One can understand all moments in the social history of rural Quebec as transitional.* Furthermore, the continuity of change has been matched by an equally unbroken attempt to deny its reality. As some of the folk have gradually, continuously, and with little apparent resistance abandoned their folkways, others have labored to rediscover and preserve a folkloric Quebec. The attitude of the university students who have objectified the lives of their parents is suggestive in this regard. Certainly their attitude typifies recent changes in familial values in Quebec, and it might also represent a common intergenerational slippage, a (universal?) tendency to displace or objectify in memory what were once live and unexamined routines. But for our purposes this attitude is above all interesting as a small example of the search for folkloric authenticity that has been linked to French-Canadian nationalism for well over a century. Since at least the mid-nineteenth century professional and lay field workers—folklorists, ethnologists, sociologists—have gone among the people to record their folkways. Guided by a variety of ideological outlooks, almost always nationalistically tinged, they sought rural communities that they imagined to be isolated, authentic, and self-sufficient. Yet their very presence among the folk can be taken as one among several factors that belie the naiveté and changelessness so frequently attributed to rural life. Thus we can fairly ask: How has the pursuit of the folk society by folklorists and others led to the demise of the folk society—or, better, to the creation of traditions which, though imagined as authentic, are from our perspective objectifications of traditional culture, hence different from what they are believed by the objectifiers to be?

Quebec as a Folk Society

The idea of the folk society[4] has been seductive for Western thinkers since the eighteenth century at least. In the sociological tradition alone one can point to a number of famous dichotomies that embody it: Maine's status and contract, Durkheim's mechanical and organic solidarity, Tönnies' *gemeinschaft* and *gesellschaft,* and even Marx's analysis of town and country (cf. Nisbet 1965:19–28). For our purposes I want to examine that version of this theme that has been directly applied to the Quebec case: Robert Redfield's model of the folk society. Redfield (1947:295–301) described the folk society as small and isolated; its members have no contact with people from other groups, but are on intimate terms with one another. Status is ascribed, never achieved, and "behavior is personal, not impersonal."

4. Portions of this section and the next appeared previously, in somewhat different form, as "In Search of the Folk Society: Nationalism and Folklore Studies in Quebec" in *Culture* 3 (1):103–14 (1983).

In Search of the Folk Society

Though technology is not necessarily simple it is pre-industrial. The only division of labor is that based on sex roles, and the society is economically self-sustaining. Values in the folk society are integrated, behavior follows unquestioningly from values, and all aspects of life are relevant to one another and to the actors. There are no books, no sense of history, no cultivation of science and theology, for in the folk society tradition reigns supreme. It follows that there is no self-consciousness: "Behavior in the folk society is traditional, spontaneous, and uncritical," and "there is no objectivity and no systematization of knowledge."

Redfield was careful to point out that his folk society was an ideal-type, as was its logical opposite, the urban society. In the study of empirical societies Redfield used a third type, that of the peasant society, to analyze what he called "the rural dimension of old civilizations." Peasant societies are those whose members "control and cultivate their land for subsistence and as a part of a traditional way of life" (1967:20). The solidarity of peasant society is characterized by its "folklike inwardfacingness," yet unlike the folk society, it is not isolated. Between peasant society and the larger civilization there are "economic, political, and moral" relations (1953:33, 31). In particular, the "little tradition" of the peasant society is fed by, and in turn feeds into, the "great tradition" of the cities (1967:41–42). In sum, the peasant society partakes of both folk and urban society (1963:xv).

It was Redfield's student, Horace Miner, who first applied the notion of the folk society to Quebec in his study of a French-Canadian village. In the preface to *St. Denis* Miner (1939:ix) defined one of the goals of his study as "the ethnographic description of the old rural French-Canadian folk culture in its least-altered existent form." Miner (5) believed that a folk society had developed in New France, enduring there for well over a century until urbanization, industrialization, and its own structural weaknesses destroyed it in all but the rural corners of Quebec. St. Denis, he believed, had remained a folk community, but he knew that it was changing even as he sought to capture what remained of its "folk character." Miner (234) characterized the demise of the folk society in terms of the "increasing dependence of the local society upon the great industrial civilization of which it is becoming a part." The old self-sufficient isolation had been shattered, he argued, and the parishioners of St. Denis abandoned their folkways and replaced them with urban innovations.

This mix of old and new, and the important connections that linked St. Denis to the wider society, led Redfield to see Miner's material in terms of his own model of the peasant society. In the introduction to Miner's monograph (1939:xii–xix), Redfield described those aspects of St. Denis that were folklike and those that were urban. On the one hand the villagers had a folk culture characterized by an integrated value system and behavior in conformity to it. On the other hand they participated in a money economy, were literate, and had ties to the urban world. Neither Redfield nor Miner considered St. Denis to be typical of French Canada, for they realized that Quebec in the 1930s was already an industrialized society. But they did think of their village as representative of an older, more traditional Quebec, and saw it as a baseline for the study of "social change."

Many years after the publication of *St. Denis* a series of articles by Canadian scholars reexamined the utility of the folk-urban model for the study of Quebec. Philippe Garigue (1958:5–28) attacked the Redfield-Miner model, arguing that the Quebec countryside had never been more than an extension of the towns and, in particular, that an isolated, specifically rural culture had never existed in French Canada. Several of Garigue's colleagues counterattacked, justifying the vision of Quebec as a folk/peasant society (Guindon 1960; Rioux 1964). Though some statistical data were invoked in an exploratory fashion, the argument turned on the problem of whether such-and-such a social fact could be interpreted as a sign of rurality. For example, everybody agreed that the Catholic high tradition was one of the attributes that made Quebec a peasant society instead of a completely folk society. But Garigue (1958:22) argued further that the presence of the Church "reduced the particularism of rural communities" and maintained "cultural homogeneity" between town and country. The other side contended that the Church deliberately isolated its flock (to protect them from "Anglo-Saxon" values) and enforced the kind of homogeneous, sacred worldview typical of folk and peasant societies (Rioux 1964:170–72; cf. Redfield 1939:xvii).

One of the curious aspects of this controversy, unremarked by the participants, is that the folk/peasant society envisioned by Rioux and Guindon was not the folk society that Miner had in mind. As we saw, Miner (1939:286) looked back to New France to find a folk society, and when he wrote of its demise he chose 1800 as a significant date:

> The new elements, which have entered into the pattern of life since 1800, originate almost exclusively in the cities. They are the result of urbanization and industrialization. As these processes were largely due to English stimulus, many of the new elements are characteristic of English and American life.

Guindon and Rioux, however, located their folk/peasant society in the nineteenth century. In his reply to Garigue, Guindon (1960:534) tried to show "how it was that French Canada became a predominantly rural society at the end of the eighteenth century, and remained so throughout the nineteenth century." Rioux (1964:170) similarly argued that the folk society "reached its peak in French Canada" during the nineteenth century.[5]

This temporal transposition of the folk society derives from an important current of historical revisionism elaborated by Quebec historians and social scientists after World War II (Cook 1971:114–40). The revised history has become the history accepted by contemporary nationalists; the older history is that of the clerical-conservative nationalists. The older history looked to New France as a golden age, and saw the French-Canadian people as a rural race whose survival would depend upon its will to resist modern innovations. In the revised history the rurality of French Canada is seen to result from the Conquest. In this view New France had been not a peasant society, but a trading society. The Conquest "decapitated" this society by eliminating its nascent bourgeoisie; those French Canadians who survived and stayed on were forced to surrender economic and political control to the English. As a result, French Canadians isolated themselves in the rural hinterlands, while the conquerors dominated the colony from Montreal and Quebec City. Disastrous as these circumstances have been for the social evolution of Quebec, they entailed one compensating factor: the subsequent isolation of French Canada led to its survival and, beyond this, to its development as a unique nation. This has been explicitly argued by Rioux:

> Forced to isolate themselves in a rural milieu in order to survive—for the cities of Quebec and Montreal remained predominantly anglophone until the mid-nineteenth century—the Québécois attach themselves to the soil during years and years and develop a well particularized social type; it is during this long wintering that they become Québécois for good. . . . (1974:17)

At this point the interpenetration of social-scientific and nationalist discourse becomes quite clear. Indeed, as Garigue (1964:186) later wrote, "the emergence of sociological theory about French Canada can be considered as an ideological extension of the very social reality it purposes to study." What I want to emphasize here is how well sociological models of the folk society match nationalistic visions of a rural Quebec out of which the nation has been born. Whatever the particular version of the folk society model, used for whatever heuristic or ideological purposes, all answer a

5. The terminology becomes somewhat confusing at this point because Rioux substituted the series "tribal," "folk," and "urban" for Redfield's "folk," "peasant," and "urban." However, he asserted that "peasant society *stricto sensu* is a variety of the folk-society," finding both to be characterized by smallness, closeness to nature, social homogeneity, and lack both of impersonal relations and an extensive division of labor (1964:166).

pressing need to find somewhere in the past an authentic version of the nation or society that can be used to make sense of the present situation. For Miner and Redfield the folk society represented a starting point in the historical process of social change. For clerical-conservative nationalists like the historian Groulx, Catholic New France represented both the birth of the nation and its finest flowering. For a contemporary nationalist like Rioux, nineteenth-century rural Quebec was the milieu in which a cumulative process of differentiation led to the emergence of a new nation. Each of these perspectives requires a myth of the new beginning, in which a limited group of people, isolated in a virgin natural milieu, is imagined to transform itself into a new social entity, distinctive and bounded. Each overlooks what came before by using such archetypal symbols as an ocean voyage or a military conquest to sever continuity with the past. And each then uses the new beginning to explain, justify, or condemn what followed.

The fact that different scholars and ideologues have imagined different folk societies for Quebec suggests that the model partakes more of the romantic and mythical than of the objective and factual. The questions that Garigue raised remain unanswered. Was French Canada ever a folk society? Did it exist as a collection of isolated rural communities, relatively uninfluenced by the surrounding world? In the next section I focus on two types of evidence that suggests negative answers to these questions. First, the best sociological studies of rural Quebec record what would seem to be continuous processes of social change and cultural diffusion. Moreover, change and diffusion affected aspects of life that today are objectified as typical of the folk society—folk dancing and music, for example. Second, cultural objectifiers are as traditional in French Canada as the traditions they record; we find them active from at least the mid-nineteenth century onward. These two types of evidence—continuous change in the folk aspects of Quebec life, continuous activity of folklore objectifiers—are linked, since the very researchers who recorded the facts of change were at the same time attempting to stop change and preserve the past. This will be evident in the work of Marius Barbeau, the "dean of French-Canadian folklorists." To the degree that Barbeau's career as researcher and popularizer is typical of the Québécois approach to the past, it suggests that the province has never been unreflectively anchored in tradition, with "no objectivity and no systematization of knowledge," as Redfield put it.

In Search of the Folk Society

As we have seen, Miner (1939:286–90) spoke of "new traits" in St. Denis, meaning those that had diffused from the cities since 1800. He took the trouble to catalogue them under a variety of headings indicating their ubiquity in daily life: Agriculture and Husbandry, Food and Drink, Home-Product Techniques, Games, Music and Dance. Miner's French-Canadian predecessors, Barbeau and Léon Gérin, shared his vision of colonial New France as the original French-Canadian folk society, where ancient French traditions, adapted to a new environment, had provided the basis for a folk culture. Barbeau (1936:71–96) wrote at length of the slow death of traditional handicrafts, crafts that he saw as rooted in the French Renaissance. Like Miner he believed that the advance of industrial civilization, coupled with what he saw as a lack of collective self-confidence and pride, had all but destroyed traditional French Canada. "After 1880," he wrote (1949:75), "goods manufactured in foreign cities displaced domestic handicrafts. People buy, but make little at home anymore." Elsewhere he wrote of the collapse of native crafts and styles in the face of importations from New York as early as 1825 (1936:170). Gérin believed that the "community family" of the French-Canadian peasant was the key unit in French-Canadian social structure (Falardeau 1965:277–81). Though Gérin sought rural families anchored to their farms through the generations, he often wrote of peasants who moved regularly from farm to farm, from country to city, from Quebec to New England, and back again (1938:40–41, 151–81). Gérin, who began his field studies in 1886, documented this restless, incessant movement dating back at least to the 1850s in the family histories that he collected. And, as Morissonneau (1983:16) has argued, the contradiction between the stability that Gérin sought and the mobility he found has plagued nationalist elites and, before them, colonial and Church administrators, throughout most of French-Canadian history: "They invented for themselves a people rooted in the land. But this peasant identity was more an ideal than a reality drawn from observation."

These glimpses of rural life reveal important contacts between Québécois peasants and the wider world, certainly for the second half of the nineteenth century, and probably before as well. Though the isolation of rural Quebec must certainly have been pronounced in comparison to contemporary rural areas, there was nonetheless a greater circulation of people and diffusion of foreign culture traits than one might at first expect. As a more detailed example of this, bearing directly on modern-day conceptions of the folk society, consider the evidence pertaining to folk dancing. Because dance fashions change rapidly, and because the history of particular dances is difficult to unravel, almost any form of dancing popular before World War II can today be presented to the public as traditional. Yet fieldworkers from Gérin in the 1880s to Rioux in the 1950s report that rural folk not merely passively endured, but eagerly sought city novelties in song and dance. What appears old and traditional today was at one time, often quite recently, new. Working in St. Justin in 1886, Gérin (1898:191) remarked that "the best-known dances today seem to be those introduced by young people returned from the United States. But the *gigues,* cotillions, and quadrilles are not forgotten." Miner (1939:290) listed only cotillion and *salut des dames* as old culture traits in St. Denis; such dances as quadrilles, reels, and sets he included among the new. Doyon (1950:173) reported that in nineteenth-century Beauce county young people went regularly to work in Maine, where they sought fashionable novelties as well as high wages:

> Old informants still remember countless amusing anec-
> dotes recalling the good times when, as young men, they
> would go haying in the States. As soon as the day's work
> was done, they looked for fun, and danced to their hearts'
> content, particularly on Saturday night. New dances or
> new ways of dancing were sought, because they made the
> young dancers still more welcome at home with their
> sweethearts.

Doyon also commented on the difficulty of determining the origins of particular dances, due to the fact that French, English, Irish, and Scottish dance elements have intermingled almost from the first years of contact among these various groups. Small wonder that the famous fiddler, Jean Carignan (Petrowski 1978:25), has declared that "Québécois folklore doesn't exist. It is a folklore made up of scraps from Ireland and Scotland." Carignan's opinion is perhaps drastic, but it does point to the intricate patterns of cross-pollination that have always characterized the folklore of France, Great Britain, and, later, North America.

We thus find that research on folk dancing—one of those culture traits held to typify the folk society and even to represent the national spirit—reveals not unchanging indigenous traditions but constant innovations and importations. Furthermore, this steady diffusion of foreign cultural material into French Canada has been matched by a continuous process of objectification intended to recover the old traditions before they disappeared. Not only did folklore collectors attempt to record fading traditions, they attempted to rejuvenate them, both among the "folk" who practiced them and among their urban compatriots.

In her history of folklore activities in Canada, Carpenter has related the style, even ethos, of folklore research to the ethnic and sociopolitical background of Canadian researchers. She traces the relative unimportance of Anglo-Canadian folklore scholarship (both within Canada and in terms of international recognition) to its dependence upon a British model, one that has stressed "the romantic preservation and propagation of survivals" (1979:162). This has resulted in a lack of interest in the living folklore of the researchers' milieu—that is, in "English Canadian" folklore—as well as in a lack of any attempt to use that folklore for social or political ends. In French Canada, by contrast, folklore studies have always been conditioned by nationalism: in particular, by the defensive stance of French-Canadian nationalists. With the emergence of an indigenous French-Canadian intelligentsia in the early nineteenth century came a conviction of the necessity to defend and preserve French-Canadian culture. "As a direct result" of this conviction, Carpenter claims, "French-Canadian folklore studies are exceptionally well developed. Both at home and abroad, they are the best known and most lauded of all Canadian folklore endeavours" (206).

As Carpenter points out, almost from the beginnings of New France European travelers recorded descriptions of the folk life of the colonists. In the eighteenth century these were to be found in the form of travelers' diaries and accounts of voyages in the "interior" or "wilds" of North America, as typical titles would have it. Such literature appeared continuously throughout the nineteenth century and into the twentieth. Later examples tended to be geographically more narrowly focused, perhaps reflecting the transition from travel to tourism that Boorstin (1961:77–117) has discussed. Most of this literature was written by outsiders to French Canada, first by British and French authors and later by Americans and English Canadians. These writings were romantic, interpreting rural French Canada in terms of "the Rousseau-inspired fascination with the primitive, exotic, and natural" (Carpenter 1979:210); their discussion of folk life stressed folk music above other aspects of custom, an emphasis that Carpenter sees as typical of British folklore studies; and it was aimed primarily at English-language audiences. What was the influence of such literature on the developing French-Canadian self-image? This is a question that I cannot answer conclusively. Obviously it would only have been known to that small (in the early nineteenth century especially) fraction of the French-Canadian population that was literate and even bilingual. But, as we shall see, these were the people who began to articulate a sense of French-Canadian national identity and to objectify French-Canadian culture, and they have never been averse to idealizing, in a romantic vein, the rural roots of French Canada. There is a time-honored tradition among nationalist historians (Groulx 1952: 1:208–9; 2:193–96; Wade 1955:6–42) of citing the accounts of European travelers in depictions of the social life of New France. Through the "standard" works of these historians, observations by certain voyagers have been built into the telling and retelling of national history. Second-hand histories, such as those of social scientists required to provide background as a prelude to some variety of synchronic analysis, dutifully cite these voyagers "as cited in" the major histories of Groulx, Wade, and others.

As an explicitly nationalist ideology developed among the French-Canadian intelligentsia, lay scholars began to record the history and traditions of their "race." By the mid-1800s,

There was an educated and influential native French-Canadian elite composed mostly of clergy and professionals but including journalists and politicians. This intelligentsia became profoundly concerned with the preservation of extant traditions, very much in a "get it before it dies out" attitude, and with the popularization of French-Canadian history and culture. Their concerns derived from a desire to promote French-Canadian identification as a defensive reaction against threatening English domination in the pre-Confederation era. (Carpenter 1979:212)

The greatest of these lay scholars was F. X. Garneau, the first of French Canada's two "national historians." (Groulx was the second). Inspired by Garneau, as well as by French romantic writers, a circle of young writers began to write romantically about their peasant countrymen in an effort to awaken national pride (Lacourcière 1961:374). The members of this literary movement did not engage in research and collecting. Among their contemporaries, however, were two musical scholars (Hubert LaRue and Ernest Gagnon) who published, in 1863 and 1865, the first "truly scholarly studies" of French-Canadian folk songs (Carpenter 1979:213–14). Carpenter claims that these studies were undertaken for scholarly rather than nationalistic purposes. Nonetheless, they took their place among other nineteenth-century collections of French-Canadian folk songs that became increasingly popular among more nationalistic French Canadians. By 1904 a French musicologist, Julien Tiersot, could write that the folk song in French Canada, "far from being despised by the educated classes, has remained in favor with them as much and even more than among the lower classes" (quoted in Carpenter 1979:217)—though Carpenter cautions that his claim was "somewhat exaggerated."

At the beginning of the twentieth century, then, there was an established literature that interpreted at least some aspects of French-Canadian folk life. That literature was influenced by both romantic and nationalistic ideology and contributed to a vision of the peasant roots of the nation that has consistently been progagated by educated elites. Carpenter argues (220) that with the advent of Marius Barbeau as a researcher and popularizer of French-Canadian folk traditions, what had been merely a "persisting interest" in folklore was transformed into a "movement."

Preston (1976:129) has written that Barbeau's "pursuit of folklore appears at once to be unswervable and yet not narrow-minded or provincial toward particular areas or traditions." Barbeau's initial interest in French-Canadian folklore (starting about 1914) was stimulated more by British and American scholarship than by French-Canadian nationalism. Affiliated throughout his career with federal institutions, he never became an advocate of an exclusively Québécois nationalism, nor has he been claimed by nationalists as a scholar-hero, as were such people as the historians Garneau and Groulx. Yet, as Preston suggests (131), "there was a tension within Barbeau" between his "cosmopolitan" career and "his primary loyalties to the roots from which he came."

Barbeau was born in 1883 in Beauce county, where he spent most of his youth. Carpenter (1979:221) describes his family as "nonpeasant, relatively highly educated," and as one "which did not commonly exhibit its peasant heritage." Yet looking back, Barbeau remarked that "I was stewed in folklore; I realize that now" (quoted in Preston 1976:124). After admission to the Quebec Bar in 1907, he went to Oxford as the first French-Canadian Rhodes scholar, where for three years he studied anthropology, archaeology, and ethnology under R. R. Marett. He was awarded a diploma in anthropology in 1910, having written his thesis on "The Totemic System of the North Western Tribes of North America," and was hired by Sapir early in 1911 for the Anthropology section of the Victoria Memorial Museum (now the National Museum of Man) (Carpenter 1979:221–22; Preston 1976:123–25).

While doing field work among Huron Indians near Quebec City, Barbeau came across much material of French origin or influence. Because he sought (in the British tradition) the most exotic and the most ancient, he ignored this material until his encounter in 1914 with Franz Boas. Boas expressed immediate interest in the diffusion of French materials among the Indians. Barbeau (1943:167) later proclaimed this encounter to be directly responsible for the folklore movement that he spearheaded:

> It [the movement] was brought about by Dr. Franz Boas in 1914 when, at an annual meeting of the Anthropological Association in New York, he invited the author of this article to collect French Canadian folktales and publish them in the *Journal of American Folklore*. This urge released new initiatives within Canada . . . that have been highly productive ever since.

Among these new initiatives was the reactivation of the Canadian branch of the American Folklore Society (animated mainly by anglophone Montrealers from 1892 to 1897), which "soon reached its maximum size of about 140 members" (Barbeau 1943:168). Barbeau became co-editor in 1916 of the *Journal of American Folklore*, which subsequently published eight issues devoted to Canadian research (1916, 1917, 1919, 1920, 1926, 1931, 1940, 1950). He recruited a number of colleagues to help him collect French-Canadian materials and, with their aid, began the work of popularizing what they gathered. Among the popularizing activities were the first folklore shows in Canada.

In 1916, at a resort hotel on the lower Saint Lawrence, Barbeau presented a folk singer who entertained his audience with songs, tales, and dances. In 1918 Barbeau gave a paper to the *Société historique de Montréal* on "The Role of Oral Tradition in the Study of Our History." This presentatiion apparently stimulated him and some of his colleagues to attempt something more ambitious:

> The songs and tales that we had cited naturally would suggest the idea of returning to the source, of hearing the singers and storytellers themselves. What particularly stimulated this urge was the realistic presentation that Miss Loraine Wyman had given—at the invitation of the Society—of some English songs that she had gathered in the Kentucky mountains. (Barbeau 1920:1)

Loraine Wyman was one of a great number of ballad collectors and cultural missionaries who were drawn to the Appalachian mountains in the first decades of the twentieth century. Whisnant (1983) has carefully documented the invention of an Appalachian tradition which was propagated both among mountaineers and the public at large. Barbeau (1920:1–5) had other models as well. He mentions a private show, under the auspices of the Folklore Society (of Great Britain), that he witnessed in 1910—"a realistic performance of 'Jack in the green,' an ancient dance . . . that our esteemed professor, M. R. R. Marett, had staged on his lawn, for selected guests, at Oxford." And he cites a performance of folk songs arranged and staged by the French musicologist Tiersot in Paris in 1885.

A combination of motives prompted Barbeau and his colleagues to attempt a similar performance in Canada. They wanted to convince "the educated classes" of the validity of their research, hoping that conviction would lead to financial support. To do this they had to overcome not merely indifference but hostility on the part of those who were ashamed of the peasant element of French-Canadian society:

> In the eyes of these critics it is futile to spend one's time gathering and publishing folk tales and anecdotes. Isn't the lower class contemptible and ignorant, its language and customs boorish? "Why do you persist in unearthing this nonsense that we have been trying to eliminate for fifty years?"—thus were we impatiently reproached, in a

> public meeting, by a colleague of the Royal Society of
> Canada. (Barbeau 1920:1)

Yet, according to the folklorists, a return to folk sources was precisely
what was needed to stimulate national culture. Their larger purpose
was to encourage the French-Canadian intelligentsia to seek inspiration in the folk culture of Canada rather than in French high culture.
As long as French-Canadian writers emulated French models the
creative élan and corresponding renown that they sought would
escape them. "Wasn't it time to attack urban prejudices and to make
known, by examples . . . that humble patrimony that the rural population conserves unconsciously for the regeneration of the race?"
(1–2).

Barbeau and his colleagues presented their examples in two
public "soirées" held in Montreal in 1919. Barbeau claimed that these
differed from their European models in that the folk themselves were
the performers. In fact, Artur Hazelius had peopled Skansen, his
open-air folk museum in Stockholm, with folk performers in the
1880s (Anderson 1984:19), while "primitive," as opposed to "folk,"
performers were common in the great universal expositions of the
late nineteenth century (Jacknis 1985:81). In any case, these folk
performers knew how to amuse the urban audience:

> The first soirée of popular traditions . . . took place March
> 18, 1919. Its success was decisive. We had to promise a
> second soirée in the near future for those who had been
> unable to find a place in the overflowing hall. "This is like
> the good old days," people said everywhere. Even before
> the Repentigny singer—dressed as a logger, wearing a high
> felt hat, arrow-sash and log-driver's boots—had raised
> some excitement with his rowing song, "Envoyons de
> l'avant, nos gens!," we were no longer in doubt as to the
> fate of our enterprise. The audience seemed won over.
> Fiddlers, singers, . . . dancers, story-tellers followed one
> another during more than two hours, while the audience
> never tired of applauding them. . . . The stage setting . . .
> represented the interior of a rural house. . . . For many of
> the spectators this reawakening of childhood memories
> was utterly delightful. Some had even come from afar to
> attend this resurrection of the past. (Barbeau 1920:3)

This passage describes a folklore *spectacle* similar to several that
I attended sixty years later. By the time of my field work this peculiar
objectification of folk culture—the intimacy of family life displayed
publicly on stage—had become an established practice. Barbeau continued to experiment with methods for bringing folklore to the attention of the urban public. Between 1927 and 1930 he organized three

"Folk-Song and Handicraft Festivals" at the Château Frontenac in Quebec City (Barbeau 1936:105). By the time of my field work these festivals too had become conventional—traditional modes for the preservation of tradition.

At this point I break off the discussion of the history of folklore studies in French Canada. Carpenter has sketched the official institutional history, but her interpretation of the relationship between folklore studies and social life in Quebec fails to disentangle itself from the conventional nationalistic interpretation. For example, Carpenter speaks (1979:205) of the role that folklore studies have played in "the evolution and maintenance of a distinct French Canadian culture." Yet her use of the term evolution can be said to privilege not change but the preservation of past social forms in an unchanging state. According to her, folklorists have helped to "maintain" French-Canadian culture because they have prevented the disappearance of traits and features essential to national culture. These elements of national culture, once secured, allow for an adaptation to modernity (evolution?) that preserves Québécois distinctiveness. But Carpenter implies, as do nationalist ideologues, that future changes will be based on the essential culture that was "fixed" somewhere in the past and "preserved" by the concern of folklorists and other culturally conscientious activists.

Recent research on particular national traditions of folklore scholarship provides extensive documentation of "the invention of tradition" (Hobsbawm and Ranger 1983) by those scholars and aficionados most concerned to preserve folk customs in their pristine purity. According to Wilson (1976:30–31)

> In Finland . . . as well as in other countries seeking historical justification for separatist policies, romantic nationalism and folklore research were initially the same thing. . . . Had it not been for the nationalists in search of a culture, much Finnish folklore . . . would have disappeared.

Yet Wilson goes on to show that Finnish folklore was not merely preserved, but largely reconstructed in what I have called objectified forms; that these objectified forms were presented as "genuine folklore" to "the common people" via "the popular media, . . . folklore festivals, and . . . the public schools"; and that, consequently, "there developed . . . a sort of folklore about folklore" that influenced Finnish national life infinitely more than unobjectified or "pristine" folklore, which for all practical purposes disappeared (123–28).

In another study, Herzfeld has examined the analytic constructs that nineteenth-century Greek folklore scholars used to persuade both their compatriots and outsiders that Greek folk life was significantly continuous with the classical civilization of Hellenic Greece. Herzfeld (1982:17) suggests that the work of these scholars quickly influenced the customs of the peasantry, despite the fact that "the formulation of a Greek national identity in terms of cultural continuity [with ancient Greece] was something of a novelty to the largely illiterate country people." Similarly, Trevor-Roper (1983) and Morgan (1983) have shown conclusively how the "traditional" Highland Scottish and Welsh cultures were constructed by aristocratic and middle-class enthusiasts and gradually sold, as an authentic national past, to the general public; and Whisnant (1983) has documented the same process for the Appalachian United States, though there the invention of a regional identity has not yet led to nationalism. In each of these three cases "pieces" of culture that the public takes to be quintessentially Highland Scottish, Welsh, or "mountaineer"—items of clothing (the kilt), musical instruments (the Welsh triple harp, the dulcimer in Appalachia), handicrafts, types of dances, and social gatherings, to suggest only a few—have been shown to be importations from areas of "high" civilization rather than indigenous elements of these purportedly folk cultures (cf. Utley 1961).

The Quebec materials presented in this chapter suggest that the work of folklorists has been one among several factors that have brought continuous change to rural Quebec. Rather than preserving pristine folkways, folklorists have helped the folk to replace them with invented, objectified traditions to which both rural and urban Québécois have responded. When Miner (1937) set out to describe the folk culture of St. Denis, he learned not only that it was disappearing, but that it was not naive in the way he had imagined. "I just got track of a story-teller in a neighboring parish," he wrote Redfield from the field, "and am arranging to get some of his old tales, anything he has not gotten out of a book." E. C. Hughes (1943:172), working in an industrial town in the 1930s, remarked that long-time residents, representatives of the "business and professional classes . . . are perhaps more concerned than others lest their recently arrived rural fellow-countrymen lose their rural orientation." Doyon's (1950:172) informants from La Beauce argued among themselves about whose version of a particular dance was "authentic." Rioux (1961:53) noted that even in a "homogeneous culture such as that of French Canada" several versions of an ancient folk song existed side by side; these ranged from the relatively naive—"sung by certain peasants who have conserved it in their oral tradition and who become less numerous each year"—to the relatively objectified—"sung by people influenced by the folklore campaign of the past twenty years" (cf. Rioux 1950). Elsewhere Rioux (1961:93) gives a glimpse of the anthropologist helping to keep alive tradition through his participation in local events: in this case, a wedding between a woman from Belle-Anse, where Rioux was working, and a man from a nearby village.

After the meal the wedding party enjoy themselves in the hotel. . . . A hotel employee accompanies on the piano a young woman . . . who sings more "cowboy" songs; a few old women listen. The men have begun to drink beer again. To create some excitement and observe the reaction, a linguist who was working at Belle-Anse, his wife and myself sing some old response-songs. We ask the crowd to give the replies; the songs are a big hit. People gather together, sing and laugh. An old man with the appearance of a peasant, a relative of the groom, even sings "La Belle Françoise." Some women from Belle-Anse find the song and singer so comical that the mother of the bride has to leave the room in order to stop laughing.

Thus have the folk come to abandon and even to ridicule those traditions that urban collectors have come among them to discover. The displacement of folk customs has long been combatted by folklorists who, like Barbeau, struggled also to awaken urbanites to the beauties of their rural roots. But in so doing the folklorists have objectified those aspects of social life that they sought to preserve; that is, they have transformed them into discrete things to be studied, catalogued, and displayed. This involves selection and reinterpretation. The objectifier looks at a familiar milieu and finds that it is composed of traditional traits, things that he carves out of a hitherto taken-for-granted cultural background and makes over into typical specimens. But to select aspects of a social world as traits, and then to isolate the chosen traits in a new context—to photograph them, inscribe them, perform them on stage, immure them in museums—necessarily changes the meaning that those traits have to objectifiers, trait-bearers and onlookers alike. Paradoxically, the attempt to preserve traditions through objectification brings change. New criteria for the classification of social experience are brought into play which discriminate as meaningful entities what were before unmarked practices, or which assign new meanings (for example, "traditional") to practices previously objectified and marked in other terms. To the degree that these new interpretations become incorporated into the "things" themselves—that is, become part of the understanding that the folk have of their lives—to that degree will the objectifiers change folk culture by creating it as "tradition."

I have illustrated this argument with examples drawn from the realm of popular amusements. During the late 1970s I discovered a great swell of public interest in Québécois folklore, traditions, and culture. Many people were attempting to make their heritage (*le patrimoine*) live again and, in so doing, became the latest actors in a long history of innovation. Through their devotion to tradition they helped transpose it, altering it where it existed among unreflective folk and introducing it in objectified form to other audiences. I would guess that Québécois folk dances have for some time been more widespread in objectified rather than naive form. In my explorations of the Quebec countryside I occasionally came across a village with a dance hall and a Saturday-night dance. The old dances, squares, and quadrilles accompanied by fiddle and accordian, alternated with modern numbers danced to primitive rock and roll. Such dances could be found in Quebec City as well, not as regular affairs but as holiday events or annual social gatherings. These were relatively unpublicized, almost invisible to one not immersed in the life of a particular parish. But these relatively unobjectified dances were less prevalent, even in rural areas, than objectified activities such as folk dance classes, demonstrations, shows, and clubs.

Folk dance exhibitions objectify the dances and associated familial milieu by placing them on stage. In the hockey rink the painted farmhouse and the sleigh bringing "neighbors" framed the demonstration and established the dancers as family. This family, its dances, and its spirit of solidarity became objects to be viewed and admired by several hundred spectators. What had once been, according to all accounts known to me, a domestic affair to which access was granted according to norms of hospitality and neighborliness was now transformed into a public spectacle to which anyone could buy admission.

Folk dance lessons carry out the process of objectification in a different manner. To a greater degree than imitation, formal instruction marks dances as objects of study and clearly demarcates the roles of teacher and pupil. Some Québécois who have learned to dance through simple imitation find instruction in "the old dances" somewhat odd. At one village festival a costumed folk dance troupe performed, then taught the crowd a simple dance, mingling in the squares to facilitate the first attempts. Later a resident told me that he had never seen such a thing, adding that "dancing—it seems to me that's as old as the earth."

The ethnological orientation of some instructors adds another aspect to objectification. The teacher of a course I took had studied folklore at Laval university, continued to participate in the university folklore club, and collected recordings of traditional music as a hobby. He identified each dance that he taught as originating in a particular village: "This quadrille comes from St. ⸻." I interpret this to mean "This dance was collected or encountered at St. ⸻." As Ellis, commenting on some spurious regionalizations of the Grimm brothers, notes (1983:26): "There is a folkish air in this practice of naming the region, a suggestion that the tale sprang from a particular area of the soil of Germany." Yet the degree to which dance forms are interpreted as being specific to individual villages or regions will depend upon the criteria that one uses to classify them, and there is no guarantee that an outsider's classification will correspond to villagers' perceptions. One woman told me that the dances of her village and all surrounding villages were identical and, when questioned, said that people did not correlate particular dances with villages, though she said that regional variations were recognized, contrasting the style of La Beauce with that of the Lac St-Jean region. In contrast, at folklore *spectacles* troupes were introduced and identified by region and village. This type of objectification is carried to its logical extreme in a popular weekly television show that for many years has presented residents of Quebec villages in demonstrations of their local dances. The few performers that I was able to question claimed that particularities of costume, style, and form had always been recognized. That regional, even inter-village differences developed seems unquestionable, but the degree to which variations were perceived, and the values attached to such perceptions, are unknown. The identification of dances with localities may once have occurred in situations of inter-village rivalry, but is today most evident in self-conscious elaborations of cultural identity.

These methods of objectifying folk dancing have contributed to its survival or resurgence among those whom the objectifiers might consider to be "folk." One Vacances-Familles family described the death and rebirth of dancing in their area. In the early 1970s the Saturday-night dances of their village were discontinued, since most people had lost interest and even forgotten the dances. However, during celebrations marking the 300th anniversary of the founding of their village, residents were invited to perform their indigenous dances on television. The few people who still knew the dances taught those who volunteered to perform, and thus the villagers relearned their dances. After that the Saturday-night dance was revived, though according to my hosts many dancers in the revived dance were tourists unknown to them. Still, the family seemed happy to be able to attend and proud to take along their *vacanciers*. But they were well aware that their dances were folklore and, as such, worthy of preservation.

That a folk tradition has been created for urban Québécois who are no longer folk seems unquestionable. That tradition has been created for the folk themselves is a less common assertion, but one that recent research supports. I have documented the activities of folklorists well back into the period when Quebec is said to have been a folk society, and suggested that the canonization of their lifeways prompted the folk to reinterpret aspects of their routine existence. To the extent that they came to conceptualize their lives as "traditional" their understanding of themselves would have been changed. In my field work I often encountered such reinterpretations among rural Québécois who had been sought out by nationalistic or romantic enthusiasts. The final irony is perhaps represented by the farm families of Vacances-Familles whose income depends more and more on tourism. By marketing themselves as farmers they lessen their economic dependence on farming. At the same time, the unobjectified round of their daily lives becomes a series of staged performances.

Boorstin (1961) has termed these performances for tourists "pseudo-events," but MacCannell (1976:102–4) argues that this term trivializes what is a central aspect of modern societies. Similarly, Elli Köngäs-Maranda has suggested the cultural and political significance of folklore research by pointing out that "colonizing countries have anthropology museums; colonized countries have folklore archives" (1979:187). Her observation reminds us not only that nationalism and folklore scholarship have flourished together among people seeking political independence, but that the search for a folk society, as well as its influence on the folk themselves, is one aspect of a much broader domain of "cultural politics." We turn now to a more narrowly governmental version of the politics of culture, a rationalized and bureaucratic quest for national culture and cultural development.

CHAPTER FOUR

The Founding of the
Ministère des Affaires culturelles

Quebec Cultural Politics before 1960

In Quebec and Canada systematic and sustained government action in cultural affairs has been motivated by the conviction that the state has a responsibility to buttress and develope national identity, particularly against the threat of other national cultures exerting international influence. To say this is not to deny the importance of pressures brought to bear on governments by interested individuals and organizations of various artistic milieux, nor of an elitist patronage of "high" culture by certain political and economic leaders. Yet in recent decades national purposes have dominated: on the one hand, nationalistically legitimated government intervention has greatly stimulated both artists' demands for services and their willingness to organize themselves as interest groups; and, on the other, high culture itself has been encompassed as merely one aspect of national culture. In brief, cultural "development," as well as government's responsibility for it, have come to be perceived as essential to national well-being.

Traditional cultural institutions have been supported by the Canadian government since the mid-nineteenth century. For example, the Geological Survey of Canada and its National Museum were founded in 1842, the National Gallery in 1880, the Commission of Monuments and Sites in 1914, and the Canadian Broadcasting Corporation (CBC) in 1936. Justification for the founding of the CBC was explicitly nationalistic—in the face of the perceived threat from American radio—as was the impetus to establish, in 1949, the Royal Commission on National Development in the Arts, Letters, and Sciences (Massey Commission). In the aftermath of the Second World War a renewed sense of Canadian national identity gave rise both to new aspirations and new insecurities. At least from the perspective of "British" Canadians, Canada's newfound international standing and the belief that Canadians had finally outgrown a colonial mentality were offset by a renewed French-Canadian nationalism, by demographic shifts tending to reduce the proportion of British Canadians in the total population, and by an increasing American presence (Fraser 1967:1–4). In this context the government asked the Massey Commission to examine, with "the national interest" in mind, those "institutions which express national feeling, promote common understanding and add to the variety and richness of Canadian life" (Canada 1951:xi). In response the "culture commission," as it was popularly called (Shea 1952:4), recommended sweeping federal initiatives in the "organization, financing and administration of the arts, media, humanities and social sciences in Canada" (Schafer 1976:45). It justified these recommendations in terms of a nationalist vision of independence and development:

> American influences on Canadian life to say the least are impressive. There should be no thought of interfering with the liberty of all Canadians to enjoy them. Cultural exchanges are excellent in themselves. They widen the choice of the consumer and provide stimulating competition for the producer. It cannot be denied, however, that a vast and disproportionate amount of material coming from a single alien source may stifle rather than stimulate our own creative effort; and, passively accepted without any standard of comparison, this may weaken critical faculties. We are now spending millions to maintain a national independence which would be nothing but an empty shell without a vigorous and distinctive cultural life. (Canada 1951:18)

It is only a small irony that Canadian efforts stemming from the Massey Commission engendered similar concerns in a Canadian province, Quebec. A tradition of government aid to culture had been established by the Provincial Secretary (1919–36) Athanase David, known in his time as "le mécène de la province." Influenced both by French intellectual trends and by local artists and writers, David introduced legislation to establish, for example, the Quebec Historic Monuments Commission, a provincial art museum, and fine-arts schools in Montreal and Quebec. He multiplied grants to artists and cultural associations, provided scholarships for study in Paris, brought French musicians to teach in Quebec conservatories, and sponsored such events as the "Semaine du livre Canadien" (Rumilly 1952:75–76; 1953:21–24, 241–44; MAC 1979a:9–18). This concern was sustained during the Duplessis government (1936–39, 1944–60) by the

Undersecretary, Jean Bruchési, who has written in his memoirs of his roles as "Santa Claus" to French-Canadian intellectuals and "cultural ambassador" for the provincial government (1974:74, 90). Yet by the 1950s Quebec progressives viewed such efforts as decidedly inadequate, particularly when contrasted to those the federal government had undertaken since the Massey Commission. Moreover, Ottawa's intervention itself provoked serious criticism: it violated what French-Canadian nationalists and others perceived as the constitutional balance of power, with the federal government extending its activities into social and cultural domains traditionally reserved to the provinces and thought to be crucial to the national survival of French Canada. This dual critique, of Quebec's inadequacies and of Ottawa's encroachments, was central to those currents of critical social thought in French Canada that would lead to the so-called Quiet Revolution in Quebec and to attempts to renew Canadian federalism by attending to the "bicultural" character of Canadian society.

The Quiet Revolution has acquired near mythic status in Quebec, being commonly understood to mark the sudden emergence of a self-consciously modern and "adult" society. It is not clear why the early 1960s should appear as a watershed in Quebec's history (though one suspects that postwar nationalists needed to find a potentially successful revolution somewhere in their history in order to mark the birth of a modern nation [cf. MacCannell 1976:3–12]). Many people believe that Quebec experienced a cultural and political "lag" in relation to economic development in the first half of the twentieth century. The province had become increasingly industrialized and urbanized since the turn of the century, yet clerical-conservative nationalism remained the dominant social ideology until the Quiet Revolution. Conservative nationalists—agriculturalist, anti-statist and messianic, as characterized in the title of a famous essay by historian Michel Brunet (1957)—refused to recognize that French Canada was no longer a rural, peasant society and refused to sanction the type of welfare-state legislation elaborated elsewhere to counter the perceived problems of industrial capitalism. Rocher (1973:18) has described this situation as a "strange contradiction" in which Quebec "adopted the social structures of industrial civilization, but kept the mentality, spirit and values of pre-industrial society." This may account for the perception of a revolution in the early 1960s: as Rocher, looking back at the Quiet Revolution, puts it, "this accumulation of backwardness could only become more and more explosive," leading at last to "the rapid, almost wild rhythm of the cultural mutation of the past years." Yet this view should be modified at least by insisting that it was not "the society" as a global entity that was out of tune with itself, but the vision of certain elites as compared to the daily life of the masses for whom they spoke. In other words, though conservative leaders refused to accept social change, working people, whose world was becoming urbanized, modernized, and "Americanized," were living it. More important, in the eyes of traditional elites, they were accepting it as well. And it was precisely the backwardness of the elite vision, entrenched in power during the long Duplessis regime, that stimulated the various strands of critical social thought that finally embodied themselves in the Quiet Revolution. In sum, the Quiet Revolution, triggered by an election and a change of political regime (1960), represents the coming to power of a new elite and the culmination of three decades of intellectual criticism, debate, and frustration.

In order to understand the birth of the Quebec *Ministère des Affaires culturelles,* we should look at two aspects of what Rocher described as Quebec's accumulating backwardness: first, the Church's attempts to provide the social services deemed necessary in industrializing societies, and, second, the Duplessis government's unwillingness to do so. From the late nineteenth century and particularly after 1930 the Church's reaction to urbanization and industrialization was to increase, and even to professionalize, its social-welfare activities. Levasseur has pointed out (1982:64) that in 1931 there was one cleric for every 97 Roman Catholics in Quebec. Moreover, "of this clerical personnel, it is estimated that only one half was engaged in religious work strictly speaking; the other half specialized in the [social] works of the Church: education, charity, health, welfare, leisure." This army of workers was engaged not only in the newly established urban parishes, but in "Catholic Action" in such specialized associations as scout groups, student groups, and Catholic labor unions. The Church's goal, according to Levasseur, was "to consolidate or stop the erosion of its hold on the social and cultural life of French Canada," and this at a time when modernization was creating an ever-growing gap between "religion and civil society" (64–65). In the face of federal government attempts to intervene in social welfare, the Church insisted on its exclusive jurisdiction, opposing federal intervention on two counts. First, the Church, with "the blessing of the Quebec state," controlled social services in Quebec. Thus Federal intervention "could diminish not only the power of the Quebec state, but above all that of the Church." Second, social legislation invariably introduced "Anglo-Saxon" values into those familial and educational institutions which the Church saw as the moral foundations of French-Canadian society. For example, the Church contested a 1943 federal law on physical education on the grounds that it was "naturalistic and materialistic" (61–62). And in place of state action it offered its own extensive social works.

Claude Ryan, a journalist and politician, has described lay participation in the Church's work as he experienced it:

Catholic Action was launched in Quebec in the mid-thirties in direct answer to an urgent call of Pope Pius XI for an active participation of the laity in the apostolate of the Church. . . . It was received in French Canada with that profound disposition of obedience to Rome which has been a leading trait of French Canadian catholicism throughout its history. . . . Thousands of priests . . . and laymen answered the appeal of the Pope with a fervour and dedication that could not but remind one of the spirit of the apostolic age. (1961:52)

Though these lay volunteers and specialists were carefully screened and supervised by the clergy (Levasseur 1982:66), by the 1950s it was becoming clear that the Church could not marshall the resources necessary to counter the perceived cultural erosion of French Canada. On the one hand, the problems of "modernization" with which it was attempting to cope were growing; and, on the other, its ability to recruit clergy was declining as the rural population, main source of its personnel, decreased relative to the urban (Coleman 1984:63). In this situation the Church was forced, contrary to its ideology, to seek the aid of the provincial government, and thus to acquiesce in "the passage from the power of the Church to that of the state" that is generally accepted as the institutional grounding of the Quiet Revolution (Levasseur 1982:72).

Yet the demise of the Church was more than a matter of inadequate resources. Many clergy and lay persons engaged in social work were brought to question the conservative nationalism of the hierarchy: "the gap between the Church's official ideology, which defined Quebec as a Catholic, French and rural society, and its pastoral work in urban settings generated tensions between the high and low clergy, between clerics and laity" (Hamelin and Montminy 1981:39). Many of the Catholic Action workers who rose to positions of secular leadership during the Quiet Revolution had been influenced by such "Neo-Catholic" philosophers as Maritain—who, as Guy Frégault wrote in his memoirs (1976:154), "seemed to us to situate St. Thomas somewhere on the left." Neo-Catholic thought was concerned to make the Church's vision relevant once again in the twentieth century, and from this point of view the Quebec Church's renewed attempt to penetrate civil society was suspect. As Ryan put it, "by the younger militants . . . the Pope's call to the apostolate was understood as a challenge to build a bridge, rather than widen the existing gap, between the Church and the modern world." Significantly, this was "the first generation of French Canadians to be marked by the modern developments of human, particularly social sciences" (Ryan 1961:53–55). Moreover, as Coleman has remarked

(1984:52–55), Catholic Action organizations "tended to be administered by a central office at the diocesan level" rather than at the level of the parish; hence they developed their own bureaucracy of lay professionals delivering specialized services to an urban clientele. In sum, the very involvement of the Church in social and cultural "works" helped foster a new intelligentsia that would break free from clerical control of "cultural affairs" and turn to a technocratic state and its ally, social science.

While the Church grappled with social problems the provincial government contributed to the growing unrest among intellectuals and social critics by what was seen as its comparative backwardness. At a time when other North American and European governments were developing modern welfare-state policies in response to the Depression and, later, to wartime needs and those of postwar reconstruction, the Quebec government under Maurice Duplessis clung to the anti-statism of traditional nationalism. Quinn has written (1979:6) that the maintenance of provincial autonomy against federal encroachment has always been central to Quebec's agenda within the Canadian Confederation. Yet Ottawa's expansion during and after World War II could not be countered by the old-fashioned patronage system that Duplessis controlled. In the early 1940s the federal government began to introduce new social services, to push for greater governmental centralization within Confederation and, to finance these innovations, "to monopolize the most lucrative sources of tax revenue, thus curtailing seriously the taxation resources of the provinces." After the War it continued on this course, which, from Quebec's point of view, "threatened to alter radically the constitutional arrangements of 1867." The chief concern of the second Union Nationale government (1944–60) was to fight federal centralization, and Ottawa's social legislation "met with relentless opposition from the province of Quebec" (113–15).

Yet Duplessis' resistance put Quebec progressives in a bind. Though they sympathized with the ideal of provincial autonomy, they believed that Duplessis' manner of pursuing that ideal harmed rather than helped Quebec. Instead of providing Quebec with the social services that progressives believed necessary, Duplessis went to elaborate lengths to refuse or sabotage those offered by Ottawa on the grounds that Quebec's institutions were adequate, if not "the best." Quebec was usually last among provincial governments to adopt social and economic legislation considered standard elsewhere (McRoberts and Postgate 1980:60–64), and Quebec progressives were forced to turn to Ottawa for examples of enlightened social policies. Their dilemma was typified in the famous case of Duplessis' refusal of federal grants to universities on the grounds that education is a provincial concern: Quebec intellectuals were torn between respect for Duplessis' constitutional position and the crying financial needs

86

of their universities—which were drastically underfunded by Duplessis, whose scorn for intellectuals was legendary (Trudeau 1957). Finally, Duplessis' opposition to the growth of governmental bureaucracy and his reliance on discretionary rather than statutory grants further frustrated the emerging group of liberally educated, would-be leaders that Ryan described (Guindon 1964; Quinn 1979:136–37). As McRoberts and Postgate point out (1980:64), there were few social scientists in Duplessis' administration.

Three Philosophies of National Culture

In this context, federal initiatives stemming from the Massey Commission—such as increased grants to universities and the establishment, in 1957, of Canada Council[1]—evoked an ambivalent reaction among Quebec intellectuals and progressives. The Massey Commission had justified its recommendations for federal cultural policies by distinguishing between "formal education," which it recognized as a solely provincial concern, and the "general non-academic education" that citizens experience throughout life, and for which, it claimed, governmental responsibility was not constitutionally circumscribed.[2] Since the Massey Commission defined culture as "that part of education which enriches the mind and refines the taste . . . through the arts, letters and sciences," it could argue that the federal government was morally bound to contribute to general education in order to promote cultural development:

1. Schafer (1976:45) gives this summary account of Canada Council: "Patterned after the Arts Council of Great Britain, but with a much enlarged scope and a more demanding mandate, the Canada Council has acted as a source of inspiration and assistance to thousands of individual artists, scholars and organizations. To satisfy its objects—'to foster and promote the study, enjoyment and production of works in the arts, humanities and social sciences'—the council is empowered to make grants and awards; sponsor competitions, exhibitions and performances; facilitate international exchanges; and undertake research."

2. Père Georges-Henri Lévesque, founder of the Faculty of Social Sciences at Laval University, and an important leader among what I have called the progressive forces in Quebec during the Duplessis era, was frequently blamed by French-Canadian nationalists for formulating the subtle distinction between formal and general education that was held to legitimate federal action in cultural affairs (Parisé 1976:60). In contrast, recent federal documents (Canada 1982) on cultural policy retrospectively dub what had been known as the Massey Commission "the Massey-Lévesque Commission," thereby creating the impression that a government commission of the 1950s was more explicitly "bi-cultural" than people at that time would have liked to admit. In both cases, Lévesque's participation has been taken to be symbolically crucial.

87

> If the Federal Government is to renounce its right to asso-
> ciate itself with other social groups, public and private, in
> the general education of Canadian citizens, it denies its
> intellectual and moral purpose, the complete conception
> of the common good is lost, and Canada, as such, becomes
> a materialistic society. (Canada 1951:7–8)

This argument never convinced French-Canadian nationalists.
In an editorial in *Le Devoir*, André Laurendeau complained (1959a)
that "the central government has established institutions whose primary function is cultural," adding that "the [constitutional] regime is
thus slowly changing." By contrast, sociologist J. C. Falardeau (1960)
credited what he saw as French Canada's postwar cultural awaken-
ing to such federal institutions as Radio-Canada and the National
Film Board, which, he claimed, gave work to artists and helped to
create a public for them. Beyond the constitutional question, many
politicians and intellectuals agreed that government must assume
greater responsibility for cultural affairs. The Montreal Junior Chamber of Commerce suggested the establishment of a provincial arts
council "to develop and aid French-Canadian cultural life" through
grants for theater, "films illustrating French-Canadian culture,"
orchestras, and libraries (*Le Devoir* 1959). Writing on the editorial
page of *Le Devoir*, Laurendeau (1959b) and Pierre Vigeant (1960) called
for state aid for theater and historic preservation, while G. E.
Lapalme, leader of the Liberal opposition in the Quebec legislature,
asked the Union Nationale government to change the title "Provincial
Secretary" to "Minister of Cultural Affairs" (*Le Devoir* 1960a). And
though after the death of Duplessis (September 7, 1959) the Union
Nationale government seemed more receptive to granting cultural aid
(Laporte 1960), Quebec's "backwardness" compared to Ottawa
remained obvious to many. An anonymous commentator in *Le Devoir*
wrote that Quebec's tradition of support for "cultural undertakings"
seemed to die under Duplessis, an impression reinforced by Canada
Council's presence: "an arts organization knew that there was hope
for aid from Ottawa, but none from Quebec" (*Le Devoir* 1960b). And,
as Guy Frégault wrote in his memoirs (1976:157), many new graduates
of Quebec universities left to work for such federal-government
organizations as Radio-Canada once they realized that there would be
no posts for them in the straitened institutions where they had been
trained.

On the eve of the Quiet Revolution, then, the question of government involvement in national culture was being widely discussed. Yet people disagreed not only on the constitutional question,
but on the meaning of the term "culture" and, especially, on what
constituted "French-Canadian culture." It will be useful at this point
to consider in some detail the differences among three well-articu-

lated positions, each of which analyzed the constitutional problem and the political context from the perspective of a particular theory of nation and culture.

The Tremblay Commission

Durocher and Jean (1971) and Coleman (1984:72–75) have argued that Duplessis was pressured to create the Royal Commission of Inquiry into Constitutional Problems (Tremblay Commission) by an unlikely coalition of business leaders and nationalists. Coleman suggests that Quebec entrepreneurs were anxious for a stronger provincial government to aid indigenous businesses that were competing against outside firms expanding into Quebec, while the nationalist intelligentsia sought, as always, to preserve what was seen as Quebec's constitutionally mandated provincial autonomy. According to Durocher and Jean (337), the "unprecedented prestige, power and authority" of the federal government after World War II seemed to nationalists "to relegate the provincial governments to the shadows," and justified, in their eyes, Quebec's "desperate struggle against Ottawa in the domain of federal-provincial relations." In this situation many saw Duplessis' "negative" autonomism as utterly inadequate, and convinced him to appoint the royal commission. He did so with reluctance in March 1953 and expected nothing more than a brief report. But the commissioners saw their mandate differently; they held 97 public hearings, received 217 briefs, and ultimately published a four-volume report which is nothing less than an inventory of the national situation.

Reread thirty years later, the Tremblay Commission *Report* presents a sometimes confusing blend: a theory of culture which combines Neo-Catholic philosophy and traditional French-Canadian nationalism, as well as an endorsement of Canadian federalism side-by-side with a call for more responsible government at the provincial level. Much of this material can be found in the extensive discussion of "The Problem of Culture" with which the second volume begins. There the Commission presented its vision of a French-Canadian culture grounded in Roman Catholicism as this was defined in the Neo-Catholic point of view. Nonetheless, though they cite Maritain's *Man and the State* and draw on his understanding of the relationship between religion and culture, their commitment to nationalism leads them to utilize Maritain selectively, overlooking his subordination of nationalism to religion.

For Maritain, culture belongs to the temporal, natural order and thus is subordinate to religion, which emanates from the eternal and supernatural order (1945:15–17). True religion—Roman Catholicism—is universal and confined to no particular culture, though its divine spirit freely assumes culturally specific forms in order to make itself available to humans (42–43). By contrast, when a society particularizes its religion by subordinating it to nationalism, religion deviates from both natural order and supernatural truth:

> Pagan antiquity admirably understood the city's need for religion; its error was to absorb religion in . . . local civilization . . . by deifying the city, or, rather, by nationalizing the gods. . . . (18)

Maritain does not slight such eminently human communities as the city or the nation, but he sees them to be "natural," in contrast to political society, which is the work of reason. Thus for Maritain the nation is not an absolute value: though political society must be organized in such a way that national realities are respected, its goal is man's temporal well-being, not the glorification of the nation (1951:4–11). And in the service of earthly welfare the polity remakes the nation:

> A genuine principle of nationalities would be formulated as follows: the body politic should develop both its own moral dynamism and the respect for human freedoms to such a point that the national communities which are contained within it would both have their natural rights fully recognized, and tend spontaneously to merge in a single higher and more complex National Community. (8)

For Maritain, then, the state creates nations of a higher order. But this "principle of nationalities" has been perverted in modern nationalisms which conflate "nation" and "state": "the State, when it has been identified with the Nation . . . has presumed to impose by force of law the so-called type and genius of the Nation, thus becoming a cultural, ideological, caesaro-papist, totalitarian State" (7).

How do the authors of the Tremblay *Report*,[3] who cite this section of Maritain's book, treat his clear statement of the nation's natural limits? In discussing both the Catholic foundation of French-Canadian culture and the place of French Canada within Confederation they shy away from the universalism of Maritain's philosophy. According to the *Report*, "culture may be defined as an organic collection of knowledge, of means of expression and of values." Knowledge and values tend towards the universal—knowledge because "the data of learning know no frontier," values because they provide each culture with "a metaphysic" or interpretation of ulti-

3. The section of the *Report* treated here was written largely by Esdras Minville, one of the pioneers of a nationalist thought that embraced economic as well as political and cultural concerns. Minville was a "close supporter" of Abbé Groulx (Coleman 1984:72; Durocher and Jean 1971:342, 351).

mate reality (Quebec 1956: 2:8–10). By contrast, the forms of culture are particular:

> Every national culture is a[n] . . . interpretation of a philosophy either universal or tending towards universality. What there is of *national,* and consequently of difference in it, is not the thought but its form; on one side the expression and, primarily, the language; on the other side . . . usages, customs, traditions, etc. (15)

This distinction between universality and particularity is also expressed in the discussion of religion and culture with which this section of the *Report* dutifully begins: culture, we are told, receives from religion "its general inspiration and directive thought; while religion borrows from culture such and such means of integration within . . . daily life" (6).

Evaluated with respect to the individual's needs, culture should help human beings achieve spiritual fulfillment, even salvation; this was the "personalist" dimension of Neo-Catholic philosophy (Coleman 1984:50). But human beings are social as well as spiritual creatures and, according to the Tremblay *Report,* culture is available to them only as national culture, "the totality of the rational and spiritual values forming the collective patrimony of a determined human group" (15). With the introduction of the concept of national culture, the Commissioners' argument changes, for the discussions of universality and individual fulfillment are now subordinated to the idea of a national culture taken as an absolute value. We are told, for example, that despite ceaseless change a communal "cultural type" must be based on unchanging values: "if the underlying thought itself changed, there would be substitution of one culture for another" (29). Or again, though there is some discussion of diversity within a communal culture, the authors assume that a healthy culture, which affords its members the greatest chance for self-development, springs from a unified collective milieu: "to be efficacious, the ethnic environment should be homogeneous" (21).

According to the Commission, the homogeneity and immutability of a healthy national culture have characterized French-Canadian culture in the past. The *Report* defines this culture in terms of "its Christian inspiration and its French genius" (33); and it summarizes this French and Christian content in neo-Thomist terms: "natural law," "supernatural human vocation," and so on (33–38). Despite this abstract formulation, the authors affirm that such concepts are "lived spontaneously as a tradition" by French Canadians. They add that individuals can "achieve their cultural type" only when they live according to these cultural principles (35), an argument which clearly subordinates individual fulfillment to national character.

As we should expect, there is a negative vision offsetting this confident account of cultural content. Everywhere in the modern world Christian culture is threatened by the new culture of scientific materialism which "has retained nothing of [the] fundamental postulates" of "the old Christian humanist culture" in which it originated. Both the content and the homogeneity of French-Canadian culture are threatened by the existence of those French Canadians who have strayed from traditional values and adopted attitudes of the English-speaking world:

> Primarily it was the practice of economic and political institutions of British origin which resulted in the creation of an individualistic and liberal mentality among a people whose religious . . . intellectual . . . and social traditions had within them nothing either individualistic or liberal. . . . Men think along certain lines, but they are induced to live along certain other lines, and they end up thinking as they live. It is not otherwise that assimilation proceeds. (72–73)

Arrived at this assessment, the commissioners call simultaneously for modernization and for the preservation of traditional values. They acknowledge that assimilation is proceeding apace, yet assert that the unchanging principles of French-Canadian culture "retain their full value." What is needed, then, is social and cultural "restoration" (73) that will modernize French Canada while respecting ultimate values. And only the state can carry out reforms of this magnitude:

> The time is long since past in which we could trust ourselves to the spontaneity of instinctive reflexes for the preservation and renewal of a particular culture. . . . Every government must, from now on, have a cultural policy, in the full sense of the word. (68)

This brings us, then, to constitutional problems. Government must assume responsibility for "cultural restoration and expansion" (71) by formulating an overall cultural policy to consider not only specifically cultural institutions (educational, scientific, artistic) but the cultural impact of legislation in all domains. The task facing French Canada is particularly urgent—nothing less than the reintegration of French-Canadian culture into the modern milieu. According to the Commission, a society's institutional system is an expression of the collective culture, and if institutions become outdated they must be remade so that they can continue to express national culture while satisfying human needs in a changed, modernizing world. It is time, the *Report* urges, "to completely 'rethink' the whole social order" (73).

Yet such rethinking must be carried out by the nation itself, or by the government that represents it, both because creativity and progress depend upon autonomy and because only indigenously designed and executed plans can express the spirit of national culture. What, then, is the national government of French Canada that is to be called on to lead the restoration? Here the authors make a dual claim. First, they argue that Quebec should be considered the national government of all French Canada, both within and beyond Quebec's borders:

> If the Anglo-Canadian culture . . . can count on the orga-
> nized life of nine out of the ten provinces to live and
> develop itself, the French-Canadian culture can count
> only on the organized life of the Province of Quebec, the
> sole centre where . . . it can freely express, renew and
> enrich itself. . . . And that province . . . remains the verita-
> ble cultural focus . . . of all French Canada. (70)

Second, and as a consequence of the first argument, the Tremblay Commission claims that Ottawa by itself cannot be considered the national government of French Canada. They argue that "the 'national' government of Quebec is the federal government and the government of the Province acting together." Ottawa therefore has no right to violate the constitutional division of responsibilities by undertaking cultural projects "on the grounds that it is a 'national' government" (77). In sum, in order to reserve for the Quebec government a "national" autonomy in the global domain of culture, the *Report* claims that Quebec—having pan-Canadian responsibilities—is more than a provincial government, and that Ottawa is less than a national government with respect to French Canada as a whole. Finally, the Commission sketches a role for the federal government. First, it must leave the provinces the resources and freedom they need to fulfill the cultural mission that is constitutionally theirs; and, second, it must ensure that all federal institutions, and particularly those (such as the CBC) which are primarily cultural, respect the specificity of each of Canada's two nations.

The Tremblay Commission *Report* both looks forward to the Quiet Revolution—indeed, the provincial Liberal Party adopted many of its views as its own in the campaign of 1960—and backward to clerical-conservative nationalism (Trofimenkoff 1982:275–76; Durocher and Jean 1971:357–63). It seeks to combine both modernization and preservation. It calls for a global cultural policy on the part of a national government in order to restore an unchanging culture which is changing, in order to integrate into the modern world values

93

that are not of the modern world. Just as the Massey Commission had stressed Ottawa's responsibility for Canadian national culture—a global reality that could not be constitutionally confined to one level of government—the Tremblay Commission suggested that Quebec, as the national government of French Canada, had responsibility for French Canadian culture throughout Canada. But by denying the existence of a Canadian nation and culture—since it saw Canada as a bi-national state with no unitary culture— it could dispute federal government claims to global cultural action, and particularly to cultural action on behalf of French Canada. The Commission did not reject Canadian federalism, but subordinated it to the preservation of the two nations which compose it. And their vision was not so lofty as that of Maritain, who spoke of the merging of national cultures "in a single higher and more complex National Community" (1951:8). By contrast, the Tremblay Commission advocated a full contribution from French Canada to the life of the Confederation, but envisioned that contribution as the fullest possible development of its separate, particular culture. In brief, for the Commission "the transcendence of . . . particularisms" is ultimately a less valued goal than the development of each of them (81). Much more comprehensive than Duplessis had envisioned, the Tremblay Commission *Report* is a typical nationalist inventory which tries to summarize the situation of the global society. It was the first such attempt sponsored by the provincial government (Durocher and Jean 1971:358), and as such was indicative of things to come.

Pierre Elliott Trudeau

Pierre Trudeau has consistently opposed anti-Canadian versions of French-Canadian nationalism since his days as a political journalist and academic among the tiny group of Quebec progressives publicly critical of the Duplessis administration. As a major figure in Ottawa— first as assistant to the Liberal Prime Minister of Canada, then as Minister of Justice, and finally as Prime Minister (from 1968 to 1984, with only a brief interlude [1979–1980] out of power)—Trudeau has had an historically unusual opportunity to put his ideas directly into practice. In chapters 5 and 7 I will touch on federal cultural policies elaborated under his leadership, but for now I confine my attention to essays written in the late 1950s and early 1960s.

Citing such scholars as Weber and Kedourie, Trudeau defines nationalism as a historically particular political philosophy that specifies which units of population and territory might properly claim to form a sovereign state (1964:190). He dismisses any concept of the nation as a biological or natural reality (1962:156–57), arguing that in Europe centralizing states were at first territorial and only subsequently—with the development of the idea of popular sovereignty—

national. Moreover, since nations are not natural units, states rely on "the gum called nationalism" to manufacture consensus just as would-be nations rely on it to form states. For Trudeau the argument is "circular":

> The idea of nation which is at the origin of a new type of state does not refer to a "biological" reality . . .; consequently the nation has constantly and artificially to be reborn from the very state to which it gave birth! In other words, the nation first decides what the state should be; but then the state has to decide what the nation should remain. (1964:190)

Thus "nationhood [is] little more than a state of mind" based on an arbitrary philosophy, and within the logic of this nationalist world view, "every sociologically distinct group" can claim nationhood and hence the right to form a sovereign state (189). For Trudeau, then, "the very idea of the nation-state is absurd" because it is indefinitely fragmenting: every nation, however its borders are drawn, will encompass groups which can in turn constitute themselves as national minorities claiming the right to self-determination (1962:158).

Absurd and irrational, nationalism is, in Trudeau's view, an emotional force, and to it he opposes federalism as representative of reason in an unreasonable age:

> Federalism was an inescapable product of an age which recognized the principle of self-determination. For on the one hand, a sense of national identity . . . was bound to be generated in a great many groups. . . . But on the other hand, the insuperable difficulties of living alone and the practical necessity of sharing the state with neighbouring groups were in many cases such as to make distinct statehood unattractive or unattainable. For those who recognized that the first law of politics is to start from the facts . . . the federal compromise thus became imperative. (1964:192)

Thus federalism, which recognizes what to Trudeau are the true facts of ethnic heterogeneity, is superior to political systems based on nationally exclusive self-government, which sacrifice good government to spurious natural facts. And good government is measured above all by the freedom and opportunity for self-development which the state makes available to human beings. From this point of view nationalistic states are again suspect, for it is the business of the state to meet the needs of all citizens regardless of their ethnic or other particularities: "the aim of a political society is not the glorification of

95

a 'national fact'" but "the establishment . . . of a legal order that will safeguard the development of its citizens" (1965:4, 21). In terms of economic and social welfare this imperative translates into policies which balance the greatest possible increase in per capita income against the redistribution of wealth among all classes and regions.

With respect to the Canadian situation, Trudeau excoriates both French- and English-Canadian nationalisms. His denunciation of Duplessis' clerical-conservative nationalism, and his steadfast blaming of Quebec for Quebec's ills, make it easy to overlook his countervailing denunciation of English Canada as the cause of French-Canadian isolationism. According to Trudeau, the Confederation of 1867 was meant as a practical solution to a Canadian reality in which neither French Canada nor English Canada would yield to or assimilate the other. Yet English Canadians have stubbornly refused to accept their French-Canadian compatriots. Exercising a tyranny of numbers, they largely excluded French Canadians from the federal bureaucracy and promoted an exclusively British-Canadian nationalism at home and abroad. As the central government grew more powerful compared to the provincial governments, the fact that Ottawa seemed to represent British Canada but not French Canada became increasingly galling to French Canadians. Moreover, provincial initiatives, stifled by Ottawa when they threatened continental economy and unity, were unopposed when they negated the rights of French-Canadian minorities outside Quebec (1964:198–200). In sum, the original (and, from Trudeau's perspective, reasonable) compact that had united French and English Canadians in Confederation was gradually replaced by a federal state based on a nationalism inimical to one of the two groups: "during several generations, the stability of the Canadian consensus was due to Quebec's inability to do anything about it."

For Trudeau, the understandable though tragic result of English-Canadian arrogance has been a defensive French-Canadian nationalism that has stifled Quebec. Trudeau stresses the reactionary, oppositional nature of Québécois nationalism—which he calls an "overdeveloped" security system—in terms that suggest the objectification of culture which is a central theme of this book:

> Our nationalism, to oppose a surrounding world that was English-speaking, Protestant, democratic, materialistic, commercial, and later industrial, created a system of defence which put a premium on all the contrary forces: the French language, Catholicism, authoritarianism, idealism, rural life, and later the return to the land. (1956:7)

Trudeau argues that French-Canadian social thought, exclusively preoccupied with this nationalism, has ignored twentieth-century

96

social science and turned instead to "the social doctrine of the Church." Yet papal calls for social justice have been narrowly interpreted in French Canada to support "authoritarianism and xenophobia" while the Church's concern for progress, democracy, and the emancipation of workers has been sytematically overlooked (13–14). Finally, the anti-statism of the nationalists has led to internal paralysis—a situation in which all social reforms have had to come from Ottawa.

Trudeau's recipe for reform requires both English- and French-Canadians to sacrifice their narrow nationalisms and the "self-destructive idea of nation-state in favour of the more civilized goal of polyethnic pluralism" (1962:165). He envisions Canada as a "federation grouping two *linguistic* communities" (1965:31) and, in contrast to the Tremblay Commission, rejects French-Canadian claims to a special status for Quebec as the "national" government of French Canada. Trudeau thus advocates a "constitutionalist" rather than "separatist" option for French Canadians, urging them to participate fully in democratic processes at both the federal and provincial levels and thereby to make Canada *their* country:

> French Canadians must . . . abandon their role of oppressed nation and decide to participate boldly and intelligently in the Canadian experience. It is wrong to say that Confederation has been a total failure for French Canadians; the truth is rather that they have never really tried to make a success of it. In Quebec, we tended to fall back upon a sterile, negative provincial autonomy; in Ottawa our frequent abstentions encouraged paternalistic centralization. (31)

By the same token, English Canadians must accept French-Canadian participation and abandon their exaltation of "the *English*-Canadian nation" (32).

With respect to the cultural policies needed to ensure a Canadian national identity and consensus, Trudeau advocates, first, vigorous federal initiatives "for the defence and better appreciation of the French language" (32), with special care taken to insure that federal services be available in French to all francophone citizens; and second, a federal campaign to bolster nationalism *"at the federal level."* The latter effort is necessary for pragmatic, not philosophical, reasons; a federal state—which is a reasonable compromise among various emotionally motivated nationalisms and regionalisms—must invest whatever is necessary to counterbalance the loyalties focused on its constituent units: "a national image must be created that will have such an appeal as to make any image of a separatist group unattractive" (1964:193).

Finally, French Canadians must assume responsibility for their own cultural excellence by making full use, within Quebec, of the control over cultural institutions granted the provinces by Confederation. According to Trudeau, "the mere survival of the French language and of the cultural values relating to it" are "already assured" by demographic realities; the challenge, then, is

> to stimulate our language and culture so that they are alive and vital, not just fossils from the past. We must realize that French will only have value to the extent that it is spoken by a progressive people. (1965:30)

Thus in Trudeau's essays of the late 1950s and early 1960s we find what has been described above as the progressives' critique of Quebec's backwardness. Yet Trudeau's position can be distinguished from that of other social critics in terms of the focus of his individualism: where French-Canadian nationalists typically privilege the collective individual, Trudeau's social vision concentrates on the self-development of individual citizens aided by a state whose main task is to ensure that competition among them proceeds in a just manner. Trudeau is equally critical of English- and French-Canadian nationalism and chauvinism. According to him, French Canadians should cease complaining about English-Canadian injustice and look to their own betterment, and, above all, they should expect excellence to stem from competition on the pan-Canadian stage rather than from protection within a Quebec reserve. Thus despite his concessions to pragmatic cultural investment on the part of a federal state, Trudeau advocates above all "an open culture," and suggests "that cultural protectionism, like its economic counterpart, would tend . . . to produce a weak, 'hot-house' culture" (29).

Georges-Emile Lapalme and the Quebec Liberal Party

Georges-Emile Lapalme has been called the "father" of Quebec's Ministère des Affaires culturelles, and many of the people with expertise in cultural affairs whom I interviewed praised Lapalme as a politician who brought vision and integrity to Quebec cultural politics. As one government official told me, he was "an esthete who was ubiquitous in the cultural domain"—"Quebec's Malraux." This comparison (which some find a bit strained for, as one well-known writer asked me, how can a simple provincial politician be expected to be a Malraux?) is perhaps motivated by the intense admiration for André Malraux that Lapalme expresses repeatedly in his memoirs, as well as by the influential example that Malraux, the first French Minister of State for Cultural Affairs, set during the early years of the Quebec Ministry. For not only was Lapalme an "esthete"; he was an advocate of French "high" culture, and Malraux's definition of culture as "the best of what survives in men's works" was particularly congenial to him (Lapalme 1973:96; cf. Malraux 1953:630–42).

After serving in Ottawa for five years as a federal deputy, Lapalme returned to Quebec in 1950 to head the provincial Liberal Party. His was the unenviable task of organizing the opposition to Maurice Duplessis and the reigning Union Nationale. He began by building a party organization that was clearly separate from the federal liberals, for the encompassment of the provincial liberals by the "centralizers" in Ottawa was a favorite campaign theme of Duplessis. Lapalme's Liberals were defeated by the Union Nationale in 1952 (winning 23 of 92 seats) and 1956 (20 of 93 seats), though the popular vote was closer than the distribution of seats indicates (Quinn 1979:173). In 1958 Lapalme was succeeded as leader of the Party by Jean Lesage, who had been Minister of Northern Affairs and Natural Resources in the federal cabinet of Louis St. Laurent. Lapalme remained leader of the opposition in the Quebec assembly from 1952 until 1960, when he became Minister of Justice in the Lesage cabinet.

Like Trudeau, Lapalme was a progressive who blamed Quebec's backwardness on the negative autonomism of Duplessis, and who looked to Ottawa and abroad for examples of enlightened social policy that he wished to see enacted in Quebec by a modern provincial government. Campaigning in 1952 under the slogan "Social Justice"—at a time when such rhetoric inevitably engendered accusations of "communism" from the Duplessis camp—the Liberals addressed such issues as social security, free public education, academic freedom, labor legislation, provincial control of natural resources, and the legal status of married women (Lapalme 1970:22–70). By 1956 natural resources and education had been singled out as central campaign issues, both typifying the progressives' concern to use the provincial government to bring Quebec and the French-Canadian nation fully into the twentieth century. Citing his own campaign speeches, Lapalme recalls in his memoirs the electoral themes of 1956:

> "In an era of unprecedented wealth, in a world where physics, mechanics, chemistry and electronics are becoming masters of matter put in the service of man, what have we produced since 1947?" And I gave some statistics: mechanical engineers, 0; physicists, 0; mining engineers, 56; geologists, 40; managers, 0; aeronautical engineers, 0; agronomists, 0. This preoccupation was that of the Americans who were conquering the world. . . .
>
> Everything seemed clear to us: to respond to increasingly complex problems, a modern liberal state had to become at least partially technocratic. (208)

Here was the quintessential Quiet-Revolution attitude, shared by politicians like Lapalme and intellectuals like Trudeau: the belief that good government based on technical knowledge was the key to social progress. But unlike Trudeau, Lapalme was profoundly nationalistic, and his political activities were devoted to French-Canadian national development. As he writes in his memoirs (1970:241), "the French Canadian must recognize that the most all-embracing aspect of his milieu is not democracy but the French fact. The child lives by the language that he learns long before he utilizes democracy." For Lapalme, then, French-Canadian nationality—epitomized and grounded in its [high] culture—was a fundamental reality that democracy must respect, a position which is, as we have seen, precisely the opposite of Trudeau's but which accords well with the cultural nationalism of the Tremblay Commission. Like the Tremblay Commission, Lapalme advocated a pan-Canadian development of French-Canadian culture, with Quebec seen as the "mère-patrie" of all French Canada. On the other hand, in contrast to the commissioners, Lapalme defined French-Canadian culture in purely secular terms as "French and Canadian in its essence" (1973:85). For him culture, education, and the French language were indissolubly linked; he considered the last of these to be most fundamental, and he explicitly excluded religion from this triad.[4] This secular vision of culture was characteristic of certain intellectuals and artists, active during the 1940s and 1950s, who opposed the clerical-conservative vision of a Catholic national culture but were nevertheless appalled at the spread of American mass culture or even a "Québécois" popular culture. Lapalme would have agreed with his counterpart in the Duplessis government, Jean Bruchési, who proclaimed repeatedly in the postwar years that Quebec must remain faithful to "French intellectual culture," to "one of the most brilliant forms of human civilization: French civilization," and that Quebec "needed above all a French soul" (1974:103–11).

Lapalme played a key role in establishing the quasi-diplomatic relations between the governments of France and Quebec that would loom so large in nationalist politics of the 1960s and 1970s. Duplessis had been famous for speaking of French Canadians as "des français améliorés" (improved Frenchmen), an expression suggesting the pious dismissal of post-Revolutionary France by the clerical-conservative nationalists of Quebec.[5] For Lapalme, however, such an attitude was almost suicidal: without the continual aid and influence

4. Interview with G. E. Lapalme, Montreal, January 1984.
5. The strength of Catholicism in Quebec has always made it possible to justify the Conquest of New France by Great Britain in retrospect, for the British victory can be said to have preserved Canada from the anti-clericalism and atheism of the French Revolution. On such "providential conquest" theories, see Cook (1971:99–113) and Galarneau (1970).

of French high culture, French-Canadian culture would only degenerate, a process that Lapalme saw above all in the *"franglais"* spoken not only among the masses but in the "high-cultural" institutions of education and government:

> Session after session I spoke without effect in favor of language and culture . . . but above all, of a Franco-Québécois rapprochement. (1970:238)

> . . . it had always seemed to me aberrant not to attempt to obtain water from the source in order to ensure our survival by administering an injection of . . . *francophonie*. (1973:42)

These ambitions could not be realized as long as Duplessis remained in power, but they became central to Lapalme's mission once he became a cabinet minister in 1960.

As a politician and strategist Lapalme advocated the growth of the Quebec "state" as the most appropriate tool for the social and cultural development of the French-Canadian nation. For Lapalme cultural policy was but one aspect "of an overall policy of economic and social progress" (Frégault 1976:17), yet he stressed the priority of the cultural domain:

> During ten years, without ever denying the linkage between economics and culture, I always put culture in first place, always privileged our spiritual or intellectual rather than material wealth. The texts are there, by the hundreds: "It is not by money that we will win against the Americans or the English. It will be by culture. The economy will necessarily follow, because no one will then be able to take away anything from our culture." (1973:29)

Such rhetoric suggests the clerical-conservative distinction between French-Canadian spirituality and Anglo-Saxon materialism, and this echo of older nationalisms will appear repeatedly in Quebec cultural policy-making. Yet Lapalme was a secular esthete who looked to France rather than Rome. From the time of his entrance into Quebec politics he had advocated that the "pieces of culture divided among six or seven departments" be brought together in one coordinating agency.[6] Thus when De Gaulle named Malraux State Minister for Cultural Affairs in 1959, Lapalme asked the Canadian Embassy in Paris for information about the new post, and demanded in the Quebec assembly that the post of Provincial Secretary be retitled "Minister of Cultural Affairs" (*Le Devoir* 1960a). But France and Malraux provided more than the example of their bureaucracy:

6. Personal Interview, Montreal, January 1984.

Lapalme was particularly drawn to the type of French intellectual culture that Malraux epitomized, and, as we shall see, the Cultural Affairs Department that he established in 1961 bears to this day Lapalme's high-cultural orientation.

The Founding of the
Ministère des Affaires culturelles

The Liberal Party that came to power in the Quebec Assembly in June 1960 has been retrospectivley characterized as both nationalist (McRoberts and Postgate 1980:95) and "resolutely antinationalist" (Clift 1982:18). The concern of the Party for progress and technocratic reform has sometimes been taken to represent a liberal and individualistic, as opposed to a nationalist, orientation, as has a favorite catch-word of the period, *rattrapage,* or "catching up": "the ideology of catching up is by definition federalist, for it envisages the . . . integration of the Quebec people in a greater American world, through the intermediary of Canada. It is essentially a negation of Quebec as a nation" (Rioux 1971:79; cf. Clift 1982:19–23; Levasseur 1982:73–80). Yet a progressive and individualistic ideology can be combined with nationalism, which is itself an individualistic ideology, and this the Liberals did by pledging themselves to both collective and individual self-development and, indeed, by equating the two. Moreover, among the Liberal Party's leading lights were nationalists like Lapalme and René Lévesque (though the nationalisms of these two differed in important respects), technocrats like Paul Gérin-Lajoie, who engineered the State's takeover of education (Clift 1982:25), and a pragmatic politician like Jean Lesage, whose task, as Party head and Premier, was to hold the party and the cabinet together. It is thus misleading to portray the Liberals as representing a homogeneous point of view, for, like most political parties whose goal is to win elections, they tried to appeal to as many people as possible while maintaining an image of consistency (Quinn 1979:171–81).

In the 1960 electoral campaign, the Liberals opposed the "negative" nationalism of Duplessis; yet, as Lapalme has pointed out (1970:40–41), Duplessis' nationalist rhetoric set the tone for all political debate in the 1950s (much as the Parti Québécois would do in the 1970s). The Liberals countered the Union Nationale not with an antinationalist doctrine, but by articulating what they saw as a progressive nationalism—that is, by seeking technocratic development for the collectivity as well as for individuals. They drew heavily on the Tremblay Commission's suggested reforms (cf. Lesage 1959), which allowed them to advocate change without appearing to challenge the

Church, but they drew as well on Lapalme's more secular progressivism. The Liberal program of 1960 (reproduced in Roy 1971: 2:378–88), written mainly by Lapalme, stressed "national" development as much as liberal reform and progress, as the following declaration, attributed to Lesage and placed at the head of the program, indicates: "It is the duty of the Government of this Province to evaluate what we possess . . . so that it may be developed in such a manner that Quebec may . . . grow in the path of its traditions, its spirit and its culture" (378).

The first section of the platform was entitled "La Vie nationale" in the French version, but simply "Education and Culture" in the somewhat different English-language version (reproduced as Appendix C in Quinn 1979:313–23). Eight articles concerning educational reform—free and compulsory public education, free textbooks, appointment of a royal commission on education, and so on—were preceded by the first article of the platform calling for the establishment of a "Ministère des Affaires culturelles" or "Department of Cultural Affairs." This was to include five agencies: L'Office de la Langue Française (ou de la linguistique), Le Départment du Canada Français d'outre-frontières, Le Conseil Provincial des Arts, La Commission des Monuments Historiques, and Le Bureau Provincial d'Urbanisme. The English version provides the following translations: A Provincial Arts Council, An Historic Monuments Commission, A Provincial Office of Town Planning, A Provincial Linguistic Office, and An Office for Cultural Relationships with French-speaking groups outside the Province. These translations, and the ordering of the items, suggest an attempt to minimize for anglophone readers the nationalistic implications of cultural affairs, which are spelled out explicitly in the French version as a "commentary" on Article 1:

> The French fact (*le fait français*) constitutes the most all-embracing element of the Quebec context, and it is one that we owe it to ourselves to develop in depth. It is by our culture rather than by numbers that we will prevail. Conscious of our responsibility to the French language, we will endow it with an agency that will be both protective and stimulating; conscious of our responsibilities to the three or four million French Canadians and Acadians who live beyond our borders in Ontario, the Maritimes, the West, in New England and Louisiana, Quebec will become the mother country of all. In the arts, while participating in universal trends we will try to develop a culture specific to us; at the same time, we will use urban planning to enhance what remains of our French character. It is in terms of language and culture that our French presence in North America can assert itself.

This is clearly Lapalme's rhetoric but, as we have seen, his was not the only vision of French-Canadian national culture or of the proper governmental role in developing it. Perhaps if voters had attributed as much importance to the idea of national culture as did nationalist leaders like Lapalme, the first article of the Liberal program and its relationship to the various competing definitions of French-Canadian culture would have attracted more attention than it did. In the nationalist (and decidedly "highbrow") newspaper, *Le Devoir,* the Liberal proposal for a cultural affairs department made the headlines (1960d), but in the more popular and much more widely read *La Presse* (1960) it was barely mentioned as one among many more important proposals of the Liberal program. None of the Liberal Party leaders, other than Lapalme, was particularly attached to the idea, and its prominent position in the program was due only to the fact that Lapalme was the principal author. Lesage, the party leader, spoke frequently during the campaign and during his administration of "the French fact" and of government's responsibility to develop it, but for him, and for the public as well, the key issue was education, not culture. Lesage followed the Tremblay Commission in advocating educational modernization as a key to socioeconomic development (for both individuals and the collectivity) as well as to cultural preservation (1959:81–82, 119–20). Yet he was willing to modulate his nationalist rhetoric to meet the needs of the moment. Speaking to conservative audiences, for example, he made Catholicism an important element of French-Canadian culture (1961a, 1961b), but omitted it at other times (1961c). He was similarly willing to include or exclude, as the occasion dictated, favorable references to the French-Canadian cultural contribution to Canada.

Within eight months of taking office the Liberals moved to create a cultural affairs department. Lesage's presentation of the cultural affairs bill to the Quebec legislative Assembly combines traditional nationalist themes, progressivism, and a cautious federalism into a politically acceptable package. Lesage stressed that a cultural affairs department was "a vital necessity" for national preservation, national progress, and international reputation (1961c:1; extracts reprinted in MAC 1976:11–13). He calls on the nation "to remain faithful to itself" while developing its cultural heritage to meet the challenge of modernity:

> There exists in North America something which is correctly called the "French fact." . . . The present-day French Canadian collectivity has received it as a heritage from its ancestors. But heritage creates duties as well as rights. . . . We must not only safeguard what exists and conserve what we have. We must improve and assert it. . . . We must . . . be dynamic and . . . INNOVATE. (3–4)

The necessity for cultural development (as opposed to cultural preservation) is justified in terms of the spiritualist bias of older French-
Canadian nationalisms combined with a more modern desire to
compete internationally, "to shine in the world": "We will not be the
first government to send a man to the moon. But though we will not be
in the inter-planetary race, we remain in the cultural one . . . [where]
the highest aspirations are permissible for us" (4).

Second, Lesage adds to these "sentimental" and "patriotic" jus-
tifications a "reasonable" argument: French-Canadian culture is necessary to Canada, he argues, to preserve it from Americanization:

> I am certain that our Latin culture can add oxygen to the
> air that we breathe in America. And our English-Canadian
> brothers know that the French-Canadian collectivity, if it
> continues to assert itself, will aid them . . . to counter an
> exceptionally grave danger, a sickness already present in
> us which constantly menaces our Canadian identity: the
> American cultural invasion. . . . (5)

In sum, French-Canadian culture is "a common good" for all of
Canada, one that both English- and French-Canadians have good
(though differing) reasons to protect.

Next, Lesage carefully specifies the proper limitations to government's role in cultural development:

> Let us understand one another clearly. The Govern-
> ment does not create culture, not does it control it.
> The Government seeks simply to create the climate
> which will facilitate the flowering of the arts. (5)

In a world where materialism is increasingly threatening to spiritual
values, Lesage emphasizes "spontaneous cultural expressions" (2) as
an antidote. And though government must aid "artistic creation" to
organize and manifest itself, Lesage privileges the creative initiative
of individuals. Such remarks, in the context of parliamentary debate,
are obviously meant to protect the government from charges of
"socialism." Moreover, they serve to remind people that culture exists
as the "natural" product of the nation, something which can never be
created artificially by a government.

Lesage goes on to comment on the agencies to be associated
with the new department. One of these, the Historic Monuments
Commission, had been in existence since 1922 (see chapter 6), but the
other three were new: a Provincial Arts Council, a French Language
Bureau and an Extra-territorial French Canada Branch. Lesage's
remarks on these agencies show in embryo the major cultural concerns that will occupy the Quebec government from that time on. The
Arts Council is to encourage artistic excellence and to ensure that the

cultural revival of French Canada continues. Moreover, this mission has international as well as domestic ramifications: the Council "must also try to stimulate artistic expressions which bear a seal, a sign, a trademark which calls the world's attention to them as PRODUCTS OF QUEBEC" (7).

A similar concern—almost a cultural imperialism—lies at the heart of the justification for an Extra-territorial French Canada Branch. Lesage argues that French Canada "doesn't stop at the borders of the Province of Quebec" (7); Quebec is the "mother country" of all North American French minorities, and, as such, has a moral responsibility to help them "to safeguard their identity." Moreover, all of Canada will profit from "the diffusion of our culture," as will all of North America from the "shining influence [*rayonnement*] of French culture" (8). And Lesage mentions that the government intends to pursue an analogous course with respect to immigrants within Quebec, that is, to those who, though not extra-territorial, are nonetheless not "within French-Canadian cultural borders." We must, says Lesage, "tempt them to integrate themselves by choice into our culture" (9)—a theme that will become increasingly urgent in Quebec cultural politics, as we shall see in chapter 7.

Finally, Lesage devotes almost a quarter of his speech to the government's role in the protection and development of the French language. These arguments too will become increasingly urgent in Quebec cultural affairs, and we will consider them more extensively in chapter 7. For now it is enough to point out that Lesage bases his argument on the "sociological" fact that language, culture, and nation are inseparable. If the government does not take steps to fortify the French language in the face of anglicization, the French-Canadian nation will run the risk of death: "we could no longer be French Canadians if we spoke another language" (10). The government will therefore join with the many people who have been engaged in "the struggle in favor of good language" (11), and its French Language Bureau "will become the tangible and omnipresent expression of the conscience of French Canada" (12)—a neat statement, perhaps, of the increasingly secular vision of French-Canadian culture being offered to the public (cf. Coleman 1984:132–35).

The Liberal government's cultural affairs bill was a "motherhood" proposal that few could oppose. The leader of the Union Nationale opposition announced that his party was in favor of the "principle," but added that they would rather the government not involve itself in the cultural domain because a leftist government could misuse a cultural agency for propaganda and indoctrination (*Le Devoir* 1961a). André Laurendeau (1961) ridiculed this criticism: according to him, the proposed law, of obvious "nationalist inspiration," was necessarily vague, for only experience would enable the government to specify the modalities of its application. But if one took seriously the Union Nationale's fears, all government action would be ruled out. Writing also in *Le Devoir*, Jean-Marc Léger (soon to be appointed to a post in the French Language Bureau) offered a comprehensive summary of the reasons for the establishment of the new department and the expectations that French-Canadian nationalists had of it. "We find ourselves," he wrote (1961), "in the singular situation where the central government has tended to play an ever greater role in the cultural domain, and notably in favor of French culture in Canada." For Léger this was aberrant for several reasons. First, a state must have primary responsibility for its "national culture"—and the appropriate guardian of French-Canadian culture was the Quebec government. Second, Ottawa's cultural action was suspect on constitutional grounds. Finally, the increasing alienation of French-Canadian intellectuals from the provincial government and their orientation toward Ottawa had to be remedied. As a response to these problems, the new department would be "a ministry of cultural well-being [*salut culturel*] as well as a ministry of foreign relations"—an expectation that epitomizes the nationalists' dream of a strong national state and a renewed national life.

One Culture, Many Contents

At the time of the creation of Quebec's *Ministère des Affaires culturelles,* there was no consensus as to what constituted French-Canadian culture. The clerical-conservative ideal of a Catholic national culture was still being vigorously promoted by the Church hierarchy. For example, during the 1960 electoral campaign the Montreal archdiocese was planning its parade for Saint-Jean-Baptiste day (June 24), the "national" holiday of French Canada. It announced a parade with some 20 floats illustrating the theme of "the French-Canadian presence" in Canada: six floats were to be devoted to the pioneers of New France, "cradle" of Canada (first settlers, peasants, colonial government, fur traders, explorers, and founders of the Church); six to French Canada's "determining influence on Confederation; and nine to the role of French-Canadian culture "as guarantor of Canadian identity" (*comme sauvegarde de l'entité canadienne*) (*Le Devoir* 1960c). Here was a tangible symbolization of their culture, conservatively defined, that thousands of people would witness (cf. Coleman 1984:219–20).

By contrast, an anti-nationalist intellectual like Trudeau, with his dismissal of the concept of a national culture and his definition of cultural progress in terms of individual achievements, had only a small audience at this time, as did his colleague, the sociologist Marcel Rioux (1955), who drew on Ruth Benedict's notion of cultural integration in one of the rare anthropological accounts of French-Canadian culture published in Quebec before the 1960s. By the mid-1960s the secular social science that people like Trudeau and Rioux espoused would achieve a preponderant influence in the Quebec government, but before 1960 social science in Quebec was still Catholic. Throughout the 1950s the influential school of social science at Laval University (Quebec City) was criticized by conservatives for its secularism (Trofimenkoff 1982:291–92), yet its self-definition seems tame enough today: "the School applies itself to scientific instruction, in conformity with Catholic doctrine, devoted to French culture and designed to meet Canada's needs" (Tremblay and Faucher 1951:199).

Finally, the Quebec Liberal Party, on the eve of the Quiet Revolution, was about to advance the cause of secularization in Quebec by substituting bureaucracies of the state for those of the Church in education, health, social welfare, and cultural affairs. Their definition of French-Canadian culture centered on language and French high culture and tended to ignore religion, and they included in the state's role in cultural affairs the creation of an international presence for French Canada.

Yet despite these differences concerning the content of national culture, most politicians and intellectuals in Quebec agreed that the existence of that culture, however defined, must be defended at all costs. With respect to this issue, Trudeau appears almost wildly iconoclastic. Arguing that national cultures were not natural entitites, he championed cultural competition among individuals rather than a collective defense of national culture. Few would follow him to this conclusion, for, as we have seen, French Canada's cultural uniqueness—and, therefore, the existence of a French-Canadian nation—were fundamental presuppositions of social theory and political strategy in Quebec. As Lapalme put it, in Quebec the "French fact" is more important than democracy itself (1970:241). It remained for Lapalme, and the Department of Cultural Affairs that he founded, to define the responsibilities of a democratic government towards the national culture that he cherished.

CHAPTER FIVE

Holistic Culture, Bureaucratic Fragmentation

The 1975 organization chart (*organigramme*) for Quebec's Ministère des Affaires culturelles shows not the straight lines, boxes, and plain block lettering that one expects to find in a chart, but an eighteenth-century French-Canadian town (see figures 5.4, 5.5). The ministry's administrative units are represented as buildings or sections of buildings, and the organizational links between units appear as the roads and paths that connect the buildings of the town. The picture is labeled in an elaborate but easily readable script, suggesting tradition and modernity harmonized. It is printed as a fold-out on heavy brown paper, thus doubly contrasted to the glossy white pages of the annual report in which it is published. These brown fold-outs recur five times more in the report, marking the beginnings of the chapters that describe each of the ministry's five major administrative units. The secondary fold-outs picture only those buildings and roads associated with the particular administrative division under review: all other sections of the town are whited out (MAC-AR 1976; figure 5.6 shows a similar chart taken from the report of the following year, MAC-AR 1977).

This organization chart, including the series of partial charts into which it has been analyzed, suggests a contradiction in the cultural policies and aspirations of Lapalme and his successors at the Ministère des Affaires culturelles (hereafter M.A.C.). On the one hand, most advocates of state participation in Quebec's cultural development have argued for a global approach, one that would encompass the totality of a Québécois culture which increasingly has been defined in holistic, anthropological terms. On the other hand, governmental administration of culture seems unable to proceed except by fragmenting what is conceived to be the cultural domain, dividing it among dozens of bureaucratic units both within and

109

beyond the M.A.C. Thus an organization chart, normally an abstract representation of bureaucratic rationality, is translated into the image of a total community, but only momentarily: for the purposes of a routinized annual report, that image of totality must be fragmented anew to reveal clearly the elements that compose it.[1]

In this chapter and the two that follow I will argue that this contradiction, between holism and fragmentation, is neither an accident nor the result of bureaucratic mismanagement. Rather, as we saw in examining the search for the folk society (chapter 3), attempts to capture or preserve a total culture must fail—because the objectifying approach to culture implicit in and fundamental to such attempts inevitably fragments the cultural totality sought.

Bureaucratic Fragmentation

The Quiet Revolution initiated a spectacular development of Quebec's governmental bureaucracy. Although by the end of the 1960s economic factors began to constrain the absolute growth of the public sector, there has been no end to the proliferation, reorganization, mutation, and elimination of the departments, divisions, committees, and commissions that comprise it. Within this vast bureaucracy the M.A.C. has been relatively unimportant. Its annual reports reveal continual reorganizations and a succession of fresh starts that never develop. The ministry has been considered to be marginal by successive administrations, by the media, and even, at times, in its own estimation. Moreover, it has been unable to hold on to its best ideas, that is, to establish itself as the predominant governmental actor in Quebec's cultural affairs. Thus the *Office de la langue française* originated in the M.A.C. but passed to the *Ministère de l'Éducation* in 1971. Lapalme and the M.A.C. were instrumental in establishing Quebec's quasi-diplomatic relations with France and other francophone countries, yet these prestigious governmental functions have largely been absorbed by the *Ministère des Affaires intergouvernementales*. The Quebec government's concern with immigration and "ethnic minorities" was initiated within the M.A.C. but led to the creation of an immigration ministry in 1968. The arrival

1. Friends with experience in business to whom I showed the chart remarked immediately that the full chart blurred those distinctions of rank which, they felt, were an important message of more orthodox organization charts. In their interpretation, then, the total community pictured in the drawing would have been egalitarian. They noted, however, that the partial charts restored the image of organizational hierarchy, since in those simplified versions the chain of command from the "houses" of the minister and deputy ministers to the highlighted divisions was clearly revealed.

in power of the Parti Québécois saw the creation of "super-minister" or *ministre d'État* for Cultural Development to plan global cultural policy and to coordinate cultural policy-making throughout the government. During its first term the Parti Québécois government established the *Société québécoise de developpement des industries culturelles*, to provide risk capital for cultural entrepreneurs, and the *Institut québécois de recherche sur la culture*, to coordinate long-term research on the cultural development of Quebec. And so on: thus has the dream of a policy designed to foster a cultural totality led both to fragmentation within the M.A.C. and to the creation of new bureaucratic units beyond it.

Focusing for the moment on the internal organization of the M.A.C., we can form some idea of the continual reorganization it has been subject to by reviewing its annual reports. As we saw in the last chapter, even before the Liberals came to power Lapalme had argued that all existing "pieces of culture" in the provincial government be brought together to form one agency. He also wanted that agency to include new offices to deal with language, cultural relations beyond the province, and governmental assistance to the arts. Accordingly, after its first year of operation the M.A.C. found itself administering a French Language Bureau and provincial Arts Council, both newly created, as well as a host of cultural institutions that pre-dated its establishment: an archive, a library, a museum, musical and dramatic conservatories, artistic and scientific competitions, the *Commission des Monuments historiques* (to which was attached a newly created *Service d'Archéologie*), the *Inventaire des Oeuvres d'Art,* and the *Service d'Astronomie*. The problem that Lapalme and his Deputy Minister Guy Frégault faced was how to rationalize the administration of these offices and activities. As the M.A.C.'s third annual report put it,

> Quebec's cultural activity is of such diversity and its blossoming [épanouissement] entails such pressing exigencies that the ministry's divisions must be ready to design the necessary programs, establish priorities among them, and assure that they are carried out.

To do so, the report continued, requires "systematic inventories," realistic planning, adequate funding, and competent personnel (MAC-AR 1964:11).

By 1964 a major administrative division, the *Direction générale des arts et des lettres*, had been established. Its subdivisions (*services*) were devoted to letters, music, theater, research (to study the needs of organizations applying for grants, and the uses of funds granted), and *Aide à la creation et à la recherche* (to organize competitions for grants). A second major division, the Extra-territorial French Canada Branch specified in the 1961 law, was also established. Noting such initiatives, a commentator in *Le Devoir* concluded than the M.A.C. was "on its way to becoming an important ministry [un grand ministère]" (de la Tour Fondue-Smith 1963:11). Yet little more than a year later, in September 1964, Lapalme resigned both his position as Minister of Cultural Affairs and his seat in the Quebec legislature to protest the M.A.C.'s lack of funding and clout. Lapalme bitterly compared his impoverished ministry to the newly created *Ministère de l'Éducation*, which he considered no more crucial to cultural survival than the M.A.C., yet whose share of the provincial budget was vastly greater (MAC 1976:14–15; cf. Lapalme 1973:226). Commenting on Lapalme's resignation in *Le Devoir,* Claude Ryan (1964) noted that "At the M.A.C. hope and disappointment have followed one another." According to Ryan, such agencies as the Arts Council and the Extra-territorial French Canada Branch were launched with fanfare but quickly became moribund.

Lapalme was succeeded by Pierre Laporte, who appointed a committee to prepare a *livre blanc* or white paper[2] "to formulate in a systematic fashion the principles that should inspire the cultural activity of the Quebec State." Laporte intended his white paper to "trace the M.A.C.'s policies for several years to come" (MAC 1965:i, iv). At the same time, Laporte began to reorganize the M.A.C. according to its functions, as these could be inferred from the 1961 law. Under Laporte three main divisions (*directions générales*) were established: arts and letters, conservation and diffusion of culture (responsible for museums, libraries, archives, historic monuments, the Extra-territorial French Canada Branch, and so on) and arts education (conservatories). The *Office de langue française* continued as a separate unit within the M.A.C. In addition, the *Centrale d'artisanat* was moved from the Ministry of Tourism, Hunting, and Fishing to Cultural Affairs in order "to accentuate the cultural character of handicrafts," while the M.A.C.'s *Service d'astronomie* was sent over to the *Ministère des terres et forêts* (MAC-AR 1965:14–17, 142).

In one of his first speeches after becoming head of the M.A.C., Laporte explained to the Montreal Chamber of Commerce how difficult it was to rationalize the administration of culture:

> It isn't possible in a domain such as this one to speak of efficiency as it is in other domains, nor to produce results immediately tangible and perceptible by the people. (quoted in Leger 1965:4)

> The accomplishments of the M.A.C., though magnificent, are less visible than the construction of bridges, the har-

2. White papers are "official announcements of policy" on the part of a government, and are usually followed by legislation. Between 1960 and 1979 the Quebec government issued twenty-five white papers (Gélinas 1980:1–3).

nessing of a river, the maintenance of the roads. However, they are there, numerous, unprecedented, and useful to Canadian life. (MAC-AR 1965:27)

Despite such enthusiasm Laporte was unable to pursue his ambitious course, for the Liberal Party was defeated by the Union Nationale in 1966. Laporte's white paper was viewed as too nationalistic and too ambitious by his successors as well as by those among Quebec's cultural establishment who were committed to pan-Canadian institutions and to federal funding (Frégault 1976:165–92). The new administration never recognized Laporte's white paper as a white paper, hence as an official statement of policy. It became a dead letter.

For the next ten years, under administrations of the Union Nationale (1966–70) and the Quebec Liberal Party (1970–76), the M.A.C. cultivated little more than its own marginality, despite the growing strength of cultural nationalism among the population. The ministry's weakness was demonstrated both by its inability to stick to a plan of internal organization and by the growing criticisms of its clientele. As to the former, we can make the following general observations concering the M.A.C.'s successive administrative reorganizations between 1966 and 1976: 1. Administrative sub-divisions continued to be added to and subtracted from the M.A.C. A unit for immigration, recommended by Laporte's white paper, was established in 1966, then transferred out of the ministry in 1968. The *Centrale d'artisanat* was transferred out in 1967, returned in 1971. Units dealing with film were added in 1967 and 1968, transferred out in 1975 (and returned in 1980). An *Institut national de la civilisation* was created in 1967 to combine some of the functions of an ethnographic museum with all the disciplines engaged in the study of "the civilization of Quebec," from "ethnography (including demography, classic and peasant popular art, popular traditions, etc.) to Québécois Amerindian ethnology and archeology" (MAC-AR 1968:79). The Institute was defunct by 1971, though an archeology and ethnology unit survived "to promote the study of the Indian and Eskimo cultures, past and present, of Quebec" (MAC-AR 1971:68). The *Office de la Langue française* went to the Education Department in 1971. Various autonomous or semi-autonomous agencies were created and placed under the care of the M.A.C.: the National Library (formerly the Saint-Sulpice Library), the *Grand théâtre* in Quebec City, the *Place Royale* (Quebec City) historic preservation project (see chapter 6). Also created were units dealing with cultural decentralization and regionalization. (These were often intended to counterbalance regional cultural projects sponsored by the federal government to mark the centennial of the 1867 British North America Act.) 2. During the Union Nationale administration, there was a gradual unraveling of the major administrative divisions established by Lapalme and

Holistic Culture, Bureaucratic Fragmentation

Laporte. By 1970, when the annual report included for the first time an organization chart (figure 5.1), the M.A.C.'s image of itself showed a collection of seemingly independent *services* without organizational ties to one another: arts and letters (including museums), film, *Office de la langue française*, national library, public libraries, music, theater, historic monuments, *Institut national de la civilisation*, national archives (MAC-AR 1970:51). The gradual fragmentation of Laporte's major units seems to have been motivated both by a desire for administrative rationality and by internal power struggles. Thus the 1968 report, commenting on the division of the *direction générale de l'enseignement artistique* (arts education) into two units, music and theater, explained that

> this dichotomy between theater and music . . . is designed to give music the place it deserves and to make sure that the spread of culture [la diffusion culturelle] will be more thoroughgoing and more efficient in each of these domains. (MAC-AR 1968:13)

3. With the Liberal Party back in power, the M.A.C. was again reorganized during 1970–71 (figure 5.2). Following UNESCO policies concerning "the essential functions of a cultural affairs department," four major divisions (*directions générales*) were created to cover *création, diffusion, conservation,* and *formation* (education) (MAC-AR 1971:13). The ministry was reorganized again during 1972–73, this time in conjunction with the adoption of new budgeting methods for the entire provincial government (figure 5.3). Major divisions were now those devoted to *lettres et arts plastiques* (including libraries and museums), *patrimoine* (including archives, historic monuments, archeology and ethnology), *cinéma et audio-visuel, arts d'interprétation* (including music and theater), and *relations culturelles* (MAC-AR 1973:11–16).

With regard to the dissatisfaction of the M.A.C.'s clientele, early complaints about Quebec's inadequate attention to cultural affairs blamed not the M.A.C. but the government that had created it and then refused to fund it. It will be recalled that Lapalme bitterly resented the insignificance of his ministry compared to the *Ministère de l'Éducation*. Three years after Lapalme's resignation, filmmaker Jacques Godbout offered a similar comparision in an article entitled "Pour un ministère de la Culture": "by 1980 . . . the Quebec Ministry of Culture [ministère de la Culture de Quebec] will have the dimensions of the Ministry of Education *or the Québécois will no longer exist*" (quoted in MAC 1976:39; emphasis in original). However, once the M.A.C. became established as a minor governmental department whose role was to administer grants to various cultural institutions, criticism was aimed more and more at the ministry itself. Typical in this respect was the report of the *Tribunal de la Culture* published by the journal *Liberté:*

> In Quebec scholarships are given and grants distributed, around 200 million dollars worth since the creation of the M.A.C.
>
> But because of delays . . . ; because grants are awarded haphazardly and without continuity; because the criteria for obtaining grants have been modified without consultation and without warning . . . ; because cultural organizations and cultural workers [travailleurs culturels] as well as creators have suffered from the bad faith of the M.A.C.; because excellent programs have disappeared without a trace and without replacement, the feelings of creators and cultural workers towards the M.A.C. are not very affectionate. . . . The eternal fresh starts born of the discontinuity of the M.A.C.'s policies has led to the lack of confidence, hatred, resignation, or schizophrenia of creators and cultural workers.
>
> After 12 years of existence, the M.A.C. is responsible for a veritable institutionalized morass. (Tribunal de la Culture 1975:27–28)

For its part, the M.A.C. criticized "certain artistic enterprises [which] count too readily on grants to balance a badly planned budget," and defended its use of administrative norms to regulate state aid to cultural affairs (MAC-AR 1969:12).

In the fall of 1975, one year before the election of the Parti Québécois, Jean-Paul L'Allier was chosen to head the M.A.C. (The fact that he was the seventh person to hold the post since 1961, and the fourth since the Liberals had regained power in 1970, is yet another indication of the weakness and disorganization of the M.A.C.) L'Allier represented the most nationalistic wing of the Liberal Party, and he was also, according to people whom I interviewed, the first head of Cultural Affairs to be able to stand up to his counterparts in other ministries.

Under L'Allier the M.A.C. published a *livre vert* or green paper[3] in May 1976 entitled *Pour l'évolution de la politique culturelle.* The first 90 pages reviewed the history of the ministry by publishing lengthy sections of various documents, including Lapalme's letter of resignation, Laporte's white paper, and the report of the *Tribunal de la culture.* Drawing on these sources, the green paper presented a critical summary of the M.A.C.'s first fifteen years of existence. It

3. Green papers are "working papers" intended to stimulate debate; they do not commit a government to a specific course of action. Between 1960 and 1979 Quebec issued six green papers (Gélinas 1980:1–3).

suggested that Laporte's white paper presented a coherent long-term plan that was abandoned because it was deemed too nationalistic. After Laporte, according to the green paper, the ministry's leadership acquiesced in its "marginality" (MAC 1976:93). Noting the extreme inadequacy of the M.A.C.'s funding—"it has at its disposal less than one half percent (½%) of the total budget of the Quebec government"—the green paper argued that the ministry had become little more than a patron of the arts. Moreover, its patronage was controlled largely by the minister who, often disregarding whatever expert advice was available, awarded grants to those best able to make known their interests. Thus the ministry had failed to formulate coherent long-term policies, to establish sufficiently autonomous organizational structures, and to develop personnel with both expertise and the power to act. Above all, according to the green paper, the M.A.C. had failed to conceive and implement cultural policies that would be binding for the entire Quebec government:

> . . . it has been unwilling or unable to establish itself as the *cultural conscience of the State,* making clear to all what must be done and what limits must be respected in order that government action of every type and in every domain favor the protection and development of Québécois culture. (95; emphasis in original)

With such a global approach in mind, the green paper went on to make detailed proposals for the reorganization of the M.A.C. However, like Laporte, L'Allier was unable to act on his ideas because of a change of administration. But unlike Laporte, L'Allier and the Liberals were succeeded by a government that was heavily committed to state intervention in cultural affairs. With the accession to power of the Parti Québécois, the M.A.C. expected at last to be taken seriously. But the new administration created a new position, that of Minister of State for Cultural Development, and named Camille Laurin, a powerful figure within the party, as its first occupant. L'Allier had mobilized his staff around the green paper, but Laurin thought that its proposals were too narrowly focused on the M.A.C. He believed that a Parti Québécois government was bound ideologically to enact cultural policies that would permeate all government action.

During its first administration (1976–1981), the Parti Québécois devoted significant political resources to cultural affairs, above all with its 1977 language law (Bill 101) and with the publication of Laurin's 1978 white paper on cultural development. However, neither of these projects was sponsored by the M.A.C., and though the Parti Québécois administration paid it more attention than previous governments had, the M.A.C. was no more responsible for global policy-making than it had been before. Its internal organization continued to mutate, though its major preoccupations remained arts and letters and heritage (*patrimoine*). However, under the Parti Québécois two major nationalist concerns were translated into the organizational structure of the M.A.C. One involved the regionalization of cultural affairs. This had always been of interest to cultural policy-makers intent on "democratizing" culture, but the nationalists of the Parti Québécois were more concerned than their predecessors to establish distinctive regions that could be seen to make up the nation.[4] The other major concern of the nationalists was to endow the nation with "world-class" cultural institutions. This was described in the 1981 annual report as "the strengthening of national institutions that every country must organize and develop: national archives, national library, state museums, conservatories" (MAC-AR 1981:7). Thus the 1982 organization chart shows the following units as major divisions at the same level within the M.A.C.: arts and letters, heritage, museums, national archives, national library, musical and dramatic conservatories, and regional offices (MAC-AR 1982:7). In sum, for official purposes national culture now included art, heritage, and a set of generic cultural institutions similar to those of most nation-states (figure 5.7).

The cultural policies of the Parti Québécois have given rise to much debate, which will be touched on in the chapters that follow. Confining our attention to the M.A.C., we find it subject to the same criticisms in 1982 that have plagued it throughout its existence. An extensive consultation among its clientele led the ministry to publish a 442-page report summarizing the complaints, opinions, and requests of some 710 "*intervenants culturels*" (MAC 1982:3). Commenting on the release of the report in *Le Devoir,* one reporter wrote that

> one must take note of the magnitude of the dissatisfaction,
> and hope that the minister develops his talents as a com-
> municator vis-à-vis the "cultural intervenors," many of
> whom do not mask their disillusionment, even cynicism.
> (Trudel 1982:9)

The report itself admitted that "when intervenors speak of the M.A.C.'s actions with respect to creators, they rarely congratulate it." Nonetheless, continued the report, "that doesn't stop them from

4. Nationalists want the nation "to have" regions, exactly as they want it to have a culture (see chapter 6) and to have minorities (see chapter 7). The idea of a region has powerful naturalistic connotations, suggesting rurality and rootedness in local landscapes. In addition, regions can be interpreted as the "parts" of the collective body, and thus their existence can be made to imply the existence of the nation to which they belong. But regionalism also threatens nationalism, since a region is a nation writ small: hence, from a regional perspective, an emergent nation.

expecting a great deal from the State" (MAC 1982:39–40). Or, as I was told by a prominent artist, one involved for many years in the politics of Québécois and Canadian culture: "The M.A.C. makes enemies both in giving and in not giving. More than other agencies, it needs sophisticated personnel to deal with a slick audience who are, after all, professional critics."

Toward an Anthropological Conception of Québécois Culture

The preceding sketch, based on interviews and government documents, gives only a hint of the organizational development of the M.A.C. I present it not as a finished history, but as the first step in an analysis of how competing conceptualizations of "culture" both shape and are expressed in governmental policy. Reviewing the constant changes in the M.A.C.'s bureaucratic organization suggests, first, that policy-makers have had difficulty in deciding what is to be included in the domain of culture, and, second, that whatever their notion of culture, they can administer it only by fragmenting it. That ongoing fragmentation contrasts strikingly with the explicitly holistic philosophies of culture that have guided Quebec's cultural policy makers.

The Cultural Affairs Department Act (*Loi du ministère des affaires culturelles*) had defined the M.A.C.'s responsibilities in one sentence: "The Minister shall promote the development of arts and letters in the Province and their diffusion abroad." At first glance this narrowly high-cultural orientation seems to contrast sharply with the grandiose vision of cultural development articulated for the Quebec Liberal Party in 1960 by Lapalme and Lesage. It will be recalled that for them, preservation and development of the national culture, or "the French fact," were seen as fundamental necessities because national existence was said to depend on them:

> The French fact [le fait français] constitutes the most all-embracing element of the Quebec context, and it is one that we owe it to ourselves to develop in depth. It is by our culture rather than by numbers that we will prevail. (Roy 1971: 2:378)

However, the proposed structure of Lapalme's cultural affairs department suggests that his vision of the French-Canadian cultural totality was compatible with the narrow definition of cultural affairs given in the law: for Lapalme, high culture (the arts) and the French language were the heart of national culture, hence the Arts Council and French Language Bureau were postulated as central components

118

of the new ministry. Urban planning and historic preservation would protect and develop the material and sociogeographic manifestations of French civilization in Quebec. Finally, Quebec's reputation—the existence of its personality—was to be promoted internationally through initiatives intended "to stimulate artistic expressions that bear a seal, a sign, a trademark which calls the world's attention to them as PRODUCTS OF QUEBEC" (Lesage 1961c:7). In sum, though Lapalme's concerns went beyond the arts to include language, history, and material culture, his notion of French civilization (and his tendency to equate culture with civilization) suggests an elitist rather than anthropological conception of culture.

During the early years of the M.A.C., Lapalme, still heavily influenced by Malraux, continued to define national culture in terms of French civilization. The opening, in 1961, of the Quebec delegation in Paris (*Maison du Quebec à Paris*) was intended to promote economic and cultural development under the aegis of France rather than "Anglo-Saxon North America." As Lesage put it, in a speech in Paris in October of that year, "we do not want to be the cultural satellite of the United States" (*Le Devoir* 1961b). Two years later Malraux visted Quebec to celebrate the opening of an exhibition of French science and technology in Montreal. In formal speeches, Malraux spoke of France's efforts to find an alternative to the dominant imperialisms of the post war world, those of the United States with its Protestant right-wing culture, and of Soviet Russia with its Byzantine communist culture. France's mission, according to Malraux, was to renew the cultural heritage of occidental Catholic civilization in order to counter an emergent world culture that had lost its soul. He defined culture as "that power within us which has survived death, . . . the only force capable of fighting against the dream machines [of mass culture]" (*Le Devoir* 1963a, b). For his part, Lapalme declared that "the French Canadians are North Americans of French origin, French culture, . . . [with] a way of being, living, and creating in French in the New World" (*Le Devoir* 1963c). And editorialists, enchanted with Malraux, wrote of the universality and superiority of French thought, to be carried on in a new French humanism that would stand up to Anglo-Saxon materialism (Ethier-Blais 1963).

The fears that Malraux entertained with respect to the "dream machines" of modern culture and their apparently unlimited power to seduce the masses had been felt in Quebec since the early twentieth century. In the first years of the M.A.C. such fears led to a concern for the "democratization" and "decentralization" (*deconcentration*) of culture. To rescue the masses from their popular amusements, culture—high culture, artistic culture, French civilization— was to be made available to all citizens (democratization) throughout the nation (decentralization). This accords well with the primacy accorded the arts in the Cultural Affairs Department Act. As Deputy

Holistic Culture, Bureaucratic Fragmentation

Minister Frégault put it, in speech after speech, artists "express what is truest and best" in the people, and thus "the role of the State is to make the artist aware of the fact that his work is important . . . for the good of the entire community" (*Le Devoir* 1962, 1963d). The democratization of culture was also discussed with reference to article 27 of the United Nations Universal Declaration of Human Rights, which stated that "Everyone has the right freely to participate in the cultural life of the community." Thus, as Frégault told a meeting of music teachers:

> At a time when artists address themselves not only to a refined and leisured elite, but to an entire collectivity in which culture is no longer a privilege but a right, [part of] the mission of music teachers is . . . to awaken the interest of the general population in good music, by forming the taste of youth [en formant le gout de la jeunesse]. (MAC-AR 1964:28)

Such rhetoric makes it clear that the democratization of culture meant bringing high culture (*good* music) to the masses, or the masses to it.

The ministry's orientation to high culture and the arts began to change under Lapalme's successor, Pierre Laporte, whose white paper explored anthropological definitions of culture in addition to the established elitist discourse. As we saw, Laporte, with the help of Deputy Minister Frégault, wanted to formulate a coherent long-term policy for the M.A.C. Like Lapalme, Laporte advocated a nationalism similar to that of the Tremblay Commission: he saw Quebec as the "mère-patrie" of all French Canada, with special responsibilities that made the government of Quebec more than a provincial government. But Laporte was more willing than Lapalme or the Tremblay Commission to speak of the Quebec "state" as though it were an independent entity. And he was more willing to challenge what were seen as federal encroachments into the French-Canadian cultural domain.

The nationalism of Laporte's white paper is evident in its consistent presentation of a negative vision: the sweeping program embodied in its sixty policy recommendations is said to be necessary due to the "débilité de la culture nationale des Canadiens français du Quebec" (MAC 1965:28), threatened both by world-wide mass culture and by the dominance of English-language culture in North America. Nonetheless, those sixty recommendations pertain almost exclusively to such high-cultural domains as letters, fine arts, theater, music, museums, heritage, archives and libraries. Though several new areas—such as science and film—are suggested as appropriate targets for cultural policy-making, immigration is the only one that goes beyond traditional or elitist notions of culture. In other words, "culture" is still not treated as an all-encompassing category. But the white paper also draws, though only tentatively, on an anthropological definition of culture. Moreover, it abandons Malraux's concept of "French civilization."

The text begins with a brief definition of "nation" followed by an extensive discussion of "culture." According to the white paper, a nation cannot be defined in terms of birth and ethnic origins. Rather, "a nation is based on the consciousness it has of forming a distinct entity animated by a common will, and on the power it holds to shape its own destiny" (3). In this characteristic definition of the nation, notions of boundedness and independence are conveyed in personifying metaphors. Equally characteristic is the link that the white paper goes on to establish between the national entity and the content of national existence, its culture: "it is essentially by means of culture that a collectivity expresses itself, translates its mentality, learns to identify and recognize itself" (3). Thus, according to the white paper, "the Quebec State" has the right "to take charge" of national culture in order to assure a healthy national existence—"to offer the collectivity a controlling intellect [cerveau directeur] and a life-giving self-consciousness" (4–5). Here the rhetoric of personification accords well with high-cultural elitism: culture has to do with intellect and spirituality, or, as the text puts it in another passage, culture involves the "higher organs [organes supérieurs]" of the collectivity (4).

There follows an eight-page section on "The Concept of Culture." The white paper defines individual culture, national or collective culture, mass culture, and universal culture. Individual culture is equated with spirituality and the life of the mind: "A cultivated man . . . is able to lead an autonomous, original, even creative intellectual life" (6–7). The text next defines collective or national culture:

> The second principal sense of the word culture comes from anthropology. . . . In this case, culture is no longer attributed to the individual, but to the whole of a society. Culture thus understood encompasses the language, the system of values, beliefs, myths, knowledge, techniques, and social institutions that make up the heritage of a society. All collectivities, advanced or archaic, possess such a culture. . . . (10)

To this positive vision is opposed a negative vision, contained in the discussion of mass culture, which is equated with electronic media and is said to have the power to transcend frontiers and destroy local cultures (11–12). Finally, universal culture is defined as the sum-total of human artistic and intellectual accomplishments (12–13).

In this series of definitions national culture is privileged, exactly as it was in the corresponding sections of the Tremblay Commission report (see chapter 4). For example, the "cultivated man" is said to "nourish himself from sources that know no frontier," yet in the same passage we are told that the accomplishments of individuals belong above all to their collectivities:

> Culture as the life of the mind, the fruit of individual efforts, constitutes in the end the totality of intellectual and spiritual conquests that a given community considers as its heritage. (7)

Similarly, a Herderian discussion of the relationship between national culture and universal culture draws on the imagery of the negative vision to argue that cultural contributions to humankind can come only from a healthy national culture:

> A national cultural policy must open itself to the humanist and universal goals of all truly creative thought, inspiration, and art; and it will contribute to them precisely by . . . the abundance . . . of the autochthonous spiritual resources. Any society that . . . loses its distinctive character . . . would see its creative powers rapidly dry up. (13)

In sum, in the series individual culture/national culture/universal culture, the middle term is endowed with the greatest historical reality: while neither the individual nor the universal level is to be ignored, both depend upon the health of national cultures.

But how does the white paper identify the national culture of Quebec? Such a question is difficult to answer, for the text draws on a bewildering array of terms: "French-Canadian nation" (4), "French-Canadian culture" (10), "French-language Québécois" (24), "French culture" (24), "French culture in Quebec" (25), "francophone Quebec" (27), "the Québécois of 1965" (31), "French-Canadian literature" (67), "Québécois society" (85), "Québécois artist" (88), "musical traditions of French Canada" (106), "French Canadians of Quebec" (128), "Québécois heritage" (159). Or, consider the ambiguities of a passage like the following:

> We take it as a principle that the Quebec State . . . must occupy itself with everything touching on culture in the anthropological sense. This duty is crucial to the present and the future of the civilization of French expression [civilisation d'expression française] in Quebec. If Quebec wishes to define itself as a French territory in America, its government must be preeminently responsible for the destiny of the French-Canadian collectivity of Quebec. (35)

By the time of my fieldwork in the late 1970s, Québécois would look back and explain that during the Quiet Revolution an older "French-Canadian" identity had been replaced by a modern "Québécois" identity focused on Quebec as a French-language society different from the rest of Canada (cf. Rioux 1974:5–21). Laporte's white paper would seem to document a transitional moment in this process: following the Tremblay Commission, political leaders of the Quiet Revolution worked to make the "Quebec State" a modern bureaucracy responsible for the totality of collective life. At first the reference group for that project was "French Canada." But within the Canadian constitutional scheme, the growing Quebec government was bound to remain the government of a province; thus the totalizing pretensions of the leaders of that government could be focused only on the population and territory over which it had constitutional jurisdiction—the province of Quebec.

In that context, "French Canadian" no longer seemed the correct term to describe the national population. The terminology of Laporte's white paper suggests that policy makers no longer knew quite how to refer to "the nation." Their participation in the provincial government meant a territorial focus on Quebec and a diminishing of pan-Canadian aspirations. Their nationalism was by definition devoted to "French" or "French-language" culture. Moreover, this culture was now seen to be the property, the life, of a particular society, the society for which the provincial government could claim responsibility—that is, the society found on the territory of Quebec. The white paper's recommendation to add immigration to the M.A.C.'s responsibilities suggests a growing recognition that the government of a total society had to consider all the citizens of that society, whatever their ethnic origins. But this new spirit of pluralism (cf. Coleman 1981:461–63) had to remain subordinate to French-Canadian or French-Quebec nationalism. As the white paper put it, "The vitality of a culture will depend . . . on the harmony established among the subcultures that compose it" (10). Or, as Lesage had put it four years earlier, referring to "neo-Canadians" on Quebec soil: "they are not properly speaking beyond our frontiers [d'outre-frontière], but nor are they within French-Canadian cultural borders" (1961c:9). In sum, cultural policy-makers began in the early 1960s to envision Quebec as a culturally diverse society. But despite their cautious recognition of pluralism, they expected cultural unity to prevail.

Finally, the introduction of an anthropological conception of culture fits logically with the growth of a governmental apparatus whose leaders were increasingly thinking of Quebec as a total society— a territorially bounded unit that had replaced the pan-Canadian (hence unbounded with respect to a provincial government) entity suggested by the term "French-Canadian nation." In that political context, it made sense for policy makers to discuss culture as an anthropological totality corresponding to the total society for which they wished to assume responsibility. Moreover, expanding cultural affairs to include immigration also suggests an anthropological definition of culture, for the problem that "neo-Canadians" posed to nationalists had to do not with art and high culture, but with "acculturation" (206), a question of total culture.

Mutually Exclusive Totalities

As we have seen, Laporte's white paper was largely forgotten, due to a change of administration, and for several years thereafter the M.A.C. continued to orient itself to an elitist conception of culture. However, by the mid-1970s, with the Liberal Party again in power, the nationalist desire for more comprehensive cultural policies was linked to more explicit reference to anthropological culture. Consider, for example, the following remarks, from an April 1974 speech by the Minister of Cultural Affairs, Denis Hardy, to the *Assemblée nationale*:

> The modern notion of culture has been considerably enlarged. Though it remains tied to progress in the arts, letters, and intellectual accomplishments in general . . . culture also represents the totality of symbols, models, patterns of behavior, and even rules which permit a society to recognize and define itself. (MAC-AR 1975:9; cf. MAC 1976:53)

Following from this definition, Hardy announced his intention to extend the M.A.C.'s activities to the "leisure, way of life [and] environment" of all citizens. As he put it, "all are elements which make up our personal and collective identity, and their enhancement is an integral part of the M.A.C.'s work."

Hardy was succeeded by Jean-Paul L'Allier, whose green paper of 1976 pointed to the more vigorously nationalistic cultural policies soon to be undertaken by the Parti Québécois. The green paper, meant to stimulate discussion rather than announce policy, did not formulate a theory of Québécois culture. However, by quoting extensively from a chronologically arranged series of policy statements, it reproduced, and implicitly endorsed, the movement from high culture to anthropological culture. Its policy suggestions, while focusing for the most part on high-cultural sectors (which it called *secteurs traditionnels* [179]), nonetheless touched on the environment, leisure, tourism, education, and mass media.

Moreover, L'Allier's green paper articulated a scathing critique of federal cultural policy. It will be recalled that the Tremblay Commission, followed by Lapalme and Lesage, argued that the Quebec government had pan-Canadian responsibilities with respect to French-Canadian culture, responsibilities that Ottawa had no constitutional right to assume. Laporte's white paper maintained this position though without stressing it (MAC 1965:24). However, for the 1976 green paper Ottawa's presence in the cultural domain was a central issue. This was undoubtedly due to greatly increased federal attention to cultural affairs that grew out of the 1967 centennial celebrations and, more particularly, to the federal policy of *multiculturalism* which took shape in the early 1970s.

The history of multiculturalism is well known. In the early 1960s the federal government under Lester Pearson perceived a crisis in Canadian national unity, manifested above all in the rise of Quebec separatism. Pearson responded by creating the Royal Commission on Bilingualism and Biculturalism. But what emerged from the long process of consultation was bilingualism and *multi*culturalism. The federal government endeavored to give the French language equal status (with respect to English) within the Canadian government and in its dealings with all citizens. However, Canada's ethnic groups— people claiming non-British, non-French origins who had become an important demographic and political force in Canada since World War Two—objected to an official definition of Canada that excluded ethnic cultures. Thus in 1971 Prime Minister Trudeau declared multiculturalism as the official government policy:

> It was the view of the royal commission . . . that there cannot be one cultural policy for Canadians of British and French origin, another for the original peoples and yet a third for all others. For although there are two official languages, there is no official culture, nor does any ethnic group take precedence over any other. No citizen or group of citizens is other than Canadian, and all should be treated fairly. (Canada 1971:8545)

As we saw in the last chapter, Trudeau had once argued that a federal government should attend to cultural policy for pragmatic reasons, to offset the ability of regions or units within the federation to attract the allegiance of citizens. In the 1960s and 1970s Canada faced such a threat from Quebec, as well as from other sections of the country (especially the Western provinces) reacting in part against Quebec's special claims, and in part in imitation of them. Moreover, like their counterparts in Quebec, Canadian nationalists feared what was perceived as the increasing invasion of American culture conveyed by the mass media. Multiculturalism was intended to ground Canadian nationhood in an identity that could be differentiated from threatening Others both within and without. First, multiculturalism would domesticate internal diversity by rendering all ethnic claims

125

Holistic Culture, Bureaucratic Fragmentation

equally relevant—or irrelevant. As Trudeau put it, "no citizen or group of citizens is other than Canadian." Second, the multicultural Canadian "mosaic" was said to distinguish Canada from the United State of the "melting pot." In a sense which is superficially paradoxical, but fundamentally in accord with the logic of nationalism, multiculturalism was projected as the homogeneous "content" of Canadian national culture.

Multiculturalism angered Quebec nationalists, who saw it as a direct attack on themselves. The green paper put the matter bluntly:

> Ottawa's action appears to us to proceed . . . from a firm
> . . . will *to creat a Canadian culture*. To do this it is logically
> impossible for the federal government to . . . recognize . . .
> the existence of a distinct, homogeneous, and dynamic
> Québécois culture. Rather than [biculturalism] it has pre-
> ferred *multiculturalism*. It is thus not surprising that it
> wishes . . . to absorb the components of Québécois culture
> into the great Canadian totality [le grand tout canadien].
> . . . Since, from the federal point of view, Québécois
> culture *cannot* exist as an autonomous *totality*, . . . it tends
> to be denied. However, Ottawa recognizes with evident
> satisfaction the . . . contribution that each of the compo-
> nents of Québécois culture—such as theater, song, and
> literature—makes to *Canadian culture*. (MAC 1976:98–99;
> emphasis in original)

Here is a clear statement of what we might call the theory of mutually exclusive totalities. In the logic of nationalism, a nation cannot contain within itself another nation, or any total culture other than its own. (First, all subcultural differences within a nation are said to be overridden by the salience of the primary national culture, a condition of internal homogeneity that would be violated by the existence of some other national, or total-cultural, entity inside the nation. Second, from the point of view of the encompassed or minority nation, the right to self-determination would be violated.) As the green paper pointed out, a nation attempting to encompass another nation cannot admit the existence of the other as a totality, but seeks instead to decompose it and then to absorb the pieces. At the same time, an encompassed nation seeking independence—Quebec from the nationalists' viewpoint—cannot allow itself to be dismembered. The implications for jurisdictional disputes over cultural policy-making are obvious, and the green paper concluded that "there can be . . . only one political overseer" of Quebec's cultural domain: the government of Quebec (100).

Despite this unambiguous demand for political control of Québécois culture, the green paper made no attempt to define the distinguishing traits of that culture. We find only, as the conclusion to the document, a characteristic affirmation of national existence, with the assertion of an irreducible identity:

> Québécois culture is at bottom nothing other than that projection of ourselves, the people from here [gens d'ici], starting from what we have been and what we are and including what we wish to be. It is no better or worse than the culture of others; it is *we* [elle est *nous*].
> Throughout Quebec, often without knowing one another, we have a culture in common. (221).

When the Parti Québécois took power, it attempted to fill in the "empty" symbolism (cf. Parsons 1975: 65) of this statement of identity by providing a comprehensive theory of Québécois culture. The 1978 white paper of the State Minister for Cultural Development (Camille Laurin), entitled *A Cultural Development Policy for Quebec*, took for granted an anthropological conception of culture. It also suggested that the term "Quebec culture" was taken for granted as well:

> Culture designates certain ways of speaking, thinking, living, and, as a corollary, languages, beliefs and institutions common to a given group of people, small or large. French culture, English culture, American culture, Quebec culture—these are all everyday expressions. (Quebec 1978:11)

Thus the fluctuating terminology of the Laporte white paper was no longer in evidence. Moreover, Laurin's white paper argued against the existence of a Canadian culture—a term omitted from the list quoted immediately above. The green paper had merely implied such a position, in its remarks about Ottawa's attempt to create a Canadian culture. By contrast, the white paper mounted a direct attack against Canada, which, we are told, "is obliged to use a certain ingenuity to define itself as a distinctive culture" (22). The white paper went on to accuse Canada of using Québécois culture in its attempt to differentiate itself from the United States (a popular argument at the time of my field work), while at the same time folklorizing or provincializing Québécois culture in order to assert Canada as a total culture. Like the green paper, though more forcefully, Laurin's white paper concluded that the government of Quebec had to "repatriate" jurisdiction over culture: "We must draw up and promote a cultural policy which will be . . . *québécois*. We must reappropriate the means that enable a culture to endure and to grow" (36; ellipses and emphasis in original).

The white paper is divided into two volumes, the first of which is sub-titled "The Culture under Consideration." This volume is a sustained attempt to specify the characteristics of Quebec culture. The central problem it poses is the relationship between cultural integration and pluralism. "Sub-cultural" differences associated with class, region, and ethnicity had concerned French-Canadian nationalists since the Second World War, which had been accompanied by the demise of French Canada's apparent Catholic unanimity and the visible rise of Quebec's immigrant population. The issue was symbolically crucial to the Parti Québécois, for it did not wish to appear to persecute minorities in the same way that it claimed Quebec to be persecuted by Canada, yet it sought to demonstrate national autonomy by establishing Quebec as a patron to its own "minorities" (these issues will be discussed in detail in chapter 7). Thus the white paper set out to articulate a theory of Québécois culture that recognizes diversity but grounds it in unity.

The demonstration begins with "two initial questions": "Is there such a thing as a Quebec culture? If so, how can it be characterized?" (41). To answer the first question, the white paper asserts that the French language is the "focal point" around which Quebec's subcultures must unite to form a common culture. Here the reasoning is convoluted. The white paper claims to accept cultural diversity but argues that "everyone [in Quebec] should at least be able to communicate by means of one common language." (Note that this way of putting the argument presupposes that Quebec is "a" society, that is, a total social unit within which integration must prevail.) Since French is the language of the majority, it must be the common language of all citizens, of whatever ethnic origin and mother tongue. But shared language creates shared culture. Indeed, the white paper argues that since French has remained the common language of a majority for three centuries, it must be based in "a culture which in turn is the product of a permanent and organized social group." Or again: "A language cannot survive in a foreign cultural milieu; French has held its own in Quebec because it expresses the way of life of the community." The white paper concludes, in answer to its first question, that "Quebec is the fatherland of a French tradition in culture" (43–44).

What, then, are the characteristics of that culture? According to the white paper, Quebec presents "the paradox of a culture largely dependent on borrowings, yet basically original" (47). A "casual observer" might see little that is "typically *québécois*" in Quebec. Rather, he would find French language and civil law, an Amerindian "ability to live close to nature," British political institutions and criminal law, Roman Catholic religion, and United States technology and industry (45). Yet underneath such borrowings there is, we are told, an inner "originality," a distinctive "mentality" which, though it has been forced to express itself through borrowed institutions, is undeniably real. In sum, Quebec culture is "Like an artist in exile," and Quebec society suffers from cultural "underdevelopment" (47). Such a condition will lead to "suffocation" (51), a danger to be averted by political (leading to cultural) independence.

Can Empty Culture Be Filled?

In some respects this description of the characteristics of Québécois culture is as "empty" as the concluding statement of the 1976 green paper. In its search for "originality," that is, for undeniable proof of individuated existence, the white paper can find only "a certain mentality, a special spirit," something that is "not tangible but [that] can be sensed" (47). Commenting on this vagueness, some analysts claim that the long-predicted demise of French-Canadian culture has at last occurred. For example, in a useful study of cultural politics and *indépendantisme*, William Coleman draws this conclusion after comparing the Tremblay Commission's account of French-Canadian culture to that of the 1978 white paper. Coleman points out that the Tremblay Commission was able to define French-Canadian culture in terms of Catholicism and "the French national genius," as well as a set of social institutions that were "characteristically French Canadian" (1984:133). The sharp contrast between this detailed account and the vague terminology of the 1978 white paper leads Coleman to the following conclusion:

> A reading of these two documents would suggest that the processes affecting the existence of traditional French-Canadian culture and feared by the Tremblay commissioners have won out. In 1978, the traditional culture is no longer pointed to and no longer an issue of concern. Yet it would also appear that a new distinctive culture has not arisen to take the place of the old. No institutions or practices can be identified as distinctive or peculiar to the francophone community. The new way of life has come from the outside; it has been borrowed. (135)

Coleman goes on to argue that since the Quiet Revolution the Quebec government's rhetoric of cultural nationalism has hidden the fact that its economic policies, designed in the interests of the business and capitalist classes, have functioned to integrate Quebec into the mainstream economy of the North American continent rather than to maintain its distinctiveness outside it. According to him, the government's cultural policies have been used "to foster acquiescence, acceptance, or even support for policies that are against the better interests of the population" (156). This has happened in two ways: first, reforms in education and social welfare, and even language policies, have replaced the distinctive Catholic social institutions of traditional French-Canadian society with the welfare-state infrastructures necessary to advanced capitalism. Second, the government's more narrowly cultural policies, as administered by the M.A.C., have been used to co-opt the voices of cultural and political dissent: "The artistic community was gradually made more dependent on support from the state and experienced the constraints of its expression that normally comes from this dependence" (155).

However, though there is merit in Coleman's arguments concerning Quebec's integration into modern culture and the co-optation of artists and other cultural workers, I reject his appeal to a class analysis, not in itself, but as an explanation for the "emptying" of Québécois culture. Quebec did not "lose its culture" during the last forty years, nor were the government's cultural policies designed to cover up hegemonic economic policies that were culturally destructive. Like so many students of nationalism, Coleman succumbs to nationalist culture theory, collapsing the distance between its rhetoric and his analysis of it. He fails to see that the search for an integral identity, or the attempt to formulate an undeniable interpretation of the true national culture, can never succeed—and hence must be repeated indefinitely. He forgets that the negative vision is as much a part of nationalist discourse as the positive assertion of identity; forgets, that is, that the Tremblay Commission's ominous prediction of cultural death was merely one more among the voices of doom that have been heard in Quebec since the early nineteenth century. In other words, Coleman has read the Tremblay Commission's account of national culture not as interpretive ideology but as factual description. He assumes that traditional culture existed just as its advocates have claimed (cf. Handler 1985).

Coleman also misses the interpretive element in the vision of the 1978 white paper. The white paper argued that since the Conquest, Québécois culture has existed within and in spite of borrowed social institutions. It included the Church among those borrowed institutions. For the authors of the white paper, the integral, irreducible identity of the Québécois nation was no more expressed in the imported structures of the Church than it was in British political institutions or American technology. All were equally alien to the authentic Québécois, whom the white paper described as "rooted in their land, close to nature and the real meaning of life" (Quebec 1978:55). Coleman might defend the validity of the Tremblay Commision's vision of traditional culture by arguing that a distinctive institutional system—the schools, churches, and social works of Catholic French Canada—indeed existed to nourish that culture. But this merely displaces an untenable proposition—that of distinctiveness—onto another level thought to be "closer to the ground" than the "superstructural" realities of culture. In other words, Catholic social institutions indeed differed from those of the surrounding provinces, but they were also similar to them in many respects. Difference is relative, not absolute: compared to the "educational system" of, let's say, the Navajo or the Balinese, the educational systems of Quebec and Ontario in 1920 would appear quite similar. Institutions that are "different" give rise to, or (for those who privilege symbolic instead of materialist theory) are expressions of *relatively different but not absolutely distinctive* cultural processes. But neither the Tremblay Commission nor the 1978 white paper (nor Coleman) are interested in relative differences and similarities. Rather, they seek cultural entities, isolated, bounded, naturally distinctive: "close to nature and the real meaning of life."

Coleman also fails to realize that the white paper's "empty" definition of Québécois culture is politically motivated: it permits the assertion of national existence without denying what is seen as cultural underdevelopment. The notion of underdevelopment is crucial here. The "borrowed" institutions (one might well wonder what an original or authentic institution is) described by the white paper belong to the rhetoric of national immaturity examined in chapter 2. As we saw, nationalists claim that a dependent, adolescent nation is unable to create an original culture and life; political independence is said to be necessary precisely to allow for creativity, choice, and the rational control of national destiny (cf. Quebec 1978:51). Taking such arguments into consideration, we can see why the 1978 white paper insisted on the lack of originality of much of Quebec life, even in those domains (religion) where the Tremblay Commissioners saw authenticity. An inauthentic institutional life could be blamed on Quebec's dependency on Canada, and political independence could be offered as the cure for it. In other words, the white paper can have it both ways; it can assert the existence of irreducible identity, but can point as well to the constraining political circumstances which threaten that identity. The positive and negative visions are inextricably linked.

Coleman concludes his discussion of the M.A.C. by judging it to have failed:

> The working classes in the 1950s . . . were becoming a French-speaking section of North American mass-consumer society. The Department of Cultural Affairs represented a possible basis for the spawning of new institutions that would reflect the spiritual and communal roots of French-Canadian culture and perhaps arrest these trends. Its opportunity to play this role has now passed. (142)

In the next two chapters we will rethink this argument by looking at cultural policies of the Quebec government in two domains, heritage preservation and language. Those chapters will show that, like the search for the folk society, the attempt to administer cultural authenticity is doomed to failure. But that failure is not due, as Coleman (and many nationalist critics of the M.A.C.) would have it, to the demise of an authentic culture coupled with ill-designed, ill-intentioned, or badly managed government policies. The failure to create an authentic culture stems from the impossibility of the project, or, put another way, from the epistemological inadequacy of the notion of authenticity. It is no accident that increasingly holistic theories of culture have gone hand in hand with a never-ending fragmentation of the bureaucratic structures designed to promote culture. Much of the history of nationalism since the French Revolution has been the history of an objectifying logic which seeks totality but inevitably fragments the realities it constructs.

MINISTÈRE DES AFFAIRES CULTURELLES

ORGANIGRAMME

MINISTRE

Conseil des arts du Québec

Commission des bibliothèques publiques

Comité consultatif de la Place Royale

Comité consultatif des Ciné-parcs

Bureau de surveillance du cinéma

Commission des monuments historiques

Comité consultatif du livre

SOUS-MINISTRE

Service juridique

SOUS-MINISTRE ADJOINT

Information

SERVICES GÉNÉRAUX

ADMINISTRA-TION	PLANIFICA-TION	DIFFUSION	RELATIONS CULTURELLES
Budget	Recherche	Programmation Animation culturelle	Service de coopération avec l'extérieur
Personnel	Subventions		
Service central: matériel et documentation		Aménagement du territoire	Service du Canada français d'outre-frontières
			Délégation culturelle à Paris

SERVICES CULTURELS

Arts et lettres

Lettres

Arts plastiques

Musées

Office du film

Office de la langue française

Bibliothèque nationale du Québec

Bibliothèques publiques

Musique

Conservatoires

Théâtre

Conservatoires

Monuments historiques

Institut national de la civilisation

Archives nationales du Québec

Figure 5.1. Organization Chart from Ministère des Affaires culturelles, *Rapport annuel, 1969–1970*, p. 51. Courtesy of Ministère des Affaires culturelles, Gouvernement du Québec.

LE MINISTÈRE DES AFFAIRES CULTURELLES

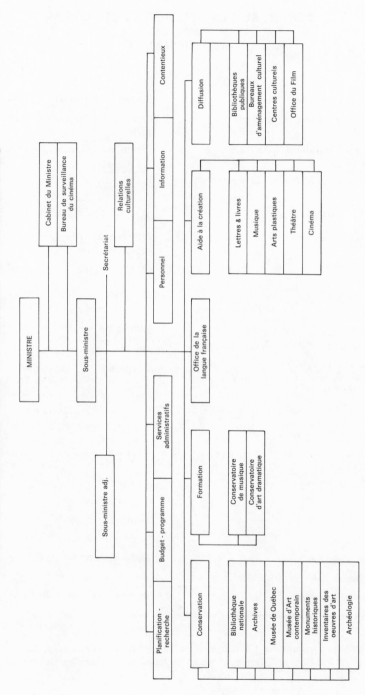

Figure 5.2. Organization Chart from Ministère des Affaires culturelles, *Rapport annuel, 1971–1972*, p. 10. Courtesy of Ministère des Affaires culturelles, Gouvernement du Québec.

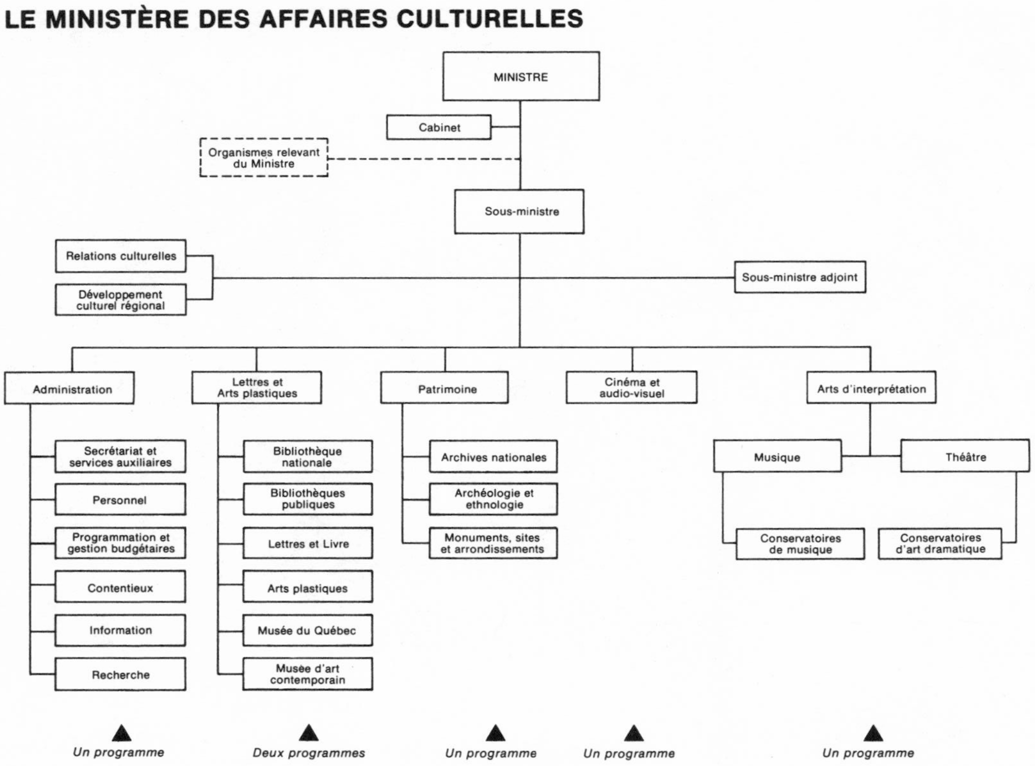

LE MINISTÈRE DES AFFAIRES CULTURELLES

Figure 5.3. Organization chart from Ministère des Affaires culturelles, *Rapport annuel, 1972-1973*, p. 16. Courtesy of Ministère des Affaires culturelles, Gouvernement du Québec.

Figure 5.4. Organization Chart from Ministère des Affaires culturelles, *Rapport des activités, 1975–1976*, foldout after p. 10. Courtesy of Ministère des Affaires culturelles, Gouvernement du Québec.

Figure 5.5. Organization Chart from Ministère des Affaires culturelles, *Rapport des activités, 1975–1976*, foldout before p. 21. Courtesy of Ministère des Affaires culturelles, Gouvernement du Québec.

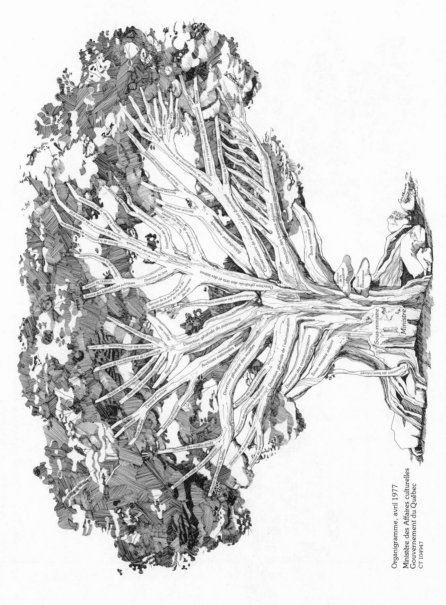

Figure 5.6. Organization Chart from Ministère des Affaires culturelles, *Rapport des activités, 1976–1977,* foldout after p. 12. Courtesy of Ministère des Affaires culturelles, Gouvernement du Québec.

Organigramme, avril 1977
Ministère des Affaires culturelles
Gouvernement du Québec
CT 104947

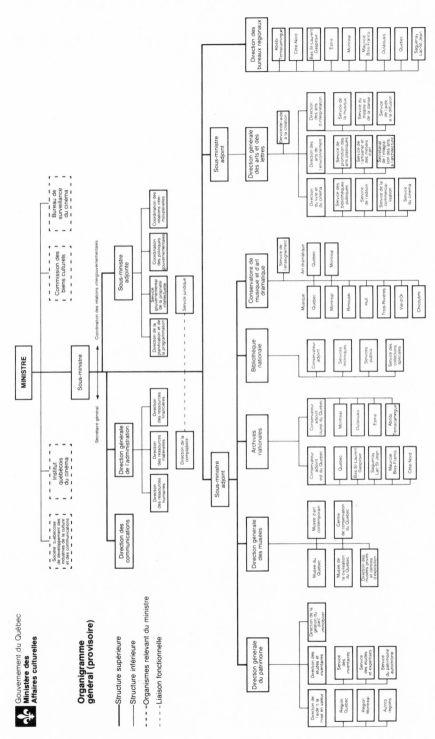

Figure 5.7. Organization Chart from Ministère des Affaires culturelles, *Rapport d'activité, 1981–1982*, foldout after p. 6. Courtesy of Ministère des Affaires culturelles, Gouvernement du Québec.

139

CHAPTER SIX

"Having a Culture": The Preservation of Quebec's *Patrimoine*

"The *patrimoine,*" a fourth-grade pupil explained, "is old things. Like that chair—if that chair is maybe 25 years old, it's part of the *patrimoine.*" An elderly farm woman to whom I told this story found it as amusing as I had. Yet her notion of the *patrimoine* was perhaps little different from that of the boy. With the current popularity of the *patrimoine,* she told me, she was now saving old pieces of furniture and farm implements that before she would have discarded. Nowadays they're worth money, she said, and besides, they don't make things as sturdy as they did.[1]

Old things are the most tangible aspect of what is know as *le patrimoine,* and in common usage the term refers to historic buildings and monuments, antiques, ethnographic objects, and works of art. Yet more than inanimate objects of some antiquity are included in the *patrimoine.* In 1978 the *Société des éleveurs de chevaux canadiens* asked the government to elevate the *cheval canadien* to the status of "national breed." The *Société* argued that the few remaining "representatives of the horses of our ancestors . . . constitute by themselves an important part of our national *patrimoine*" (Duhamel 1978a). And during a memorial service for Lionel Groulx that I attended, one speaker described the historian as part of the *patrimoine.* Having contributed so much to the study of Quebec history, he said, Groulx was now part of that history. Having given so much to the *patrimoine,* he now belonged to it.

Thus the *patrimoine* can be said to include animate objects and famous people as well as inanimate objects, merely tangible antiq-

1. A shorter version of this chapter appeared as "On Having a Culture: Nationalism and the Preservation of Quebec's *Patrimoine,*" in G. W. Stocking, ed., *Objects and Others: Essays on Museums and Material Culture. History of Anthropology* 3: 192–217 (1985).

uities. Beyond these, general national traits and larger cultural ensembles can be considered part of the *patrimoine*. Groulx spoke of patriotism as a *"patrimoine moral"* (1924:16). A critic writing in *Le Devoir* praised a literary encyclopedia that he felt would renew interest in a "forgotten literary *patrimoine*" (Royer 1978). And the French language is often described as an important part of Quebec's heritage:

> In the same way as our history and the men who have made it, to the same degree as buildings, furniture, tools, works of art, songs and tales . . . *language is an important part of our patrimoine*, of the common property of the Québécois. (Cameron 1978:16; emphasis in original)

The natural world too can be envisioned as part of the *patrimoine*. One editorialist, writing about the state-owned utility, Hydro-Quebec, spoke of the development and management of "our hydroelectric *patrimoine*" (Leclerc 1978). The *Commission des biens culturels*, arguing for the urgent necessity to protect Quebec's "natural *patrimoine*," has claimed that a tree deserves as much attention as a monument (Duhamel 1978b). Another writer describes the land itself as part of the *patrimoine:* "the territory that we inhabit, the crucible of this culture that characterizes us . . . belongs to the *patrimoine*, to the collective property of the Québécois" (Gagnon 1978:18).

Finally, the broadest definition of the *patrimoine* equates it with all of national culture. During a parliamentary debate in which the narrow versus the broad meaning of the concept was specifically at issue, one member of the Assemblée nationale offered the following definition: "The word *patrimoine* designates the totality of what we possess, and what is added to it. Thus it refers to the conservation not only of what we call traditional goods, but of everything that can be called cultural property" (ANQ 1972: 12:4585). And a government minister, speaking at a public presentation of the 1978 white paper on cultural development, described the *patrimoine* in similar fashion:

> The *patrimoine* does not represent only old stones, old houses, old mills. Our description of the *patrimoine* is a description that goes back to the very origin of the word— that is, to the word *patrie*—which is to say, the cultural heritage in its entirety, whether it be a question of our traditions, our crafts, or the fruits of the labor of all those who have preceded us. (transcribed by the author)

As several of the preceding examples show, to speak of the *patrimoine* is to envision national culture as property, and the nation as a property-owning "collective individual." Thus the concept typifies what I have called an objectifying logic. It allows any aspect of human life to be imagined as an object, that is, bounded in time and space, or (amounting to the same thing) associated as property with a particular group, which is imagined as territorially and historically bounded. Moreover, possession of a heritage, of culture, is considered a crucial proof of national existence. "We are a nation because we have a culture—given the importance of this idea in nationalist ideology, it is hardly surprising to find that heritage preservation was one of the first projects undertaken by the Quebec government as it took up work in "cultural affairs."

Cultural Property Legislation

Historic preservation legislation in Quebec has followed European trends, and though the Quebec case is thus derivative in one sense, it can also be seen as typifying a world-wide interest in cultural property that is if anything more acute in peripheral or "emerging" polities than in older metropolitan centers where people are culturally self-confident. In direct emulation of European fashions, private efforts to preserve Quebec's heritage can be found in the mid-nineteenth century (Frégault 1963), but the provincial government first acted in this domain in 1922 when it passed the Historic or Artistic Monuments Act. That law called for the "classification" of "monuments and objects of art, whose preservation is of national interest from an historic or artistic standpoint." Once classified (in the *Quebec Official Gazette*), immovable property could not be destroyed, repaired, restored, or otherwise altered without the consent of the Provincial Secretary, who was to be advised by a five-member Historic Monuments Commission (hereafter H.M.C.) established by the law. The law was vaguer with respect to the classification of movable objects. Except for those owned by the Province or by local governmental bodies, movables could not be classified without the consent of their owners. Classified objects were not to be alienated without the consent of the Provincial Secretary, but sanctions against violators were only vaguely specified.

The 1922 Act was followed in 1935 by An Act respecting the Island of Orléans. There were six rural villages on *L'Ile d'Orléans,* just down the St. Lawrence River from Quebec City. The law was intended to preserve the historic character of the Island by regulating its touristic development. It called for the improvement of roads, the creation of parks, and the erection of historic markers, and it placed restrictions on the construction of restaurants and gas stations as well as "the putting up of posters [i.e., billboards]." In 1952 the Historic or Artistic Monuments and Sites Act replaced the 1922 legislation. It added (but did not define) "sites" to the monuments and objects of art of the earlier law, and specified that the category of "immoveables susceptible of classification" was to include "prehistoric monuments, land containing remains of ancient civilization and landscapes and sites having any scientific, artistic or historical interest," as well as "immoveables the possession of which is necessary to isolate, clear or otherwise enhance a classified monument or site." It further specified that the H.M.C. could acquire and either demolish or restore properties in the last category.

The laws of 1935 and 1952 foreshadowed later developments in historic preservation legislation. The former focused not on a single object but on a sociogeographic area. The latter marks the first expansion of the category of properties deemed worthy of protection, as well as an attempt to give government a more active role in historic preservation. Both trends continued with the passage of a new Historic Monuments Act in 1963, one of the first pieces of legislation sponsored by the M.A.C. In addition to the monuments, objects, and sites covered by previous legislation, the new law provided for the "historic locality," defined as "any municipality or part of a municipality where a concentration of immoveables of historic or artistic interest is situated." Construction, alteration, or demolition within a historic locality was forbidden without a permit from the H.M.C., which was also authorized to regulate "posters and signboards." The export of classified property was prohibited without the permission of the H.M.C., and sanctions against violators were defined more precisely than in previous legislation, including provisions for fines up to $500. The M.A.C. was authorized to acquire classified property, as well as to aid private individuals and organizations to maintain or restore classified property in their possession. Finally, the law established the Historic Monuments Service within the M.A.C. to provide bureaucratic and academic expertise to both the Minister and the H.M.C. The creation of the Service institutionalized expertise within the government, and changed the H.M.C. to a more purely advisory, rather than administrative, body (MAC-AR 1965:172).

Although the M.A.C.'s third annual report (1964:52) called the provision for historic localities "the most radical modification" of older laws, the institutionalization of expertise and the creation of a governmental bureaucracy to deal with heritage was as significant as the widening of the category of what could be protected. Though the Service, like the M.A.C. generally, had difficulty in the beginning finding personnel (MAC-AR 1966:153), by the late 1960s Quebec universities were turning out enough social scientists to meet the government's demand for their expertise (cf. Tremblay and Gold 1976:26). The 1960s also witnessed a rapid increase in the number of items classified. Frégault (1963) listed 122 properties classified between 1922 and 1963, whereas the tenth annual M.A.C. report puts the total at "nearly 700" (MAC-AR 1971:79). The same report mentions that the

Service studied more than 1000 requests for construction permits that year, as compared to the 67 mentioned seven years earlier (MAC-AR 1964:53–55). Finally, the Service consciously sought to rationalize its procedures, in order to improve efficiency and to put itself "in accord with the most progressive formulas being studied or applied in other countries" (MAC-AR 1968:56).

The expansive effect of the institutionalization of heritage preservation is evidenced in sweeping new legislation, the Cultural Property Act, which the M.A.C. sponsored to replace the 1963 Act. The 1972 law opened with a list of definitions, including those for "cultural property"; "work of art"; historic property, monument, site, and district; archaeological property and site; "natural district" ("a territory . . . designated as such . . . because of the aesthetic, legendary or scenic interest of its natural setting"); and "protected area" ("an area whose perimeter is five hundred feet from a classified historic monument or archaeological site"). This array of cultural properties was complemented by intricate regulatory provisions, including two methods for controlling heritage objects: "recognition" and "classification." The M.A.C. could regulate alienation, export, and alteration of both recognized and classified property; it was to keep an official registry of all such property and would hold a right of preemption in case of alienation. Objects worthy of classification (as opposed to those merely "recognized") were additionally protected by giving the Minister the right to classify property without the owner's consent, to grant tax incentives to help individuals maintain patrimonial property, and to establish a "protected area" around a classified object— an area within which the same restrictions applied as were applied to an object itself. The M.A.C. was empowered to "make an inventory of cultural property that might be recognized or classified," to authorize inspections by experts, and to block other government agencies when their actions endangered protected cultural property—as well as to issue "archaeological research permits" and to be notified of archaeological discoveries. The maximum fine for violations was raised from $500 to $5000, and then to $25,000 by a 1978 amendment.

Nationalism, Government Regulation, and the Creation of Cultural Property

The nationalist world view permeates both the letter and the spirit of cultural property laws in Quebec. Consider the work of the H.M.C. shortly after passage of the first Historic or Artistic Monuments Act (1922). The various activities that it initiated or championed indicate that its primary mission was to make both French Canadians and the members of other nations aware of the existence of French Canada's historical and cultural possessions. Crucial to this goal was the work of "inventorying" cultural property in dossiers with extensive photographic documentation in order to preserve "at least the memory" of patrimonial objects and to aid in the "practical task" of "conservation and preservation" (H.M.C. 1923:xi). For similar reasons the H.M.C. advocated the creation of a historical museum and an ethnographic museum. The first could serve as "a temple of national devotion" (xiv) and the second would at least enable French Canadians to secure "specimens of each of the objects that our ancestors used" against the increasingly voracious appetite of American tourists for French-Canadian antiques (1925:xvii; but cf. Arcand 1984).

Other duties included the unveiling of patriotic statues (1923:xi–xii) and the erection of new monuments and commemorative roadside markers. According to the H.M.C., to increase historical awareness—"of what we once were and what we must be today"—was among the surest means to "develop the patriotic spirit of a people" as well as to give tourists a better image of the nation (1925:xiv). Finally, the H.M.C. made its inventories available to the public in such works as *The Old Churches of the Province of Quebec, 1647–1800* (1925) and *Old Manors, Old Houses* (1927), both attributed to P. G. Roy, provincial archivist and member of the H.M.C. In its third report (1926:vii) the H.M.C. called the publication of the volume on churches "the event of the year," and reprinted an appreciative review from the London *Times Literary Supplement* (27 January 1927). The H.M.C. suggested that such praise from abroad should make French-Canadians more respectful of their national heritage.

In its inventories the H.M.C. divided cultural property into ten categories: (1) commemorative monuments; (2) churches and chapels; (3) forts of the French Regime; (4) windmills; (5) roadside crosses; (6) commemorative inscriptions and plaques; (7) devotional monuments; (8) old houses and manors; (9) old furniture; and, somewhat vaguely, (10) "les choses disparues"—things that have disappeared (HMC 1926:xii–xiii). This classification, privileging buildings dating from New France, monuments referring to that period, and religious architecture and relics, shows that the H.M.C. defined national culture in terms of the conservative, clerical nationalism that dominated Quebec in the first half of the twentieth century. Roy (1927:vi) mentions a second and related categorization for buildings which may properly be considered "patrimonial": (1) those possessing "both historic character and antiquity," (2) those "whose merit lies entirely in their being of another age" and (3) those "typifying Canadian architecture." In other words, cultural property can arouse veneration because of age alone or age combined with historically important events, or because it epitomizes national existence. For Roy, buildings which were rooted in a historically specific past, or which typified a national-cultural style, "possessed originality and symbolised truly the soul of

145

an entire people" (v). By contrast, newer houses were not "really of our tradition," nor could French Canadians be "truly at home in them" (vii). In sum, what is historical and typical is authentic, truly French-Canadian. And it is assumed that authenticity is objectively ascertainable, even though, as we shall now see, the criteria to determine what is historical, typical, or patrimonial can change.

As we learned in the last chapter, since the Quiet Revolution the Quebec government's bureaucratization of cultural politics has increasingly been accompanied by appeals to anthropological definitions of culture. The concept of a national culture anthropologically defined was better suited than a definition restricted to high culture for justifying the provincial government's growing desire to intervene in all aspects of Quebec society and culture. Thus the list of "cultural property" covered in the 1972 law was much more extensive than the "historic and artistic monuments" of previous legislation, a fact that generated much discussion among the members of Quebec's Assemblée nationale who discussed the bill before its passage.

The Minister of Cultural Affairs introduced the bill by stressing the insufficiency of the 1963 law with regard to the natural and archaeological *patrimoine* and movable cultural properties. The new bill, she explained, was based on the most progressive concepts from Mexico, France, Israel, Italy, and UNESCO, and was designed to protect Quebec's *patrimoine* from the ravages of economic development (increasingly threatening to traditional architecture), from the booming art market, and from "museums outside the province" (ANQ 1972: 12:1844). All deputies who responded to the Minister valued the aims of the projected law, and all recognized the validity of the expanded notion of cultural property. As one remarked, the interdependence of all social and cultural phenomena had become increasingly obvious in past discussions of the M.A.C.'s role, and thus in the proposed law "the notion of culture has just taken a step forward" (1845).

Despite, or perhaps because of, the evocation of a broad, anthropological notion of culture, the deputies were concerned to be able to specify what properly belongs to Quebec's heritage. All agreed that "nowhere in the world is there an architecture more Québécois, that corresponds better to us, than that which we are aiming . . . to protect" (1855)—but the problem was to determine the content of such categories as "Québécois architecture" or "national heritage." For example, one deputy objected to the vagueness of the term "cultural property"—did it indicate Québécois, Canadian, or North American properties, or items from around the world housed in Quebec museums (1845)? Other discussants pondered the cases of persons maintaining dual residences, of immigrants, and of others who change nationality—when and how could the M.A.C. classify property belonging to them? How long must a person reside in

Quebec before his property could be counted as part of Quebec's *patrimoine* (4617–20)? One deputy, arguing for ethnic diversity in the composition of the new Cultural Property Commission (which replaced the H.M.C.), stressed that all who live in Quebec are Québécois, hence their property is part of the *patrimoine* and they too should be able to "rediscover [their] identity" in the official heritage (1863–64). In contrast, other deputies discussed grounds for excluding items from the national heritage. One speaker bemoaned the fact that Québécois art is lost to the nation when, as often happens, it comes to rest in the private collections of "English" Québécois (1861). And ever recurrent was the problem of separating the Québécois and Canadian heritages—how could Ottawa be prevented from claiming as Canadian pieces of Quebec's *patrimoine*, either by acquiring Canadian national monuments in Quebec or by bringing Québécois movables to Ottawa museums?

A related issue was that of the temporal limits of the *patrimoine.* Some deputies were puzzled by the broad definition of archaeological property (any object "indicating . . . human occupation"), coupled with the provision that "whoever discovers an archaeological property or site must inform the Minister." Did that mean that anyone discovering anything would have to inform the Minister (4589–90)? How old must something be before it could be considered archaeological or historical property? "History begins at what date?" (4640). They also questioned the fifty-year limit specified in the article concerning the Minister's right of preemption in the case of classified property offered for sale. Mightn't it be desirable for the Minister to acquire objects less than 50 years old; for example, those associated with persons holding important offices (4625–29)?

In response to such questions some discussants were willing to rely on the advice of experts. The Minister of Cultural Affairs refused to change the broad definition of archaeological property because archaeologists had insisted on it; and to the question about the limits of history she responded, "you have to ask the historians" (4590, 4640). Another speaker, who wanted even more reliance on expertise written into the law, argued that only anthropologists, historians, and archaeologists—as opposed to "amateurs"—could "identify a cultural property and . . . place it in the category corresponding to [its] reality" (1847). But another deputy contested expertise, arguing instead for the necessity of citizen involvement in heritage preservation: "who knows better than the citizen of a particular region the history of his region" (1863)?

The potential consequences of the 1972 law were signaled almost immediately by the newly created Cultural Property Commission (hereafter C.P.C.). In its first annual report the C.P.C. (1973:7) stressed that the law went beyond conservation to promote systematic development of heritage properties and sites. In later reports the

147

"Having a Culture"

C.P.C. elaborated its view of the Cultural Property Act as a tool to prevent urban destruction. For example, it meant to fight against the "visual" pollution of historic buildings by new construction, and it urged respect for "sociological" as well as archaeological riches (1975:133,143):

> In the absence of local action, can we . . . go so far as to regulate zoning indirectly by classifying an entire street in order to save not only buildings . . . but a sociological milieu? (1976:125)

Nor was the C.P.C. the only organization to envision such possibilities, for citizen groups increasingly turned to the 1972 law to fight pollution and to defend neighborhoods against real estate speculation as well as to preserve their local heritage. In brief, the anthropological conception of culture embodied in the law could be used in defence of lifeways as well as material property.

Nowhere were these new concerns more salient than in the debate over "Place Royale"—a name coined in modern times to designate several blocks of Quebec City's oldest section. The interest of the provincial government in Place Royale dates from the late 1920s, when the H.M.C. declared the church of Notre-Dame-des-Victoires to be a historical monument. Little more was done until the late 1950s, when the H.M.C. and then the M.A.C. began to restore isolated buildings near the church. In 1967 the government passed an Act Respecting Place Royale at Quebec City, which created a geographically delimited Place Royale (as, in effect, an historic locality) and authorized the M.A.C. to undertake its development. By 1970 the M.A.C. had acquired some forty of the sixty-four buildings in the locality, while this decaying section of Quebec City was partially evacuated. At that time the M.A.C. (1979b:18–19) intended "to privilege the French character of the locale." It would preserve buildings and parts of buildings dating to the French Regime, demolish those from later epochs, and replace them with reconstructions "as faithful as possible, in their external appearance, to those which existed in the 17th or 18th centuries." The project was to combine historical restoration, urban renewal, and touristic and economic development.

Because the Place Royale project was the largest of its kind ever undertaken in Quebec, it was seen as epitomizing the M.A.C.'s approach to heritage preservation. By the mid-1970s, however, "authentic" restorations focusing exclusively on French-Regime heritage were increasingly called into question. With the displacement of clerical-conservative nationalism by a secular nationalism oriented to the present and future, and the newfound equation of *patrimoine* with anthropological "culture," the Place Royale project became the target of an array of citizens groups and cultural-affairs

148

activists who disputed both the politics of historic preservation and the constricted view of the national past that it represented.

In late 1978 the M.A.C. sponsored a conference to bring together all parties interested in Place Royale. Specialists from the Historic Monuments section of the M.A.C. presented the case for the reigning restoration philosophy. They described four stages in the architectural history of Place Royale (Amerindian, French, British, and twentieth century) and justified their decision to focus exclusively on the French period. The architecture of that period, they explained, housed a homogeneous and original style of life which succumbed, not at the Conquest, but in the mid-nineteenth century, to the "abusive intensification of commercial activities" associated with British and American architecture. Because Place Royale represented the most important "concentration of [architectural] elements from the French period," it was crucial to the identity of the entire (Québécois) nation. Thus the specialists reaffirmed their commitment to the reconstruction of a French-Regime Place Royale. As they put it, for Québécois seeking their national identity, Place Royale "becomes a privileged tie between the French Canada of yesterday and Quebec of today." To walk through Place Royale is "to be transported into the past," and such contact with "our deepest roots" *(nos origines profonds)* is crucial to the ongoing vitality of national culture (165–69).[2]

Criticism of this position came from architects, social scientists, citizen groups, and cultural-affairs facilitators *(animateurs)*, almost all of whom agreed on two complaints. First, in privileging French-Regime architecture to the exclusion of all else, the project had favored fakery at the expense of the authenticity of an evolving system of styles. Second, the Place Royale project had arbitrarily isolated part of a neighborhood, turning it into an artificial museum while destroying the authentic social life that once existed there.

Taking the architectural critique first: critics argued that restoration at Place Royale had proceeded on the basis of an arbitrary judgment as to the superior value and authenticity of French-Regime styles. In their view such judgments were relative, subject to shifts in historiographical fashions. Furthermore, "restoration itself is merely one more action to which a building is subjected . . . in the course of

2. An American specialist has given this evaluation of the philosophy of the project: "Nationalistic motivations are explicit in current restoration activities in the Canadian city of Quebec. A direct expression of the Québécois determination to reassert the presence of French culture in contemporary Canada, the Place Royale is being radically restored. Most physical evidences of the earliest seventeenth-century settlement . . . had been blurred or destroyed by subsequent development. The current campaign involves a hard-edged mix of demolition, restoration, and sometimes complete reconstruction of the oldest buildings to re-create the appearance of Place Royale before the British conquest" (Fitch 1982:55).

its long life" (25). Thus critics urged that restoration respect all styles and epochs represented in a site. Some even redefined authenticity as the accumulation of styles contained in the latest state of a building, "a state resulting from a normal evolution" (157). And some suggested a new reading of history to justify that position: rather than characterizing the nineteenth century as a period of commercial invasion by English speakers, they argued that nineteenth-century architecture, with its diverse influences, be seen as an expression of "the adaptive faculty of Québécois builders" (152). Finally, these critics demanded that restoration be readable and even reversible. Since the restorations of today will become simply one more phase in the life of a building, future generations must be enabled to identify them as the work of the current generation of restorer-occupants, who should leave a record of the reasoning behind their choices (25, 157).

Turning to the sociological critique, we find the same concern for the continuity of an integrated global culture. Critics argued that the law establishing the boundaries of Place Royale had created a geographic and administrative entity arbitrarily isolated from the larger neighborhood. Restoration had made a museum of Place Royale, destroying 200 years of continuous social life (49) and turning it into a "concentration camp for culture" (39). As one *animatrice* who had worked for the M.A.C. told me in an interview a few months before the Place Royale conference,

> Fifty years ago that was an extraordinary spot—the business center of Quebec—lawyers, notaries, a whole population lived there. People worked on the boats—there was really life there—a market, children in the streets. It was alive! But it began to run down. And then, when rumors were heard about the Place Royale project, this process accelerated. The owners said, "we're going to be expropriated." And they stopped keeping up their property. So the neighborhood fell into ruins—a slum. Then the Ministry comes and says, "okay, we're going to redo the whole thing, we'll remove everybody and bring them back when it's finished." But people can't live like that—people who are already disadvantaged, uprooted. That makes them doubly uprooted. And now there is nobody but tourists.

Critics at the conference also argued that the culture displayed at Place Royale was typical of what culture has become in a society that privileges economics above all else: an isolated and reduced commodity (35). In contrast, they wanted an urban renewal strategy that would privilege the residential function of the neighborhood, combined with a judicious mix of other functions such as education, tourism, recreation, and business. Only by establishing Place Royale as a "natural" social milieu could it be made to live again. Otherwise, as G. E. Lapalme noted, "at the approach of winter there would be nothing but the silence of a vast museum. . . . Only a normal life . . . can conquer winter" (12). In sum, these critics deplored what they saw as the reduction of the *patrimoine* to a fragmented, commercialized image of the past; instead, they envisioned it anthropologically, as "the mark of a community of men in a particular space"—a witness to "the continuity of a human milieu" (37–38).

These critiques, both architectural and sociological, correspond in some respects with my analysis of the nationalistic objectification of culture. I have argued in this book and elsewhere (1984) that those who seek the sources of national identity reinterpret aspects of a social world as typifying that world, which is then understood to be territorially and sociologically bounded ("the nation") and in possession of "a" culture composed of detached, object-like "traits." The critics of Place Royale contested the interpretation of authentic identity and history represented by the project. Yet they did not reject the notion of an authentic culture but merely located it elsewhere: in the ongoing life of ordinary citizens. Their argument reflects the ascendancy of a holistic, anthropological conception of culture; yet such a conception depends on an objectification at least as extreme as that of narrower conceptions of the *patrimoine,* for it focuses on life itself as the object to be preserved, documented, and sacralized. As we saw in chapter 3, folklorist Marius Barbeau took credit in 1919 for first presenting nonprofessional folk artists on stage. While the critics of the Place Royale project rejected the notion of turning the site into a museum frozen in time, they had no objection to putting the ongoing life of the site "on stage" for tourists. Even the restorers are viewed as actors, and urged to leave an objective record of their motivations!

The conflict between restoration and "real" life seen in the debate concerning Place Royale was frequently evident in interviews and discussions that I had with people concerned about the *patrimoine.* The cultural affairs *animatrice* who discussed Place Royale with me had worked in a small village where a group of farmers had asked the local authorities to realign the range *(rang)* road where they lived. According to her, this road was "all crooked, with lovely old houses and trees by the side of the road. Not at all like the dull straight streets of [suburban] Sainte Foy." Yet the farmers, who used large trucks to haul their milk over this road, found it to be more and more impractical. Their request for a straightened road aroused the opposition of another group of residents in the *rang*—young people who had bought farms and moved to the country in search of a more natural, patrimonial life. Their opposition in turn aroused the farmers, who, according to my informant,

> complain about the strangers who try to tell them what to do. It's really violent, this debate. In the village news-

paper one of the young people writes a poetic letter, full of oratorical sallies, describing the beauties of the *rang.* Then the next week there is a reply from an old *habitant,* very practical. In the final analysis the attitude of this fellow is much more patrimonial than that of the poet.

The *animatrice* went on to explain that the crooked road corresponded to her vision of the *patrimoine,* which for her signified more than old objects. It implied a life style and a scale of living inherited from the past and unmarred by the "unnatural" aspects of urban, industrial society. In straightening the road the authorities destroyed its patrimonial organization and scale: "For me, it's not right. They've changed everything, the ambiance, the organization of the life that is already there." But, as she recognized, if anyone had a claim to be traditionalists, it was the farmers, and "it was they themselves who asked for it, because that crooked little road wasn't practical for their big milk trucks. They don't see the matter the way I do, yet it's *their* attitude which is patrimonial."

As a footnote I should add that this story was told to me in the informant's nineteenth-century farmhouse, which had been classified and restored. Despite her evident delight in the house, she told me of the constraints entailed by its classification as a "bien culturel": any improvement or repairs, she said, required authorization from the M.A.C. And we wondered how the farmers of her village would have reacted to such an imposition.

On Having a Culture

The preceding review of heritage legislation in Quebec indicates a steady expansion of the category of patrimonial things—an expansion we can compare to what Durkheim called the contagiousness of the sacred. Early legislation sought discrete pieces of culture, monuments and objects of art originating in a well-defined sociohistorical era, and sacralized them by surrounding them with rules designed to isolate them from social space and historical time (cf. MacCannell 1976:42–45). In succeeding legislation the category of things that could be sacralized grew. The sacred past expanded forward and backward to include more recently created properties and the pre-French, prehistoric Amerindian civilization of Quebec. Sacred space grew as historic and natural localities were added to buildings and art objects in the category of cultural heritage to be protected. The sacralized objects themselves became contagious, spreading their sacredness into the "protected" zones surrounding them. Even the "view" attached to patrimonial sites became inviolable. Meanwhile, burgeoning scholarship in the human sciences objectified more and more "great men" or, at least, more and more occupiers of named positions in expanding public institutions, and those personages were also taken to be infectiously sacred, so that anything they touched could become patrimonial.

There has also been a proliferation in the number of social domains considered capable of generating heritage. The initial concern with religion, New France, and great men has widened to include a variety of historical epochs and sociological milieus. Today people talk about the "industrial *patrimoine*" (for example, early factories) and the contribution of ordinary people, as well as of diverse ethnic groups, to Quebec's heritage. Official attention to the archaeological *patrimoine* extended the realm of the sacred beneath the earth's surface. Finally, the 1972 law established degrees of sacredness by adding the procedure of recognition, for less worthy property, to that of classification.

To document the spread of the sacred does not, however, identify its source, which I would locate in the relationship of patrimonial property to the collective individual. C. B. Macpherson (1962) has suggested the term "possessive individualism" to describe that relationship as it was initially formulated in Locke's labor theory of value. Locke's problem was to explain how individuals could appropriate for themselves portions of the earth and its resources, which God had given to all men as common property. His solution was to treat a person's body as his property, along with the labor of his body and the "works of his hand" (1690:305). By objectifying labor as an individual's property, Locke allowed the individual to put his imprint upon natural objects. He annexes them, and they become, in effect, extensions of himself: "Whatsoever then he removes out of the State that Nature hath provided, and left it in, he hath mixed his *Labour* with, and joyned to it something that is his own, and thereby makes it his *Property*" (ibid.). Thus can self-sufficient (and, it should be noted, presocial) individuals isolate, objectify, and attach what is "common" and unbounded. In brief, in the individualist world view there is an almost mystical bond uniting the agent with the things he acts upon. Moreover, if on the one hand those things become his property, on the other hand the individual comes to be defined by the things he possesses. For example, Locke grounded society itself in the need of individuals to protect their possessions—a theory that Marx found well-suited to a society "in which relations between men are subordinated to relations between men and things" (Dumont 1977:5; cf. Marx 1867:81–96).

The preceding analysis sheds light on the relationship uniting nation and culture, the collective individual and its *patrimoine*. "We are a nation because we have a culture"—nationalists in Quebec and elsewhere have elaborated that assertion in many forms. It suggests that existence is a function of possession: "You [*on*] can live without [formal] instruction [but] you do not exist, you will leave no trace, if you are without culture" (Lapalme 1973:226). Moreover, what the nation possesses is often conceived to be part of it, so that cultural content becomes the very body of the nation; as one British museum administrator put it, in a plea for tougher export controls for cultural property:

> The artistic possessions of a country are a great part of its heritage, . . . they are part of us and their outgoing diminishes us. There is a difference between coveting something for a particular collection and saving for the nation something which is part of it. (Finlay 1977:13)

As we have seen, the most basic assumptions of nationalist ideology concern the existence of a geographically, historically, and culturally unique nation. That nation is believed to be "born of" and indissolubly linked to a bounded territory and a particular history; those links are conceived to be natural, not arbitrary. This set of assumptions is rarely questioned *from within* the nationalist perspective of a given nation; but when questioned from the outside, by spokesmen for competing national groups, it is often fervently and creatively defended. An outsider's denial of national existence can thus be interpreted as a challenge. To meet such a challenge nationalists must claim and specify the nation's possessions: they must delineate and, ideally, secure a bounded territory, and construct an account of the unique culture and history that attaches to and emanates from the people who occupy it. It is at this point that disputes about the ownership of cultural property come into play. However constituted or mobilized, and however situated with respect to given political boundaries, a self-conscious national or ethnic group will claim possession of cultural properties as both representative and constitutive of cultural identity. Yet the ability of such groups to validate ownership claims, and then to act on them, will differ widely.

We might imagine a typology of cultural property claims, constructed from three opposing pairs of features of objects and the groups that claim a relationship to them: actual possession of an object versus lack of possession; control of the cultural identity or affiliation of an object versus the lack of such control; and sovereignty versus the lack of it—that is, political autonomy versus minority status or collective encompassment. Combining these, we find six possibilities:

(1) A sovereign group possesses an object, and controls its identity (example: the Liberty Bell).

(2) A sovereign group possesses an object, but does not control its identity—that is, cannot claim that the object is unambiguously

and exclusively affiliated to its culture (example: the Elgin Marbles in the British Museum).

(3) A sovereign group does not possess an object but claims to control its identity (example: the Elgin Marbles, from the Greek point of view).

(4) An encompassed or minority group possesses an object, and controls its identity. This situation is often seen to justify the encompassed group's aspirations for political autonomy: "we are a nation because we have a culture" (example: those pieces of the Quebec *patrimoine* securely housed in provincial museums).

(5) An encompassed group possesses an object whose identity is disputed (example: those pieces of the Quebec *patrimoine* controlled by the provincial government but also claimed by the Canadian government as constitutive of Canadian identity).

(6) An encompassed group controls or claims to control the identity of an object, but does not possess it (example: those pieces of the Quebec *patrimoine* housed in federal museums outside Quebec).

We can further elaborate this typology by considering the responses of disputing parties to the claims of their opponents. For example, in the second situation—that of a sovereign group possessing an object whose affiliation is disputed—we can imagine these additional possibilities:

(a) The owning group can make no legitimate claim to control the identity of the object in question, and responds by attacking the validity of other claims to it. As one art dealer, justifying his traffic in Greek antiquities recovered in Turkey, put it: "Do the descendants of the Turks who drove out the Greeks from Asia Minor have a better right [than citizens of other nations] to the art made by the ancestors of the Greeks?" (quoted in Meyer 1973:112).

(b) The owning group can make no legitimate claim to control the identity of an object, and responds by rejecting any nationalistic or particularistic limitations on the object's affiliation. In these cases the object is said to belong to a universal human heritage, and the owners become its "self-styled guardians" (Miller 1984:2)

(c) The owning group asserts its right to control the [disputed] affiliation of an object on the grounds that it encompasses the contesting group which claims the object as its own. For example, the federal government in Canada claims that the Québécois *patrimoine,* or that of any Canadian minority or Native American group, is also part of Canada's heritage, because the minority groups themselves "are Canadian."

(d) The owning group claims that sustained ownership establishes a new cultural affiliation: "This is our heritage now."

In Canada the third of these additional possibilities has become increasingly relevant, as the Canadian federal government asserts its own nationalism in response to the claims of Quebec and other

155

"Having a Culture"

Canadian minority groups and to the changing relationship of Canada to Great Britain and the United States. For example, a recent review of federal cultural policy (Applebaum-Hébert Report) asks that Canadian national museums devote greater attention to "Native art and archival material." This involves changing the status of Native material culture from artifact to art—that is, from being viewed as the remains of a vanquished Other to being included as part of the "high culture" of the mainstream. Thus the Report recommends that a proposed "Contemporary Arts Centre" house Indian art currently collected in an anthropology museum (the National Museum of Man) in order to "remove the unfortunate and unnecessary connotation that works of contemporary Native art are understood best as artifacts and . . . are neither contemporary nor art" (Canada 1982:111, 148–49).

Yet the report also recognizes that regional and ethnic minorities within Canada are sensitive to issues of control with respect to "their" heritage:

> It is entirely reasonable that institutions in each region should develop collections and exhibitions which reflect the distinctive characteristics of that region. . . . the National Museum of Canada, in pursuing the objectives of the National Programmes, has not always been as sensitive as it could have been to provincial and regional priorities, interests and standards, and has sometimes acted in a directive rather than a reactive way toward the non-national museums. (118)

From the point of view of militant minorities, this is drastically understated. As we saw in the last chapter, Québécois nationalists have consistently attacked what they see as the Canadian federal government's attempts to annex their culture. What to federalists may seem a legitimate aspiration to include all Canadian "subcultures" as full-fledged constituents of a greater Canadian whole, is to nationalists in Quebec nothing less than cultural imperialism.

Similar arguments have been made by Native Canadian groups, and, more generally, by militant and self-conscious ethnic groups throughout the world who now protest what they see as the alienation of their cultural property by governments and museums of the West. Such examples indicate that claims on cultural property are made to an international audience. It is not enough to have culture and history; the collectivity's proprietary claims must be recognized by others. As in Locke's social contract, cultural property legislation aims to protect and demonstrate the collective individual's existence by protecting what it possesses from the claims of other collective individuals. As the Quebec case shows, to do this entails inventory,

156

acquisition, and enclosure. First the collectivity or its representatives (whether self-appointed leaders or a duly constituted government) must take stock of what it has—hence the widespread passion for the inventory in cultural property management as well as in nationalist literature more generally (cf. Belanger 1974:358–59). Next, what has been shown to be "ours" must be acquired—either by the state or by private citizens—and enclosed, whether by isolating property with special rules, constructing museums, or gathering relevant information and images within the covers of books.

Inventory, acquisition, and enclosure can involve making explicit one's implicit but undisputed claim to cultural property, disputing the proprietary claims of others, or recognizing something as national heritage that has not previously been so recognized. A francophone official of the Montreal Museum of Fine Arts told me that he would like to "nationalize" that institution by relabeling, in terms of Quebec's regions, art objects that are now labeled "Canadian." Currently, he explained, "Canadian" means "national" and anything from Quebec is merely "regional." A different type of creative labeling occurs in the construction of "heritage" out of previously unmarked bits of daily life. A patrimonial object can be created by locating its origins within the bounds of national territory and history. For example, a custom or an antique is said to "come from" a region and period, as if its "birth" characterized it once and for all: "Child's Rattle, Beauce County, ca. 1910."[3] On the other hand, for a multi-ethnic national *patrimoine,* properties become patrimonial when their human possessors-creators accept citizenship and thereby subordinate their ethnicity to their newly chosen national identity. In sum, all properties that can be claimed to emanate from the collective individual, or from the human beings who constitute it, can be included in the collective heritage.

As is inevitable in a world made meaningful in terms of our individualistic moral and legal codes, the proprietary claims of some will challenge those of others, and a successful assertion of rights to cultural property can exclude the rights of others in the same property. Yet despite often bitter disagreements, the disputants in contemporary "culture wars" share an understanding of what cultural property is; that is, all disputants—current, would-be, and former imperialists, as well as oppressed minorities, ex-colonies, and aspir-

3. To suggest that an object "comes from" a region evokes a naturalistic image (birth from the land) associated with "objective fact." Yet "comes from" is an ambiguous notion at best, often indicating no more than the locale where a researcher encountered a cultural thing. Ellis has argued (1983:26–27) that the Grimm brothers deliberately manipulated the practice of naming a region in order to disguise the fact that many of their German folktales were obtained from their middle-class relatives (who, though they indeed lived in various German "regions," were of French origin and spoke French at home).

ing new nations—have agreed to a world view in which culture has come to be represented as and by "things." More and more anthropologists tell tales of natives whose self-conscious authenticity depends on anthropological records of the lives of their ancestors (e.g., Linnekin 1983:245; Smith 1982:130), and more and more anthropologists are hiring themselves out as "cultural worker[s]" (Guédon 1983:259) to protect or reconstruct the culture that "belongs" to the groups that employ them. Thus it is not surprising that groups who succeed in repatriating items of cultural property often put them in their own museums. Indeed, one of the responses of Western museum administrators to third-world repatriation claims is to send foreign aid—to build and staff museums (Miller 1984:2). And one of the constant concerns of Quebec's Ministry of Cultural Affairs (and, before it, of the Historic Monuments Commission) has been to build an anthropology museum or "musée de l'homme" (MAC 1979c; Handler 1981).

As we noted at the end of chapter 3, Elli Köngäs-Maranda once wrote that colonized countries have folklore archives while colonizing countries build anthropology museums. She attributed that difference to "the search for a collective identity" typical of the nationalism of colonized peoples (1979:187–89), as compared to the need to justify imperial conquests by displaying (and thereby reducing) the "primitive" culture of the vanquished Others. Following that suggestion, we might interpret Quebec's desire for an ethnography museum, to take its place within a full array of "world-class" cultural institutions, as yet another statement concerning national maturity. In an anthropology museum the nation could at last prove, not only that it possesses culture, but that it has the power to minoritize other cultures. For, as we shall see in the next chapter, not only is it said that a healthy nation has a culture; it also has minorities.

CHAPTER SEVEN

A Normal Society:
Majority Language, Minority Cultures

Cross-cultural comparison shows, contrary to Western common sense, that social solidarity need not be conceptualized in terms of linguistic homogeneity. In the Northwest Amazon, for example, people in small villages routinely speak three, four, or more languages. Residents in a village, or even within a single longhouse, do not all speak the same set of languages and, most interesting from our perspective, people do not consider their multilingualism to be at all remarkable (Sorensen 1967). Yet from at least the early nineteenth century, Western nationalisms have accepted with little question the idea that linguistic homogeneity is highly desirable for the social health of the Nation-State. Thus it comes as no surprise to learn that "the bearers of [Colombian and Brazilian] national cultures," with their "unconsciously held monolingual values," find the multilingual Indians residing in their territories to be aberrant (Sorensen 1985: 148–49).

As we saw in chapter 5, the 1978 white paper on cultural development proclaimed the French language to be the central component of a solidary national identity around which Québécois of all ethnic origins could be expected to rally. In Quebec the equation One Nation, One Language has been justified and elaborated in several ways. First, until recently language has been valorized as a component of national identity in terms of its relationship to Roman Catholicism. *La langue, gardienne de la foi:* language, guardian of the faith— this is the famous formula that almost anyone can cite to describe the central thesis of "traditional" French-Canadian nationalism. As long ago as 1831, the inquisitive Alexis de Tocqueville was told by a French-Canadian lawyer that "our clergy are conspicuously nationalist" because "the English government has worked in underhand ways to change the religious convictions of the French Canadians." Tocqueville concluded from such remarks that "religion puts an obstacle in the way of marriages between the two races, and creates in the clergy an enlightened class which has an interest in speaking French" (1959:40, 190). During the remainder of the nineteenth century, with the clergy a dominating elite in French Canada, the patriotic association of religion and language was elevated to the status of a "national doctrine" which held sway until the 1950s (Filion 1984).

La langue, gardienne de la foi was the title of a speech and pamphlet presented in 1919 by the nationalist leader Henri Bourassa at Montreal. Bourassa began by asking "Are we more French than Catholic?" and answered himself with what seems to be a categorical assertion of the priority of religion over nationality and language: "man belongs to God before he belongs to himself; he must serve the Church before serving his fatherland" (1919:8, 11). Bourassa argued that language and nationality were "natural" bases of sociability; as such, they were acceptable to the Church as long as people understood them to be subordinate to "the only universal and complete society, . . . the Church" (10). Yet as he elaborated this thesis, Bourassa began to absolutize his commitment to the French language, a commitment which had been presented in theory as a relative and subordinate one. For example, he described French as a language devoted to Catholicism, one which "encourages, among those who speak and write it, Catholic ideas, Catholic mores, Catholic traditions, and Catholic culture [*ambiance*]." And Bourassa went on to denounce English as a language "of error, of heresy, of revolt, of division, of doctrinal and moral anarchy" (33). Bourassa explained this affinity between a particular language and a universal religion in historic and naturalistic terms: "the *true* French language," he wrote, "is the eldest daughter of the Christianized Latin language" (42). As we shall see, similar appeals to nature and history are made in purely secular discussions of language; and though Bourassa's main argument, subordinating language to religion, is rarely made today, informants readily presented it as an example of what their national identity once was.

A second formulation of the importance of language can be described as a simplified version of the so-called Whorfian hypothesis. In Quebec the idea is widespread that language is the "vehicle" and "motor" of thought, and that a distinctive style of thought and way of interpreting the world is the essence of a culture. Thus phrased, the claim is relativistic: Quebec's language-based national culture is seen as one among a world of different national cultures; its uniqueness is asserted, but superiority is not claimed for it.

One occasionally hears, however, a non-relativistic claim about language, one that draws on the (continental) French notion of the superior clarity and rationality of French language and thought. One man, a retired postal worker who attributed his nationalism to the teachings of Lionel Groulx, explained to me that my difficulties in learning French were due to the complex "nuances" of the language. As an example, he took the dictionary and chose a word at random (*concussion*), then attempted to show me the difference between it and several others with which it was not quite synonymous. He explained that the ability of French to express such nice distinctions was a key element in the "clarity" of the language, and that French was "very close to reality" in this respect. Such claims echo that of Henri Bourassa, who pointed to the clarity of the French language—in its pre-Revolutionary state, preserved in Quebec though abandoned in France—to explain the fact that it was, as he put it, "the only living language [which is] truly Catholic" (1919:44).

A third formulation of the relation between national identity and language amounts to a categorical equation of the two. In chapter 2 I quoted an informant who told me that "your language, that's you." And, as we saw in chapter 4, Premier Lesage made a similar argument in his speech concerning the creation of the M.A.C.:

> Of all the languages currently spoken in the world, the French language is the one that fits us best because of our own characteristics and mentality. We could no longer be French Canadian if we spoke another language because then we would adopt means of expression produced in a foreign culture. (1961c:10; MAC 1976:13)

Other people discussed language as a reflection of national essence. A well-known playwright, telling me of his attempts to represent the language of rural regions, described this language as "a manifestation of what we are as a collectivity." When people draw this equation between language and collective essence, they often resort to a discussion of origins, or to naturalistic metaphors. Thus the playwright carefully explained to me that the rural dialect of his plays was not a "barbarous language" but one descended from "Old French, itself descended from Latin." As such, it was, as he put it, "logical," a language that "held together." But that healthy language was threatened, he continued, by the corrupt dialects radiating outward from Montreal. For him, as for many Québécois, the centrality of language to national culture creates intense concern about perceived threats to the language. As we shall now see, the degeneration of language is at the heart of the negative vision in nationalist thought.

Linguistic Pollution

Though people in Quebec today readily identify their language as the key component of Québécois national culture, there is much discussion about what is seen as a situation of linguistic degeneration which, if uncorrected, will lead to the death of the nation. There is a long tradition of linguistic "purism" in French Canada (Aléong 1981), a tradition intimately related to the linguistic purism of France. A rather mortified Tocqueville gives us a vivid description of a Quebec City courtroom, where

> counsel for the defence got up indignantly and argued his case in French; his adversary answered in English. The argument waxed hot on both sides in the two languages. . . . From time to time the Englishman forced himself to put his argument in French . . . [and] the other did the same sometimes. The judge, sometimes speaking French, sometimes English, endeavoured to keep order.

According to Tocqueville, these French Canadians spoke in a "style" that was "vulgar and mixed with odd idioms and English phrases." "There is," he concluded, "something odd, incoherent, even burlesque in the whole picture" (1959:187).

Something odd, incoherent, even burlesque: since Tocqueville's time there has been in French Canada a steady stream of linguistic purists denouncing anglicization, *franglais*, and, in general, the incoherence of languages promiscuously mixed together. Their insecurity and zeal have been inspired by the criticism of visitors, both European and Anglo-American, ready, like Tocqueville, to dismiss local speech habits as a barbarous *patois*. Consider the following anecdote, recorded by Emmanuel Blain de Saint-Aubin, a nineteenth-century man of letters:

> In 1862 I had the honor of being asked by Lady Monck to give French lessons to her children. . . .
> "Sir," she asked, "you are French?"
> "Yes."
> "You speak, I suppose, Parisian French? I need to ask you this, for I am told that the French Canadians speak an abominable patois."
> "Madame," I told her, "I do not speak Parisian French, and I would be mortified if I could not speak my language better than a real Parisian."
> "You shock me (*Vous m'étonnez*)." (in Bouthillier and Meynaud 1972:166)

The author went on to explain to his interlocutor that any *educated* French Canadian spoke the same language as educated Frenchmen, but in general such comparisons have done nothing but feed what nationalists themselves would describe as collective insecurity.

Language purists have preached to the populace from the pulpit, in the popular press, and during good-language campaigns sponsored by a variety of patriotic and educational organizations. Also, beginning in 1912 there have been several pan-Canadian conventions or "congresses" devoted to analyzing the state of the French language in Canada. The most recent of such gatherings was convened in 1982. The published proceedings of this meeting contain familiar rhetoric: "we are traversing a critical period . . . and must, with regard to the 'Quebec national phenomenon,' and the French language itself, remain in a state of alert." The editors point out that Quebec is still insecure in its essential identity, being obliged to define itself "by comparison and opposition" both to its English-language surroundings and to a reliable linguistic norm emanating from France (Amyot and Bibeau 1984:11–12).

This discussion of Quebec and its language situated between North American English and the French language of France gives us the heart of the language problem as linguistically self-conscious Québécois perceive it. Language is thought to be a key component of national culture and identity because in Anglophone North America, "non-English" (if I may so designate Québécois French) distinguishes the Québécois from the masses they envision surrounding themselves. However, what, *phrased positively,* is the language of the Québécois? If it is nothing but the French language of France, then where is Québécois distinctiveness to be found? But if it isn't the French language of France, internationally recognized, even prestigious, then what is it?

From the Quiet Revolution until the time of my field work in the late 1970s, the notion of *joual* has been central in attempts to answer such questions about Quebec's linguistic identity. *Joual,* a word made famous by the book *Les insolences du Frère Untel,* refers to the supposedly degenerate language of Quebec. According to Frère Untel ("Brother Anonymous," pseudonym of Jean-P. Desbiens), the term *joual* is well chosen:

> There is a suitable relation between the thing and the noun which designates it. The word is odious and the thing is odious. The word *Joual* is a kind of condensed description of what it is to speak *Joual*: to speak *Joual* is precisely to say *joual* instead of cheval [horse]. It is to talk as one can suppose horses would talk if they hadn't already opted for silence. . . . (Desbiens 1960:23–24)

Frère Untel went on to describe *joual* as a language disjointed at the level of syntax and pronunciation, one suitable only for communication among *joual* speakers, and only for mundane topics: "For an exchange among primitives, a primitive's language suffices; animals content themselves with a few cries. But if one wants to attain human dialogue, *Joual* no longer suffices" (25). Though Frère Untel did not present a complete theory of the causes of *joual,* he suggested that the pervasive influence of English, and the willingness of French Canadians to abandon their culture for a materialistic, Anglo-Saxon civilization, were at the root of the problem.

Except for his use of the term *joual,* Frère Untel added little that was new to French Canada's perception of its linguistic dilemma. Language purists of several generations had expressed the same complaints and concerns. But the language issue, like the national question, took on new dimensions during the Quiet Revolution. As Québécois nationalism replaced "French-Canadian" nationalism, *joual* began to be regarded in a new light. Some informants explained to me that for the first time, Québécois were not ashamed of themselves: "we realized that we were no stupider and no less capable than other peoples." Several claimed that the 1962 nationalization of electricity (under the leadership of René Lévesque, at that time a leading member of the Liberal government) and the subsequent achievements of Hydro-Québec gave Québécois a confidence they had never had in their scientific and economic capabilities. With respect to language, a new generation of writers and musicians wrote in *joual* instead of succumbing to the need to imitate European models. For some this was an act of political militancy, a proclamation of collective cultural impoverishment associated with the "colonial" status of Quebec (Reid 1972:158). Others saw in *joual* signs of cultural vitality (Kemp 1984:62). By the time of my field work, the vogue of *joual* had largely passed. As the good-language columnist for *Le Devoir* wrote, "*Joual* is reabsorbed, like cancer healed. Singers sing in better French, writers regionalize less, content with having reacted at one time to prove their identity" (Beguin 1978:6).

But what, specifically, is *joual?* The best answer would seem to be that no one has adequately defined it (Beauchemin 1976; Reighard 1984:182), though purportedly scientific definitions occasionally surface.[1] In my discussions with Québécois, I found two conventional

1. For example, during my field stay two students in linguistics at the University of Montreal published a tentative definition of *joual* in *Le Devoir.* " 'Joual' . . . is a phenomenon characteristic of our Québécois dialect. It is a system of surface reductions, going from the suppression of a simple phoneme to that of a complete morpheme, functioning according to non-aleatory grammatical rules. . . . This definition implies that 'Joual' is a linguistic system as structured and complete for its users as would be a standard written language. The reductions are carried out according to rigorous rules which permit or forbid certain disappearances or reductions. Take the examples 'j'ai vu 'a [la] fille,' 'j'ai vu 'es [les] filles' and 'j'ai vu l'école.' We observe

understandings of the term. First, some said that *joual* is the variety of French spoken in Quebec: "nous-autres, on parle joual." They described this dialect in terms of bad pronunciation as compared with the French language of France. Some called attention to what they saw as a debased vocabulary—in particular, to the use of anglicisms, or even English words in a "raw" state, as well as to the constant recourse to swearing. Others said that *joual* involved not only English words but English syntax as well. Finally, people included "québecismes" in definitions of *joual*—that is, words and idiomatic expressions peculiar to the French in Quebec but acceptable nonetheless. In general, however, people agreed that *joual* was a deformed or corrupted language.

A second group of informants argued that *joual* is not the dialect of all Quebec, but only of the francophone working classes of Montreal. It is in this milieu, where people have neither the time nor the education to worry about the purity of their French, that *joual* flourishes. These informants too saw *joual* as a deformation of language, but they also spoke of *joual* speakers as victims of economic and cultural colonization. In a country where the world of work and the mass media are dominated by English, they said, ordinary people cannot be held responsible for their recourse to *joual*. People who gave this second definition distinguished *joual,* the corrupt anglicized Montreal dialect, from other Quebec dialects which they saw as unique and valuable. As the playwright told me:

> Take a trip through the rest of Quebec and listen to the people talk. . . . You'll see that it's completely different from the language of Montreal. I have listened to these people and in some places they speak a very beautiful language, French in its constructions, but at times an archaic French, with extraordinary words and images. These people do not speak *joual* at all.

And he concluded that, because of the media which originate primarily in Montreal, "*joual* now threatens to suffocate these other dialects, which used to be protected by distance and isolation."

Joual, then, according to either definition, is a degradation of

---

that the consonant 'l' of the definite articles 'la' and 'les' can readily disappear without altering the message, since the vowels 'a' and 'e' remain to oppose 'les' to 'la.' However, the consonant 'l' apostrophe cannot disappear since, once suppressed, nothing indicates its existence" (Tousignant and Ostiguy 1978:5).

One week later, a seemingly outraged reader published a reply to this attempt, arguing that such definitions, in which the science of linguistics is used to defend particular ideologies, "is contrary to any scientific and objective proceeding." "Nothing less resembles a 'structured and complete' code than two student papers written in 'Joual' " (Hogue-Lebeuf 1978:5).

language. As such, it was condemned by many people with whom I talked. Some denounced the "cult" of *joual* that they claimed existed among intellectuals and writers. Others agreed that *joual* ought to be portrayed in literature as one among several Québécois dialects, but criticized those who presented it as *the* Québécois language. In general, those who spoke critically of *joual* felt that its heyday was over. They recognized the importance of the acceptance of *joual* as an aspect of collective self-acceptance; they agreed also that at one time it had been important to renounce [continental] French models or, at least, the slavish imitation of French styles characteristic of French-Canadian intellectual life before the Quiet Revolution. However, this phase of collective maturation accomplished, it was time to "cure" Québécois French once and for all of the ills that plague it.

Thus, despite the symbolic significance of the acceptance of *joual,* as well as its consecration in some of the best of modern Québécois literature, the language purists have continued to hammer away at the theme of the degenerate condition of French-Canadian French. Consider the following recent account published by a linguist in a scholarly journal:

> While there is no scientific study available to document . . . the extent of the contamination of the Quebec vernacular by English, most linguistic observers are unanimous in describing the phenomenon as pervasive and alarming. The menace is most evident in the language of the lower strata of urban Quebec whose bilingual patois is known as *joual,* but it is also noticeable in the speech of . . . the middle class. . . . The vernacular of the province is not only saturated with recognizable anglicisms . . . it is also corrupted by countless hidden borrowings . . . that are the more injurious because they gain currency under the cloak of a French appearance. The inroads of English are most harmful when they affect the morphosyntactic system of French, a process that can critically undermine the speaker's identification with a dominant language and his ability to conceptualize and fully express reality (Sénécal 1983:53)

In this passage, phrases like *contamination, menace, saturate, corrupted, injurious,* and *cloak* recall the pollution rhetoric typical of the negative stance that most Québécois nationalists take with respect to the problem of mixture. We are reminded, for example, of Groulx's nationalistic novel, *L'Appel de la race,* in which an anglicized young woman who has decided to study French declares "as I refrenchify myself, I think more clearly and discriminate more finely *(je sens plus finement)*" (1922:125). The notion that people exposed to two cultures or two languages lose their identity and become confused and unable to function is a commonplace of nationalist rhetoric. As Einar Haugen remarks, "Bilinguals are often unpopular . . . looked on with distrust [and] viewed as mentally handicapped" (1973:56).

Linguistic degeneration is sometimes attributed to internal failings, as when Québécois blame themselves for not "respecting" and caring for their language. However, they more frequently stress external causes, dwelling on the dangers presented by the English language to a French-speaking society in North America. From this perspective there are two forms of corruption: first, the anglicization of French, and, second, the temptations of bilingualism. Québécois often remarked to me that a particular word just uttered was English, not French, adding that they ought to be more careful of such usage. When questioned as to why it was important to be careful, why it was necessary to "preserve" French, most of my informants could do no more than offer a vague formulation of national identity defined in terms of language:

> It's natural that a people should preserve its language. Nowhere in history do we find the case of a group that voluntarily gave up its language.

> Our part of the world is French and should stay that way, just as other places have their own customs and languages. It's a matter of pride.

Others were able to discuss the invasion of foreign words and consequent erosion of national language and culture in more elaborate terms, as indicated in the following example, taken from a speech that I heard during a public campaign to improve the quality of French in Quebec:

> Our language patrimony *(patrimoine langagier)* is a mass of words and expressions that we all share—all of us five or six million francophones. We have in common a patrimony that comes to x billion words. This is our treasure, like a natural resource. When six million people lose three, four, five words, our patrimony is reduced by that much: we lose ten, twenty, thirty million words.

Here linguistic pollution is discussed in the rhetoric of "cultural property" used more routinely with respect to material culture, museums, and historic reconstruction. But the replacement of indigenous words with foreign ones is more than a static loss to be recorded on some patrimonial tally sheet. Like the constant recourse to imported manufactures, of which nationalists also complain, the use

167

of English words represents the immaturity and lack of independence of the collective self. The wholesale importation of English terms in business, technology, sports, and other domains symbolic of modernity is said to take the place of the creation of new French words—and thus in linguistic, as in material, matters, the Québécois becomes a passive consumer rather than an active creator. Worse yet is the continual recourse to translated reading matter, for translation can be said to involve dependence not only upon the words of others, but upon their thought as well.

In general, nationalists see their excessive reliance on the words and thought of others as a negation of their national self. Both in published sources and private conversations, people paint a bleak picture of the loss of identity consequent upon linguistic pollution. They are concerned not only with the dependence on foreign linguistic material, but with the dangers involved in ignoring boundaries: to continue to permit the indiscriminate mixing of the French and English languages, to continue to tolerate the invasion of Quebec by foreign words and phrases, will lead in the end to a situation of subhuman linguistic chaos and barbarism. A mixture of French and English will be neither one nor the other, and those who speak it will be comprehensible only among themselves—cut off from the rest of the world. The Acadians of New Brunswick were often cited to me in this regard as a group whose French had become so overrun with English that they were now unintelligible to French speakers—and to English speakers as well.

Similar fears emerged in discussions of bilingualism. Some informants simply denied the existence of "true" bilingualism, saying that no one could master the nuances of two languages. Others claimed that a command of two languages involved possession of two visions of reality, a condition which leads to imprecise thinking or even, as one M. Leblanc, a university professor, told me, to "a disarticulation of the mechanism by which human beings confront the world." The question of bilingualism often arose in discussion of English as a second language in Quebec—particularly with regard to English instruction French-language public schools. Some people insisted that such instruction was dangerous if begun too early, for during the first years of education it is crucial that children acquire a basic knowledge of their mother tongue, as well as a solid grounding in a world interpreted in terms of French language and culture. To introduce a second language at this stage might hinder the socialization process, I was told, and produce children who, having mastered neither French nor English, would be maladjusted and unable to think clearly.

Still, many people admitted that English was useful to Québécois, but insisted upon its status as a second language. They welcomed the teaching of English in the public schools but said that it belonged in high school, not elementary school. And the many people whom I knew who wanted to learn or improve their English invariably insisted upon the fact that knowledge of a second language was a matter of "personal choice" or "individual enrichment." Several university students told me of their rebellion in high school at the presentation of English as a language necessary for economic advancement. It was this claim of economic necessity that they had rejected (and continued to reject), though many expressed willingness to learn English as an aspect of personal culture. These attitudes recall the importance of choice in nationalist ideology discussed in chapter 2: just as people could not imagine a nation voluntarily abandoning its language, so they would not tolerate the imposition of a foreign language for economic or other reasons. Only as an object of individual or collective choice—as "a cultural complement and conqueror's tool," as Groulx once wrote (1935:236)—would they consent to the study and use of English.

In sum, in the nationalist perspective the overwhelming presence of English in Quebec threatens the collective self. The continual recourse to English ways of speaking, as well as to English thought "camouflaged" in translation, is but another form of national immaturity and dependence. Like the massive use of imported consumer goods and cultural products, it bespeaks that inability to project the collective self into external forms which is a sure sign of alienation. At the same time, the pollution of French by English will lead to a situation of linguistic chaos and incomprehensibility. The ultimate result of this collapse of cultural and linguistic boundaries will be the death of the nation. M. Leblanc epitomized these fears in his account of French-Canadian emigrants to New England. The children of such people would lose their French yet never truly "possess," as he put it, English—for they could have no "profound roots" in their adopted language. This assimilated French Canadian is "a hybrid, a type of monstrosity," and ought, according to Leblanc, "to be called *Le Blank.*"

Nationalist Ideology and Language Legislation

The serious involvement of the Government of Quebec in language politics began in 1961 with the creation of the *Office de la Langue française* (O.L.F.) within the Quebec Cultural Affairs Department. There followed three language laws: Bill 63 (An Act to promote the French language in Quebec), passed by the Union Nationale government in 1969; replaced by Bill 22 (Official Language Act), passed by the Liberal government in 1974; replaced by Bill 101 (Charter of the French language), passed by the Parti Québécois government in 1977.

A Normal Society

One should also mention the Canadian Federal Government's Official Languages Act of 1969, as well as the provisions relating to language (article 23) in the "repatriated" Canadian constitution of 1982.

Analysts (Daoust-Blais and Martin 1981; Sénécal 1983; Coleman 1984:183ff) agree that the Quebec government began its work in language planning with so-called language corpus planning (Kloss 1969:80)—that is, with "policies designed to stabilize a standard-language norm and to develop new lexicons" (Coleman 1984:189). This task has remained central to the work of the O.L.F. as evidenced, for example, in its terminology banks and its publications designed to promote standardized and "correct" usage.

In addition to language corpus planning, the government has been increasingly concerned, since the early 1970s, with language status planning; that is, with improving the status of French in Quebec society in order to make it the dominant and preferred language of business, government, and education. Policies devoted to language status planning have been aimed at redressing the economic balance of power within Quebec, that is, at ending what nationalists see as the abnormal domination by an anglophone bourgeoisie of the francophone masses—the majority reduced permanently to economic inferiority. There is a clear progression from Bill 63, which timidly suggests that the government should "see to it that French is the working language in public and private undertakings in Quebec" (article 14b); to Bill 22, which spells out in some 40 articles how various domains of Quebec society are to be "frenchified" *(francisé)*, but *without* providing serious sanctions for citizens and companies refusing to follow government's lead; to Bill 101, which refines an overall strategy for frenchification *(francisation) and* formulates sanctions to enforce compliance.

These government actions and strategies reflect nationalist ideology in several ways. First, the work of the O.L.F. is a perfect example of defense against cultural pollution. In adopting a defensive stance the O.L.F. has taken its place in the tradition of linguistic purism discussed previously. As one observer puts it, "the OLF's philosophy . . . has evolved . . . from a rigidly normative and prescriptive strategy that implied a near total espousal of the canons of standard French to a slightly mitigated outlook that recognizes the legitimacy of some regional peculiarities in vocabulary" (Sénécal 1983:55).

Linguistic purism and the defense against pollution bring us back to the central assumptions of nationalist ideology, which posit the boundedness, distinctiveness, and homogeneity of the nation. These concepts are central to what has been perhaps the most controversial aspect of Quebec's language laws: that is, those sections of the laws relating to the language of instruction in the province's public schools. The language of instruction has been of central concern to nationalists since the mid-1960s, when it became apparent that the English-language sector of the public school system was assimilating many more non-French- and non-English-speaking immigrants than the French-language sector. That trend, coupled with a drastic reduction in the birthrate of Catholic French Canadians following the Second World War, led nationalists to fear that the French majority of Quebec (who had constituted about 80 percent of the population of the province throughout the twentieth century) would give way to an emerging English-language majority.

Bill 63 was enacted largely in response to this perceived threat. However, as far as the nationalists were concerned it failed miserably because it explicitly permitted parents to choose whether to send their children to French- or English-language schools. It thus reconfirmed the Canadian status quo, based on the British North America Act of 1867, which mandated that Quebec maintain both Protestant and Catholic schools. The ethnic dichotomy which in the nineteenth century had been phrased in terms of religion was by the early twentieth century understood in terms of language, and Quebec (alone among the Canadian provinces) found itself with an entrenched "minority" school system, supported by public funds and operating in the language of the minority (in this case, English).

Bill 22 attempted to modify that situation in order to neutralize the ability of the English-language school system to assimilate immigrants. Article 41 states:

> Pupils must have a sufficient knowledge of the language of instruction to receive their instruction in that language.
> Pupils who do not have a sufficient knowledge of the languages of instruction [i.e., French or English] must receive their instruction in French.

There followed two articles empowering the Minister of Education to devise tests to determine whether children entering the public schools had a sufficient knowledge of English to enable them to attend English-language schools. However, the spectacle of four- and five-year-old children of immigrants being denied access to English-language schools on the basis of their inability to pass a language test created both hysteria and anger among Quebec's English-language minorities. Nor did Bill 22 satisfy Québécois nationalists with respect to the education issue, for it failed to dispose of that issue neatly, and it left the door open to abuses and to political maneuvering.

Thus Bill 101 again reformulated the government's policy on the language of instruction. Article 73 specified that all children must attend French-language schools except those in the following categories:

(a) a child whose father or mother received his or her elementary instruction in English, in Quebec;

(b) a child whose father or mother, domiciled in Quebec on the date of the coming into force of this act, received his or her elementary instruction in English outside Quebec;

(c) a child who, in his last year of school in Quebec before the coming into force of this act, was lawfully receiving his instruction in English, in a public kindergarten class or in an elementary or secondary school;

(d) the younger brothers and sisters of a child described in paragraph c.

These specifications concerning the language of instruction must be understood with respect to the question of national homogeneity. To complete that analysis, however, we need first to consider the position that the successive laws took concerning the official language of Quebec. The British North America Act of 1867 had stipulated that English and French were to be the official languages of the Canadian federal government, as well as of the provincial government of Quebec—though none of the other provincial governments were mandated as bilingual. Bill 63 was silent with respect to the question of official language. However, Bill 22 declared in its first article that "French is the official language of the province of Quebec"—though it continued implicitly to recognize "the principle of linguistic duality" (Daoust-Blais and Martin 1981:54). Bill 101 reaffirmed, in its first article, that "French is the official language of Quebec"—but note the elimination of the phrase *province of Quebec*. Moreover, articles two through six spelled out what were called "Fundamental Language Rights," which declared that "every person has a right" to participate in all domains of social life in Quebec in French.

These language rights must be compared to the language rights envisioned by the federal government under Prime Minister Trudeau. The federal Official Languages Act of 1969 stipulated that "French and English are accorded equal legal status on the federal level." However, Trudeau wanted to go beyond that, "to extend the protection of both French and English language rights throughout Canada by adding a linguistic bill of rights to the Canadian constitution" (Gill 1980:38–39). This was finally accomplished by the Constitution Act of 1982. Article 23 of the Act provided that

Citizens of Canada

(a) whose first language learned and still understood is that of the English or French linguistic minority population of the province in which they reside, or (b) who have received their primary school instruction in Canada in

English or French and reside in a province where the
language in which they received that instruction is the
language of the English or French linguistic minority population of the province,

have the right to have their children receive primary and
secondary school instruction in that language in that
province.

Québécois nationalists bitterly opposed Trudeau on this issue
because they felt that Francophone minorities in "English Canada,"
with the possible exception of those in New Brunswick, had been so
weakened by a century of persecution that they were doomed to
disappear no matter what remedial measures the federal government
took. According to Québécois nationalists, federal guarantees of
bilingualism would serve only to protect the bilingual status quo of
Quebec, while doing nothing to alter the English unilingualism of the
rest of Canada (Sénécal 1984; Woolfson 1984:63–66). Indeed, late in
1982 Article 73 of Quebec's Bill 101 (the so-called Quebec Clause) was
declared unconstitutional because it contradicted Article 23 (the
"Canada Clause") of the new Canadian Constitution. From the perspective of Quebec nationalists, this judicial ruling threatens to nul-
lify the linguistic progress made under the first five years of Bill 101
(see chapter 8).

To relate these issues of language of instruction and language
rights to the underlying nationalist theme of homogeneity and boundedness, we should first note the progression in Quebec's three language laws, from Bill 63's acceptance of the notion of a bilingual
Quebec as a province within Canada to Bill 101's vision of Quebec as a
unilingual French *society*. This can be seen clearly in the explanatory
document that the Parti Québécois government issued to the public
when it introduced the first version (Bill 1) of Bill 101 to Quebec's
Assemblée nationale. This document speaks consistently of Quebec
as "a French-language society" and argues that "all . . . normal
societies" require "a common language [to] unite people" (Quebec
1977:52, 29).[2]

Here the battle between the federal and the Quebec governments over language rights becomes relevant. The historically crucial
examples of the American and French Revolutions established the

2. One might here point out how the terminology of social science can reen-
force the rhetoric of nationalism in this regard, by choosing to study a would-be
nation as "a society," then spawning research, journals, and scholarly associations
dedicated to, and named in terms of, that society. The scholars' efforts can be further
encouraged by nationalistic governments. For example, the Canadian and
Québécois governments provide funds for Canadian Studies and Quebec Studies in
the United States.

concept of a bill of rights as an important element in charters of national existence. Since at least the time of Locke, "rights" are what define individuals as equal, and a government's granting of rights establishes the conditions of homogeneity upon which a national existence is to be built. Moreover, the constitutional rights of individuals are conceived to be universal: they apply to everyone, and they define what a generic human being is. Of course, the generic properties of individuals envisioned by specific rights often turn out to be highly culture-specific; one need only think of Locke's conception of proprietorship as the most basic of all human rights, or of the rights to private property forced on native Americans in the United States by the General Allotment Act of 1887 (Dorris 1981:51–57). Camille Laurin (Minister for Cultural Development during the first administration of the Parti Québécois) used precisely this argument *against* the "rights" of English-speakers in Quebec: "The privileges of the Anglo-Québécois minority are the result of an historically contingent balance of power . . . but it [the minority] seeks to perpetuate that balance by presenting it as the expression of a formal right that must be maintained in the higher interests of humanity" (quoted in Murray and Murray 1978:241).

Viewed from this angle, language rights present a curious mixture of the universalistic, embodied in the very notion of rights, and the culturally specific—the idea that a *particular* language belongs to people by right (cf. Arendt 1958:293). In general, we can say that language rights establish the homogeneity of a nation by mandating that an essential cultural characteristic (language) be shared by all. Thus the battle over language rights between the Canadian and Québécois governments can be seen as a battle to establish the boundedness and homogeneity of the nation—that is, either Canada defined (in opposition to the United States) by the cultural characteristic of bilingualism, or Quebec defined as a unilingual French society (in opposition to English Canada).

Now reconsider the language of education. Quebec's three language laws move from a free choice of French or English (a right which suggests a bilingual Canada as the ultimate society of reference); to the notion that English is a right that can be achieved, by passing a test; to the notion that French is the ascribed right of a nation, while English can continue only for those individuals who can claim it as a right ascribed on the basis of criteria that are narrowed by being doubly naturalistic: one inherits the right to an English-language education only if one's *parents* enjoyed that right *on Quebec soil* (cf. Woolfson 1983:45).

In sum, the language policies of Bill 101 and, to a lesser extent, of the laws that came before it were intended to establish the province of Quebec as "a" society and "a" nation—both defined by the dominance of French unilingualism—while relegating English to a marginal position, even to a residual category. Bill 101 continues the anti-pollution measures of earlier legislation and also provides, more forcefully than previous legislation, for the boundedness and homogeneity of the national society. By ensuring that the children of Quebec's non-francophone "minorities" would learn French, the government hoped to integrate the minorities into the mainstream. But, as we shall now see, the trick was to do that without assimilating them—that is, without destroying their presence *as minorities* whose existence would testify to the presence of a "majority."

On Having Minorities

Since the Quiet Revolution the presence of immigrants in Quebec has been an important issue in nationalist debate. Almost from the beginnings of New France, the demographic growth of French Canada depended on a high birthrate rather than the assimilation of immigrants. However, by the time of the Quiet Revolution, the French-Canadian birthrate had finally come into line with that of the rest of North America. At the same time, with the post–World War II resumption of immigration to Canada on a significant scale, there developed in Montreal important new communities of Italians, Portuguese, Greeks, Jews, and others. Yet it was not the presence of these people in the "second-largest French city in the world" that disturbed nationalists, but their tendency to align themselves with the already entrenched English-language minority. Immigrants assimilated, as informants put it, to the English minority, choosing to learn English rather than French and to attend the English-language rather than the French-language public school system. Given the sudden drop in the French-Canadian birthrate, this swelling of the ranks of Quebec's anglophones seemed to some Québécois to pose the threat of an eventual anglicization of Montreal and, through that key city, of the entire province. Pierre Laporte's 1965 white paper put the matter in these terms:

> Statistical studies show that the relative importance of the francophone population is declining both in Quebec and Canada; the principal reason for this is that immigration is a marginal fact within the francophone collectivity of Quebec, whereas for anglophones it is an important demographic support. (Quebec 1965:206)

Much of the concern with language legislation, particularly with language and public education, relates directly to these perceptions and fears.

Some Québécois that I knew spoke as if Montreal had become a

175

foreign city to them. People said that it was "cosmopolitan," but in reference to Montreal the term often had a pejorative connotation. Friends agreed with my decision to conduct field work in Quebec City rather than Montreal because they felt I would not find the "real Quebec" in Montreal. Some viewed the presence of ethnic neighborhoods as a cultural advantage that made Montreal interesting, but argued nonetheless that Montreal was not a true Québécois city because of such diversity. Others could find no redeeming value in the existence of immigrant communities which they perceived to be in the process of assimilating to the English-language minority. Several people complained about the amount of English one hears in the streets of Montreal. One high-school student, speaking at a public meeting on Canadian unity, described a trip to Montreal in which he repeatedly failed to obtain directions in French from passers-by. Such experiences, he concluded, helped to account for the existence of an independence movement in Quebec. When I interviewed him later, he explained that "it's normal for a nation to have minorities. But it isn't normal for minorities to threaten the majority."

The idea that it is normal for a nation "to have" minorities was endorsed by the Parti Québécois government in its 1978 white paper on cultural development. There we read that "there can be no culture without minorities" (Quebec 1978:59). However, minority groups pose a delicate problem for the Parti Québécois, and for Quebec nationalists in general. On the one hand, nationalists seek a homogeneous, unilingual Quebec, a "normal" nation. On the other hand, having complained bitterly of the fate of French-Canadian minority groups in other Canadian provinces, nationalists do not wish to appear to impose a similar fate on non-francophones in Quebec (cf. Connor 1973:12–19). But how can the desire for a homogeneous nation be reconciled with fair treatment of those elements in the nation that make for diversity?

In nationalist rhetoric, one solution to this problem has been to deny that ethnic groups within Quebec are groups in any meaningful sense of the term. Consider the following remarks, taken from a speech delivered by Camille Laurin to an academic conference on ethnicity:

> The ethnic group refers to an ensemble of charac-
> teristics and traditions, the existence or persistence of
> which can be verified at the level of individuals and fami-
> lies. The nation, on the other hand, is a global society, a
> complete society, which possesses its own characteristics
> as a society, which has its own mode of organization and
> functioning, its own historic continuity, a political and
> juridical tradition and, finally, a clearly identified ter-
> ritory. A nation is thus not an aggregate of individuals

possessing, one by one, common cultural characteristics;
it is a human society, cultivated by history and thus having
its own culture as a distinct, identifiable society. (1977:2)

According to the somewhat confusing logic of this argument, an
ethnic group is not a collective individual, but individual human
beings who share certain characteristics. Since the ethnic group is not
really a group, it cannot interpose itself as a collectivity between
individual ethnics and the nation which encompasses them. In other
words, ethnicity cannot compete with nationality for the primary
allegiance of citizens. It is as if the ethnic traits shared by these
citizens are not relevant in the definition of their collective identification; their national allegiance can be only to the encompassing
nation—in this case, Quebec—and will be based on their participation in the common national culture. Those ethnic characteristics that
they possess as individuals are not to enter into the process of national
identification, just as any number of individual traits and talents do
not.

Laurin's argument has never been translated into government
policy. Rather, since at least the time of Laporte's 1965 white paper,
the Quebec government has favored a different solution to the problem of reconciling ethnic diversity and national homogeneity. This
alternative solution is to treat ethnic collectivities as so many equivalent individuals who belong to the nation. These individuals are to
be "integrated" into a mutual union rather than "assimilated" by an
overpowering totality. The 1978 white paper on cultural development
argued that the French language was the focal point around which
Quebec's national unity was to be built. That fundamental point
established, the white paper went on to validate the existence of
minority groups and to encourage their "contributions":

A viable society must consider the contributions from its
own diversity to be essentially enriching. Primarily a
French society, Quebec must also discover a source of
vitality in its minorities. Fortunately today the melting pot
as illustrated by American society is open to question:
hasty assimilation of all new arrivals is not considered
desirable. Any society that helps its minority groups to
preserve their heritage reaps a rich cultural reward and
achieves a better balance. This could and should be the
case for Quebec. (Quebec 1978:59)

Here assimilation is rejected outright, yet the concept of integration is ambiguous, suggesting full participation in national society
without the negation of minority differences. Such an argument
contradicts in two ways the position that nationalists of the Parti
Québécois (and others as well) have routinely taken when the issue is

the relationship of Quebec to Canada. First, the white paper suggests that people can indeed "be two things at once," a position flatly rejected by Quebec *indépendantistes,* who maintain that people cannot be both Québécois and Canadian. Second, a policy encouraging the preservation of ethnic heritages would seem to reproduce what the white paper elsewhere (28) criticizes as Ottawa's attempt to folklorize Quebec culture. In other words, the white paper (like L'Allier's green paper before it) saw in federal cultural policies an attempt to divide Québécois culture into pieces (music, poetry, folklore) that could be appropriated as elements of a Canadian cultural totality or, at least, rendered politically harmless. But its own position towards Quebec's "minorities," who are asked "to preserve their heritage" in order to contribute to Quebec society, seems exactly the same.

During the first administration of the Parti Québécois (1976–1981), there were political as well as ideological motives for the white paper's position on ethnic minorities. The government's language legislation, Bill 101, aroused intense opposition from Quebec anglophones, including a high percentage of the immigrants and neo-Canadians resident in the province, who saw it as a threat to their economic and cultural survival. More generally, *indépendantisme* and the possibility of Quebec's secession from Canada frightened many immigrants who had struggled not only to establish themselves in Quebec, but to obtain Canadian citizenship. Finally, the highly politicized nationalism of the Parti Québécois led its opponents—politically motivated, to be sure—to accuse it of racism, xenophobia, and ethnocentrism. The government was particularly blamed for what was seen as the underrepresentation of minorities in the civil service. In such a situation, the Parti Québécois government wanted immigration policies that were explicitly tolerant or, at least, that appeared to be so. Thus in 1981 Quebec's *Ministère de l'Immigration* became the *Ministère des Communautés culturelles et de l'Immigration* (M.C.C.I.). To its original mandate (to recruit immigrants likely to participate in Quebec's economy and culture) was added a second task: to plan policies "relative to the blossoming [épanouissement] of the cultural communities and their participation in the national life" (MCCI 1983:7).

The retitled ministry immediately published a position paper entitled *Quebecers Each and Every One* (in French, *Autant de façons d'être québécois*). This document announced the following policy objectives for the M.C.C.I.:

> to ensure the survival and development of the cultural communities as well as their individuality; to sensitize French-speaking Quebecers to the contribution the cultural communities have made to our common heritage;

and to promote the integration of the cultural communities into Quebec society, particularly . . . [into] the Public Service. . . . (MCCI 1982:x)

The document went on to describe Quebec as a nation of "converging cultures" in which Québécois "from all over the world" would work together in a "society which seeks to respect the cultural traditions of every group while affirming Quebec's essential nature as a francophone society" (1, 9). Paragraphs were devoted to Quebec's Italians, Jews, Germans, Greeks, Poles, Ukrainians, Portuguese, Hungarians, Haitians, Lebanese, Vietnamese, and others. The document even described France as one among several "countries of origin," implying thereby that the descendants of the French settlers, some 80 percent of Quebec's population, were simply one among the many ethnic groups that inhabit the nation (3–4). However, this presentation of Quebec's minorities was aimed above all at the "English" minority, close to 11 percent of Quebec's population who claim descent from English, Irish, Scotch, and American Loyalist immigrants. To portray the "English" as one among many ethnic groups was to deny them the special status they claimed as one of the two "founding races" of Canada; or, phrased differently, it elevated the status of all other ethnic groups to equality with the English, thereby decreasing the status of the latter.[3] As Camille Laurin had phrased it four years earlier, "English-speakers had best learn to see themselves as a minority, not as the Quebec wing of the English-Canadian majority" (quoted in Levine 1986:8).

To speak of policies promoting the "individuality" of each minority culture suggests a vision of the nation *as a collection of collective individuals.* Alternatively, it encourages us to envision minority groups as individual members of the nation, practically the equivalent of the human individuals who make up the majority. Either way, minority cultures are treated as individuated actors whose "contributions" are said to "enrich" the global society, thus completing the image in the language of possessive individualism.

A series of publicity folders, made available free of charge by the M.C.C.I. in 1984, popularizes this image of the ethnic group as an individual member of the nation (see figure 7.1). Each of the four folders that I picked up at a government publications outlet conforms to the same format. Each is entitled "Portrait: Les Italiens [Vietnamiens, Allemands, Portugais] du Québec." Each is printed in black and white with one color (green for the Italians, blue for the Viet-

3. This logic is precisely why Québécois nationalists opposed Canadian multiculturalism, arguing that it diluted biculturalism—a policy justified by the special status of French- and English-Canadians as founding races in Canada—in such a way that the weaker of the two founding races, the French-Canadians, became just another ethnic group.

namese, and so on). Each has uncaptioned photographs (either ten or eleven) intended to portray a particular ethnic identity: images of people who "look ethnic," of festivals, of food-related activities, of shop signs. On the first page of each is a photograph of a child of [by implication] the group, and an introductory paragraph that establishes the individuated reality of the group by naming some of its cultural possessions and contributions to Quebec:

> Did you know that the Italian community, with almost 200,000 members, is the third largest in Quebec after the francophones and anglophones? That the cathedral of Notre-Dame de Montréal was decorated by Angelo Piarrovi, an Italian artist? That there are no fewer that 250 Italian restaurants in the metropolitan area . . .? That almost 6,000 Italians helped build the railroad linking Montreal and Quebec?

> Did you know that a dozen years ago there were fewer than a thousand people in Quebec who were born in Vietnam? That the program of group sponsorship [parrainage collectif] by itself made possible the welcoming of about 5,000 Southeast Asian refugees, of whom more than half are Vietnamese? That the Vietnamese avoid touching the head because they believe the soul is located there? That in daily life they use first names instead of family names?

Each pamphlet goes on to describe its group's economic assets, customs, religion, values, language, family life, and contributions to Quebec society. Each group is also given a history in relation to Quebec, a rhetorical ploy which constructs the group as a *Québécois* minority. For example, a sketch of the history of Quebec's "German" population mentions people with a variety of motivations settling in Quebec over a period of three centuries—data that can be presented retrospectively as the history of the Québécois German "community." In some cases, there are obvious difficulties in presenting the group as an individual that is complete—possessing the full complement of individuating characteristics—as well as *integrated into yet clearly bounded within* Quebec society. The relatively exotic Vietnamese, for example, can easily be shown to possess a culture but, we are told, "the contributions of the Vietnamese to Quebec life are still scanty because they have not been here long enough to be sufficiently integrated." By contrast, the relatively unexotic Germans have been in Quebec so long that "there are few traces that demonstrate the survival here of the original culture [il est peu d'éléments qui permettent de voir en quoi subsiste ici la culture du pays d'origine]." Such examples suggest the persuasiveness—in the face of heterogeneous social realities—of a logic that constructs each "group" as an equivalent individual. All are in possession of culture and community, and each in turn is possessed by the nation, whose majority/maturity is demonstrated by yet another form of cultural property. If it were possible for modern individuals to possess "enough" without needing more, then the possession of a *patrimoine,* a language, and minorities might allay nationalistic insecurity. But, as the concluding chapter will suggest, modern culture demands unlimited appropriation, the unending production of cultural specificities that will at last prove the existence of a healthy nation.

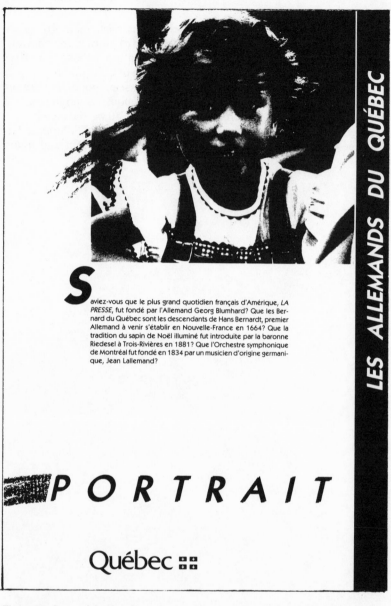

Figure 7.1. Cover of Québec *Portrait* pamphlet, *Les Allemands du Québec*, 1984. Courtesy of Ministère des Communautés culturelles et de l'Immigration, Gouvernement du Québec.

CHAPTER EIGHT

Meditations on Loose Ends: Lament and Dissent, Totality and Appropriation

*Ever since scientific work has given itself its own
proper and appropriable places through rational
projects capable of determining their procedures, with formal objects and specified
conditions under which they are falsifiable, ever
since it was founded as a plurality of limited and
distinct fields, in short ever since it stopped
being theological, it has constituted the* whole
as its remainder; *this remainder has become
what we call culture.*

Michel de Certeau 1984:6

It is difficult to evaluate the results of the Quebec government's cultural policies because, as the first administrators of the Department of Cultural Affairs recognized, culture is not readily amenable to rationalized accounting techniques. The published proceedings of the *Congrès langue et société au Québec* held in 1982 present numerous studies analyzing the effects of Bill 101, the centerpiece of the Parti Québécois's cultural policies. Most of the conference participants seem to have agreed, first, that Bill 101 had been a major step towards assuring the health of French language and culture in Quebec and, second, that continued vigilance and effort would be necessary both to prevent backsliding and to ensure further progress. Thus analysts agreed that Bill 101 had succeeded in orienting the children of immigrants to Montreal's French-language school system, but expressed concern that the Canada Clause of the 1982 Canadian Constitution could be used to reverse the new trend (Plourde 1984:42–45; Paille 1984:160; Remillard 1984:38). Some were encouraged by what they saw as moderate progress in the economic realm (Plourde 1984:44–51;

Sales et al. 1984:355), but others were more impressed by the endur-ing dominance of English in the world of business (Rocher 1984:23), while still others wondered what the economic costs of *francisation* were (Bonin 1984), or whether gains in *francisation* were due less to positive effects of Bill 101 than to the weakening of Quebec's eco-nomic situation in the early 1980s, leading to a net out-migration of Quebec's anglophones towards other Canadian provinces (Cas-tonguay 1984). One person argued that the Quebec government's immigration policies had significantly raised the relative proportion of French-speaking immigrants to Quebec and lowered the figures for English speakers (Plourde 1984:42), while another found that Quebec's attractiveness to immigrants was decreasing relative to that of Ontario, and that Quebec remained "the most under-populated country in the world" (Morin 1984:165–68).

Numerous participants spoke of the new pride that Québécois had discovered in their language: "The francophone Québécois of today has a great advantage over his counterpart of 1970; from now on he is in a position of confidence and security, knowing that he pos-sesses real rights with respect to his language and identity" (Plourde 1984:57). But others pointed out that a disturbing number of Quebec's francophone youth were powerfully drawn to the English-language culture of the United States, and that a significant minority did not consider their language to be a valued cultural possession (Georgeault 1984:398–402); that in the battle for the preservation of French new "fronts" had been opened in the domains of electronic media and computers, domains in which throughout the world French was being outclassed by English (Rocher 1984:25–26); and that in Quebec, as in the rest of the post-industrial world, there is evidence that human languages are becoming devalued and impoverished, "en perte de souplesse et de nuances [losing flexibility and nuances]" (Maranda 1984:35).

One can discover dozens of similar contrasts in the hundreds of pages that make up the proceedings of the conference. I have described such linked contrasts as the intertwining of a positive and negative vision in nationalist ideology, the simultaneous assertion of national being and nonbeing, life and death. "Nous sommes un peu-ple different"—"We are a different people," announce the headlines of *Le Devoir* for May 18, 1985, reporting the latest constitutional proposals of the Parti Québécois government to Ottawa, accom-panied by a photograph of René Lévesque in an argumentative pose. Five years after the referendum, and nearing the end of its second mandate (the Liberals would regain power seven months later), the Lévesque administration offered to negotiate ratification of the 1982 constitution (ratified by all other Canadian provinces) if Ottawa would recognize "the existence of the Québécois people" (Lesage 1985). Such a proclamation of national existence, presented as a constitutional bargaining chip, is at once positive and negative, since it seeks recognition by others of what it claims to be unassailable fact. Or consider the many "to be or not to be" statements of the 1982 *Congrès*, the "endless questioning about identity or cultural specificity," as one participant put it (Charles 1984:30), the desire to say "who we are" (Maranda 1984:38), the need to reflect upon "ce que nous sommes" (Belleau 1984:23).

This is the nationalist dilemma, the nationalist lament. It is a self-conscious lament. For decades, if not generations, nationalists have written of Quebec's schizophrenia (to use a term for the situation that came into play during the Quiet Revolution), of the agony of a people who refuse to live but refuse to die, of the mingled pessimism and optimism that must be the fate of a tiny collectivity lost in a continent of alien culture.

But there is dissent as well as lament—or, more particularly, dissent from the lament. Consider the sparring that occurred in the pages of *Le Devoir* between editor Lise Bissonnette and Fernand Dumont, a leading Quebec sociologist who was one of the principal authors of the 1978 white paper on cultural development. On September 3, 1982, *Le Devoir* published extracts from a speech that Dumont had given to an organization of French-language educators a month earlier. The extracts were entitled "Parlons américain . . . si nous le sommes devenus! [Speak American . . . if that is what we have become!]" According to Dumont, both Quebec and Canada were becoming "little satellites in an immense empire," the emerging "cultural empire" of the United States. In such a situation, he argued, the "specificity" and "originality" of Quebec had to go beyond the mere fact of speaking French, for "if that were our only difference, we would be doing nothing but translating into an odd idiom something that has nothing to do with our true being [notre être véritable]." Thus, he continued, "Let's speak American if that is what we have become; let us at least put ourselves in tune with ourselves; the French language is for us an alibi, a mask, . . . a last resort" (Dumont 1982a).

Dumont did not, however, end on this negative note, for five days later the conclusion to his speech appeared among the *Lettres au Devoir*. There he argued that "a culture is fertile only when it invents institutions," and asked whether Quebec was still capable of creating original institutions as it had in the past. (He gave Quebec's system of credit unions [caisses populaires] and Hydro-Québec as examples).[1] With respect to education, he argued, it was urgent that Quebec

1. Dumont's argument should be compared to that of Coleman discussed above, since the former is able to find at least one "original" institution (Hydro-Québec) created after 1960, whereas the latter took the lack of such institutions to indicate the death of Québécois cultural specificity. From my perspective, originality and specificity are in the eye of the beholder.

produce its own science textbooks as a step towards participation in the "international scientific community." More generally, he urged that partisan quarrels and federal-provincial haggling be put aside while a national convention ["des Etats généraux du Canada français"] met to generate "creative ideas for living in French on this continent." And he concluded with a reference to Lionel Groulx, placing Quebec among the threatened peoples who, like Poland and Ireland, "defy . . . the uniformity of empires" by "affirming . . . their difference" (Dumont 1982b).

To this argument Bissonnette responded by placing Dumont in a long tradition of nationalist thought obsessed with "the eternal existential question" about "our 'true being.'" She argued that credit unions, Hydro-Québec, and French-language textbooks had nothing to do with "an imagined ontological difference" but with Quebec's participation, via the French language, in modernity, in "an Americanness [américanité] that we share, without doing any worse than anyone else, with a large part of the planet." And she asked for a list of those cultural values that differentiated Quebec from other nations, arguing that "the discourse about values turns in circles, the crazy, missionary hope of intellectuals who watch their inevitable homogenization throughout the world and grasp at various 'others' in order to refuse to see. Ireland, Poland, Quebec . . . " (Bissonnette 1982a).

In a second editorial, defending herself from what she called the "scandalized letters" of readers who questioned her loyalty to Quebec, Bissonnette ridiculed the account of specificity given in the 1978 white paper. If Quebec's difference amounted to nothing more than a special "mentality," as the white paper put it, then, according to Bissonnette, Quebec's specificity "wasn't very specific." And she warned against politically motivated definitions of national being, describing the cultural policies of the Parti Québécois as "subventioned navel-gazing" that had stifled rather than encouraged cultural creativity (Bissonnette 1982b). Or, as she put it in the first editorial, "the suave imperialism coming from Quebec City scares me a lot more than the multinationals of culture coming out of New York" (1982a).

The fear mentioned by Bissonnette was expressed occasionally by other people I encountered, some of whom pointed out that a "narrow nationalism" can degenerate into chauvinism, racism, and authoritarianism. One woman I met in 1983 had contributed to a newly published collection of essays intended to bring philosophical perspectives to bear on a variety of contemporary topics. She had been asked to write an essay demystifying nationalism. (To maintain the informant's anonymity, I will not cite her published work.) In her essay, and in her conversation with me, she criticized the nationalists of the Parti Québécois for what she saw as their attempt to specify national "essence" in rigid and exclusive terms. What right had they, she asked, to tell us average citizens who we "truly" are, and to denounce ordinary people because they read American magazines? Like Bissonnette, she thought that the endless attempts to define national specificity revealed only that the notion of specificity was chimerical. And she found the Lévesque government's unveiling of a statue of Maurice Duplessis to be nothing less than a salute to the closest thing to fascism in Quebec's past. When I asked this woman, who was teaching in Quebec City's public schools and had completed a master's degree in political science, about the development of her outlook, she told me that in the early 1970s she had been nationalistic, but that a university course on ideologies had made her realize the narrowness of nationalist discourse. She described her disenchantment as a "normal" process of thinking things through for herself and growing up, though, I should add, she was one of the few people I interviewed who described that particular course of personal development.

Though most citizens do not articulate philosophical critiques of nationalist ideology, they manage to reject it in the practice of their daily lives—largely because they ignore its strictures. In other words, many people do not experience the mass media as cultural pollution, or the heteroglossia of their speech as evidence of mental imprecision. They can, of course, be made sensitive to such issues, particularly since all must submit to an education that equates personal success with the possession of "proper" speech habits and high-cultural "good taste." Indeed, during my first visit to Quebec, almost the first thing that was said to me by a working-class French Canadian was "On parle mal, hein?"—"We speak badly, don't we?"[2] But though sensitive, and at times responsive, to nationalistic concerns for the health of their culture, most people do not make of those concerns the guiding principles of daily conduct.

In the absence of popular commitment to their vision of a properly national way of life, nationalist ideologues have made a virtue of the people's waywardness. The notion that "ordinary people," the mass of the population, will not allow themselves to be

2. Several linguists at the *Congrès langue et société au Québec* pointed out that the ability to utilize multiple registers or dialects was more "normal" than the government's pursuit of linguistic normalization based on an international standard emanating from France. Kemp outlined what he considered to be the high social costs of the official attitude: despite rather insignificant departures from "standard" French, working class dialects are devalued, leading to "linguistic insecurity" which in turn works against achievement and success in educational institutions, themselves inflexibly committed to the standard. Kemp advocated "bidialectism" rather than "eradicationism"—a standard though rejuvenated French for written communication (a "français correct d'ici"), and a recognition of the "fundamental linguistic competencies" of working-class speakers (1984:59, 57).

defined by an elite has found its way into nationalist ideology. I often heard it said that the people showed a kind of peasant wisdom in electing both René Lévesque and Pierre Trudeau, the nationalist and the federalist. The people knew that authorities were never to be trusted totally, and that it was better to use the two levels of government, provincial and federal, as counterweights to each other than to depend solely on either one. By supporting both Lévesque and Trudeau, I was told, the people assured themselves strong leaders at both levels of government, each of whom would prevent abuses of power by the other. A more extreme version of this argument has it that the people are ungovernable anarchists, and that since the days of the fur traders they have defied their religious, political, and social elites, seeking adventure on a continental scale rather than staying submissively at home (cf. Morissonneau 1979).

After the referendum, some nationalists turned to such arguments to explain the defeat of the *indépendantiste* option. Not only did they admit to having been out of touch with popular sentiment: they decided that the Parti Québécois vision of independence depended too heavily on a monolithic state, an authoritarian institution that the people, in its wisdom, was unwilling to trust. In an essay entitled "Post-Referendum Quebec: A Geographer's Reflections," Eric Waddell, who described himself as "an ardent nationalist," suggested that by the time of the referendum the Parti Québécois government had succeeded in "reinforc[ing] the boundary around Quebec, rendering the ethnic and collective space much more secure" (1981:139, 141). The people had supported this project, he continued, but were wary of further advances by a centralizing government:

> The "modernization" of Quebec has involved the creation of a multitude of enormous, highly bureaucratized, institutions and attendant legislation that have served to radically increase the presence of the State in most domains of endeavor, and to increasingly concentrate power in the metropolitan areas, notably Quebec and Montreal. In this mutation local bureaucracies, authorities, planners and the like have become . . . simple relays in the transmission of a highly centralized and inflexible authority. Thus, for the individual in Alma, Gaspé, Richmond, Lachute or Baie-St-Paul "Quebec" has rapidly emerged as being as frustrating and elusive as "Ottawa." (143)

Waddell went on to claim that "the creative forces in Quebec society are now shifting to the regional level to reflect identities that have been . . . obscured by a generation of strident nationalism" (144). He suggested that the Parti Québécois had attempted to take account of

Quebec's "strong regional identities" but that too often its attempts at "decentralization" had led to a geographic dispersion of government offices rather than a genuine sharing of power (cf. Latouche 1979:195–214).

Thus the notion of "the region" as a privileged unit constituting the nation has come increasingly to the fore in recent nationalist discourse. For example, during a 1983 visit to Montreal I interviewed a journalist who has written extensively on *le patrimoine*. Like Waddell, he spoke of the misleading decentralization of the Parti Québécois government which had, he claimed, dispersed the State's power but not surrendered it to local communities. Quebec's true "regional identities," he explained, must not be confused with regionalized government offices. The real regions can be determined by asking people about their subjective identity. "Sorel is included in the Montreal administrative region [of the provincial government], but a Sorelian is not the same type as a Montrealer." According to my informant, the regions of Quebec have a coherence anchored in "a tradition of many generations. Quebec is such a large country that we have to use these local forces, for only locally based forces can make national policies work."

These populist critiques of the mirage of bureaucratic decentralization are well founded, but I would point out that they, like the bureaucratic ideology they attack, represent a *never-ending quest to locate authenticity in individuated units at some other level.* I am being specifically vague about what "the units at some other level" might be. Indeed, they can be many things, as long as it is possible, within the discourse of modern science and modern common sense, to envision them as naturally occurring entities. In the nationalist ideology that I have examined throughout this book, the most salient of these entities are the nation (imagined simply as the people, or as the people in conjunction with the state), the national culture, the ethnic subculture, the minority group, the region, and the person. Obviously this list must remain incomplete, for, as Hannah Arendt pointed out, such "romanticized objects . . . could be changed at a moment's notice into . . . anything else" (1958:168).

Romanticized objects—the phrase returns us to those presuppositions of possessive individualism that I have used to interpret nationalist ideology. In *The Origins of Totalitarianism* Arendt discussed "personality" (that quintessential romanticized object), anti-Semitism, and imperialism as crucial elements of a modern culture in which what she called totalitarianism became possible. Arendt's account corresponds in some measure to my understanding of possessive individualism. Her interpretation of personality suggests the modern fascination with what I have described as irreducible individualized units, bounded, homogeneous, and continuous. Arendt spoke of "the fundamental belief in personality as an ultimate aim in

189

itself," an attitude that she attributed to the German romantics—but one that remains, I would argue, central to modern culture, whatever the origins of the belief may be. Moreover, Arendt pointed out that the concept of personality was easily "naturalized," in the first instance by impoverished intellectuals seeking entrance to aristocratic society:

> Like the title of the heir of an old family, the "innate personality" was given by birth and not acquired by merit. Just as the lack of common history for the formation of the nation had been artificially overcome by the naturalistic concept of organic development, so, in the social sphere, nature itself was supposed to supply a title when political reality had refused it. (169)[3]

Arendt argued that this newfound notion of natural personality contributed to the racism and anti-Semitism of the twentieth century. In her example, as Jews were assimilated into modern culture, Jewish religion and culture disappeared and their place was taken by Jewishness—which, like personality, was taken to be innate, an inner quality characteristic of both Jewish individuals and the Jewish people. But if Judaism was a crime in the medieval world, Jewishness became a vice: "Jews had been able to escape from Judaism into conversion; from Jewishness there was no escape. A crime, moreover, is met with punishment; a vice can only be exterminated" (87). Thus, in Arendt's interpretation, inner essences, or qualities defined as natural, are taken to be non-negotiable. And once negotiation, social and political dialogue, becomes impossible, tragedy takes over.

But what is the relationship of imperialism to anti-Semitism and personality? By explicating the ideology of imperialism, Arendt focused on the possessive component of modern individualism. For her, Cecil Rhodes' assertion, "I would annex the planets if I could" epitomized the "perpetual motion" demanded by modern conceptions of property. She argued that a belief in "limitless" and "neverending" capital accumulation made necessary the unlimited, or totalitarian, accumulation of power (143–45). Unlimited power was first

3. Arendt's book has irritated positivists for whom "origins" suggests a linear narrative; hers is a work of comparative cultural analysis that sifts through three centuries of European history in order to explicate the cultural logic of ideologies that we too easily dismiss as merely irrational (cf. Crick 1979). On the other hand, anthropologists of most theoretical orientations will be justifiably offended by the ethnocentrism of *The Origins of Totalitarianism*. Just as the quoted passage presumes that one can distinguish authentic from artificial national histories, so Arendt speaks of totalitarianism as a descent to the level of savage tribes who have neither history nor civilization: "Lazy and unproductive, they [the Boers] agreed to vegetate on essentially the same level as the black tribes had vegetated for thousands of years" (1958:194).

pursued by European nations in their overseas colonies, but later turned upon the people of Europe itself. In other words, for Arendt nineteenth-century imperialism was not a direct "cause" of twentieth-century totalitarianism, but it exemplified, in a related historical context, a cultural logic that she wanted to understand. Fortunately, with respect to Quebec and Canada there is no history of violence that we can properly call totalitarian. But the nationalisms of French and English Canada generate their own perpetual motions, whether the constant doubts about national existence, the ongoing search for authentic culture, or the endless fragmentation of bureaucracies created to administer national existence and culture.

The cultural logic that brings together personality, anti-Semitism, and imperialism is the cultural logic of possessive individualism. I have argued that the nation is imagined as an individual, that is, as a bounded, homogeneous, and continuous entity. In modern culture the individual is an irreducible unit, the locus of ultimate reality. Here is a crucial point of contrast between modern and medieval culture, one succinctly elaborated by Ernst Cassirer (1932:37–41). In his account, the medieval world was understood as a cosmic order ordained and encompassed by God. It was a hierarchical whole in which humans and all other elements of the natural world were ranked, subordinate parts whose position in the system had been assigned them by God—the locus of ultimate reality. By contrast, individualism allows people to locate ultimate reality in the smallest independent units, whether the single personality or the sub-atomic particle. Hence the modern ontology of "nature," as Cassirer understands it:

> Nature . . . implies the individuality, the independence and particularity of objects. And from this characteristic force, which radiates from every object as a special center of activity, is derived also the inalienable worth which belongs to it in the totality of being. All this is now summed up in the word 'nature,' which signifies the integration of all parts into one all-inclusive whole of activity and life which, nevertheless, no longer means mere subordination. For the part not only exists within the whole but asserts itself against it, constituting a specific element of individuality and necessity. (41)

This passage does very well as a description of the nationalist vision of the world community. From that perspective, each member of the community of nations is a naturally occurring "element of individuality and necessity." Each is "specific" and each is possessed of "inalienable worth." Moreover, each nation is a "special center of activity"; that is, in my terms, each is distinguished by the content of its existence, by its culture. As we have seen, the collective individual of nationalist ideology is defined by its possessions, or, phrased somewhat differently, its existence is taken to be demonstrated by the existence of cultural property. The ability to create original or authentic cultural products testifies to the health of the nation, and national health is equated with freedom. Finally, freedom, or independence, entails the power to choose, a power which, when judiciously exercised, leads to the creation of authentic culture, of irreducible difference.

When these presuppositions of possessive individualism come alive, as it were, in social action and in history, they give rise to an unresolvable tension: that between totality and appropriation. Simply put, the individual is completed, or made whole, by property, but in modern culture the accumulation of property is never completed. The result is that modern individuals, whether persons or the collectivities envisioned in ideology, are perpetually insecure. The dilemma has been well formulated in the work of T. J. Jackson Lears on early twentieth-century American culture (1981, 1983). Lears argues that the secularization of Protestantism has created the specifically modern personality, one unceasingly seeking signs of secular salvation, defined either as a secure identity, "self-realization," or possession of what Tom Wolfe (1979) termed "the right stuff." However, the death of God has meant that the unending quest for self-realization is no longer made meaningful by a transcendental goal. The result, according to Lears, is that Americans today are driven by a work ethic exactly as their Puritan ancestors were. But lacking the Puritans' faith, our compulsive quest for "self-realization" leads only to frustration, or worse, to "neurasthenic" breakdowns (to use the turn-of-the-century term), "depression," and nihilism (cf. Handler 1986).

No one has analyzed the modern dilemma better than Alexis de Tocqueville in his *Democracy in America.* Tocqueville's great work is a relentless comparison between what he calls aristocratic and democratic societies, or, in Louis Dumont's terms, holism and individualism.[4] At the heart of the new, democratic society that fascinated him, Tocqueville found two conflicting tendencies. In a

4. *Democracy in America* is a model of cross-cultural comparison understood as an interpretive rather than scientistic exercise. The work is doubly comparative: the overall comparison between aristocratic and democratic societies is at times worked out in terms of a less general, three-way comparison between the United States, England, and France. In dozens of small chapters, Tocqueville develops his explication of particular ethnographic points—family relations, warfare, poetry, religiosity, and so on—by showing how the aristocratic and democratic versions of phenomena contrast precisely as the fundamental cultural postulates of aristocracy and democracy, individualism and holism, contrast.

democracy every human being becomes an individual, that is, equal to all others and, consequently, independent of subjection to the wisdom or authority of anyone else. However, precisely because each individual is like all others—that is, a member of a mass society no longer structured, as aristocratic society was, by hierarchical distinctions—all feel themselves to be isolated and powerless:

> When the inhabitant of a democratic country compares himself individually with all those about him, he feels with pride that he is the equal of any one of them; but when he comes to survey the totality of his fellows and to place himself in contrast with so huge a body, he is instantly overwhelmed by the sense of his own insignificance and weakness. (1835:vol. 2, p. 11)

In a brilliantly sustained analysis, Tocqueville found endless political, social, and cultural manifestations of this dilemma. Egalitarianism meant that no citizen was confined to a fixed social status. However, the theoretically unlimited social mobility that their liberation made possible condemned all to perpetual insecurity. No longer confined and defined according to their place in a hierarchical social order, all could climb the ladder of success—but none could attain a fixed and secure position where they would be content to stop. Moreover, the citizens of democratic societies became absorbed by the pursuit of "physical gratifications," since possession of private property was a privileged expression of social status:

> When . . . the distinctions of ranks are obliterated and privileges are destroyed . . . the desire of acquiring the comforts of the world haunts the imagination of the poor, and the dread of losing them that of the rich. Many scanty fortunes spring up; those who possess them have a sufficient share of physical gratifications to conceive a taste for these pleasures, not enough to satisfy it. They never procure them without exertion, and they never indulge in them without apprehension. They are therefore always straining to pursue or to retain gratifications so delightful, so imperfect, so fugitive. (137)

Tocqueville thought that this inordinate attention to trivial pleasures, combined with the isolation and weakness of individual citizens, posed a grave threat to democratic societies: the concentration of political power in the hands of a highly centralized government. The citizens of democracies, preoccupied by their pursuit of a happiness that ceaselessly escaped them, would have little time for political participation. But egalitarian ideology would not suffer hierarchical mediations; that is, the chain of "secondary powers placed between the sovereign and his subjects [that] occurred naturally to the imagination of aristocratic nations." Rather, the citizens of democracy "conceive, as it were without thinking about the subject, the notion of a single and central power which governs the whole community by its direct influence" (306). Tocqueville thought that the most potent consequence of such centralization would be "uniformity of legislation" (306). He foresaw that in egalitarian societies, politics—that is, dialogue and debate among a self-governing citizenry—would lose ground to "the science of administration" (326). Indeed, routinized administrative procedures would appeal both to citizens and to governments—to egalitarian citizens, because they "cannot understand why a rule that is applicable to one man should not be equally applicable to all others" (306), and to their government, because "uniformity relieves it from inquiry into an infinity of details, which must be attended to if rules have to be adapted to different men" (312–13). We can add that administrative uniformity contributes in its turn to the fragmentation of mass society, where everyone is a number, as a common complaint has it, but where people cannot envision themselves as part of a larger whole. And, in the administration of culture, uniformity leads away from the cultural totality that is so ardently sought, as the cultural domain (however defined) is parceled into manageable subfields, each to be developed, displayed, and sold.

In speaking of an unresolvable tension between totality and appropriation, I mean to suggest that nationalistic insecurity—the negative vision that will not go away—is incurable, a function of the logic of possessive individualism rather than the contingencies of national history. Nationalists are haunted by a vision of totality. Their modern sense of totality must not be confused with the holism of a hierarchical society. The totality nationalists seek is that of an irreducible, homogeneous unit, securely in control of its borders, self-contained, autonomous, and complete, asserting itself against a world of similar entities. The national totality will know its own essence, will control the definition of its own being. It will acknowledge the existence of other national entities, it will even be "open to the world," as a commonplace of nationalist rhetoric has it. But its identity will not depend on interrelationships and exchanges. "Our true being" can only be an inner quality, a natural essence.

To achieve the totality of a complete and self-contained existence, appropriation is necessary. The collective individual can realize itself only through constant production, through a continual objectification of what is imagined to be its authentic culture. *But objectification inevitably unbounds the bounded entity,* deconstructs the desired totality. This is because the processes of cultural objectification are as much a part of national culture as the cultural "stuff" that is objectified. At the staged performance of folk dancing, the stacks of loudspeakers and paying spectators are as much a part of the culture of the situation as the dances themselves. The museum as an institution is as authentic a piece of culture as the pieces in its collections. But if the processes of displaying, framing, interpreting culture are themselves part of culture, they cannot be bounded and controlled during the same moment in which they bound and control whatever it is that they constitute as a cultural object. We can imagine a museum of museums (such as exist already in the form of books), but its existence would then make possible a museum of museums of museums. . . .

Moreover, the "culture" of cultural objectification is shared throughout the modern world of nation-states and ethnic groups. Indeed, one might almost believe nations and ethnic groups to be the naturally bounded units they claim to be—if only one were permitted to define them as that species of social system whose function is to produce and market their own specificities. Like a row of ethnic restaurants in any North American city—all making use of a set of presuppositions that they share with their customers about what constitutes ethnic food, how, where, and when to eat it, how to pay for it, and what its value as nutrition and authentic experience is—like a row of ethnic restaurants, nations and ethnic groups participate in a common market to produce differences that make them all the same. As one critic of Canadian multiculturalism put it, "if this is 'culture,' then multi-culturalism turns out to be a choice of pizzas, wonton soup, and kosher 'style' pastrami sandwiches to which one can add ethnic radio programs" (Brotz 1980:44). Here, then, is a second sense in which the appropriation of culture deconstructs the cultural totality sought: the desire to appropriate one's own culture, to secure a unique identity, places one in the mainstream of a modern, individualistic culture to which national boundaries are irrelevant.

Tocqueville believed that the liberating effects of egalitarianism, which allowed all people to strive for their individual happinesses, reduced all individuals to sameness. He found American society to be "animated" because in the mad scramble for wealth and success, "men and things are always changing." But he went on to point out that it was also "monotonous because all these changes are alike" (239). Similarly, the appropriation of culture through administrative routines leads to standardized fragments, not totality. Quebec's Department of Cultural Affairs, with its apparently perpetual reorganizations, is indeed animated. But its activities may well lead, not to cultural diversity, but to an atomised uniformity where the state invests in pieces of a stereotypical culture that can be marketed as "products of Quebec."

As Michel de Certeau has pointed out in the passage that serves as an epigraph to this chapter, "culture" has become an ambiguous residual category. It is residual in the sense that we consider it to be a secondary phenomenon, less important than the "hard" realities of economics and politics (hence the marginality of the Department of Cultural Affairs within the Quebec government). It is ambiguous because, though a residual category, it still suggests totality. In Quebec the advocates of a strong governmental presence in cultural affairs dream of policies that would treat culture as an encompassing rather than residual category. But I suspect that the appropriation of culture by means of scientific and bureaucratic routines will never succeed in preserving or creating the natural cultural totality that symbolizes and proves national existence. Rather, those objectifying routines will become increasingly central to the life of culture in Quebec, and Quebec, like Canada, like the United States, will remain another modern place, haunted by the negative vision, the perpetual insecurity that will not go away.

REFERENCES

INDEX

REFERENCES

Aléong, Stanley
1981   Discours nationalistes et purisme linguistique au Québec. *Culture* 1 (2):31–41.

Amyot, Michel, ed.
1984   *Les Activités socio-économiques et le française au Québec.* Quebec City: Conseil de la langue française.

Amyot, Michel, and Gilles Bibeau, eds.
1984   *Le Statut culturel du français au Québec.* Quebec City: Conseil de la langue française.

Anderson, Jay
1984   *Time Machines: The World of Living History.* Nashville, Tenn.: American Association for State and Local History.

ANQ (Assemblée nationale du Québec)
1972   *Journal des débats.* vol. 12. Quebec City.

Arcand, Bernard
1984   Comment on Handler 1984. *Current Anthropology* 25:64.

Arendt, Hannah
1958   *The Origins of Totalitarianism.* 2d ed. New York: Meridian.

Athot, Gilbert
1976   René Lévesque rèpéte de façon solennelle tous ses engagements. *Le Soleil,* 16 November: A9.

Barbeau, C. Marius
1920   *Veillées du bon vieux temps.* Montreal: G. Ducharme.

1936   *Quebec, Where Ancient France Lingers.* Toronto: Macmillan.

1943   The Folklore Movement in Canada. *Journal of American Folklore* 56:166–68.

1949   La Survivance française en Amérique. *Les Archives de Folklore* 4:67–75.

Barbeau, François
1976   "Je n'ai jamais été aussi fier d'être Québécois," clame Lévesque. *Le Devoir,* 16 November: 1, 6.

Basham, Richard
1978   *Crisis in Blanc and White.* Cambridge, Mass.: Schenkman.

Beauchemin, Norman
1976   Joual et français au Québec. In *Identité culturelle et francophonie dans les Amériques,* ed. Emile Snyder and Albert Valdman, 6–15. Quebec City: Presses de l'université Laval.

Beguin, Louis-Paul
1978   La situation du français (4). *Le Devoir,* 9 May: 6.

Belanger, André-J.
1974   *L'Apolitisme des idéologies québécoises, 1934–1936.* Quebec City: Presses de l'université Laval.

References

Bellah, Robert
1983   The Ethical Aims of Social Inquiry. In Haan 1983:360–81.

Belleau, Irène
1984   Presentation de Pierre Maranda. In Amyot 1984:23.

Bissonnette, Lise
1982a   De notre agonie. *Le Devoir,* 11 September: 14.

1982b   De notre agonie—2. *Le Devoir, 18 September: 14.*

Boas, Franz
1887   The Study of Geography. In *Race, Language, and Culture,* 639–47. New York: Free Press, 1940.

Bonin, Bernard
1984   Commentaire. In Amyot 1984:77–78.

Boon, James
1982   *Other Tribes, Other Scribes.* New York: Cambridge University Press.

Boorstin, Daniel
1961   *The Image.* New York: Atheneum.

Bourassa, Henri
1919   *La Langue, gardienne de la foi.* Montreal: Action française.

Bouthillier, Guy, and Jean Meynaud, eds.
1972   *Le Choc des langues au Québec, 1760–1970.* Montreal: Presses de l'université du Québec.

Brotz, Howard
1980   Multiculturalism in Canada: A Muddle. *Canadian Public Policy* 6:41–46.

Bruchési, Jean
1974   *Souvenirs à vaincre.* vol. 1. Montreal: Hurtubise HMH.

Brunet, Michel
1957   Trois dominantes de la pensée canadienne: L'Agriculturisme, l'anti-étatisme et le messianisme. *Écrits du Canada Français* 3:31–117.

Caldwell, Gary
1976   La Baisse de la fecondité au Québec à la lumière de la sociologie québécois. *Recherches sociographiques* 17:7–22.

Cameron, Guy
1978   Un heritage précieux: La langue française. *Ma caisse populaire* 15 (4):16–17.

Canada, Government of
1951   *Report of the Royal Commission on National Development in the Arts, Letters and Sciences* (Massey Commission). Ottawa: King's Printer.

1971   *Debates. House of Commons.* 3d Session, 28th Parliament. vol. 8.

1982   *Report of the Federal Cultural Policy Review Committee.* Ottawa: Department of Communications.

References

Carpenter, Carole H.
1979   *Many Voices: A Study of Folklore Activities in Canada and Their Role in Canadian Culture.* Ottawa: Canadian Centre for Folk Culture Studies, Paper no. 26.

Cassirer, Ernst
1932   *The Philosophy of the Enlightenment.* Trans. F. C. Koelln and J. P. Pettegrove. Rpt. Boston: Beacon Press, 1950

Castonguay, Charles
1984   L'Évolution récente de la situation démolinguistique au Québec et dans l'Outaouais. In Amyot and Bibeau 1984:155–58.

Certeau, Michel de
1983   History: Ethics, Science, and Fiction. In Haan 1983:125–52.

1984   *The Practice of Everyday Life.* Trans. S. F. Rendall. Berkeley: University of California Press.

Charles, Bernard
1984   Commentaire. In Amyot and Bibeau 1984:29–31.

Clifford, James
1983   On Ethnographic Authority. *Representations* 1:118–46.

Clift, Dominique
1982   *Quebec Nationalism in Crisis.* Montreal: McGill–Queens University Press.

Cohen, Ronald
1978   Ethnicity: Problem and Focus in Anthropology. *Annual Review of Anthropology.* 7:379–403.

Cohn, Bernard S.
n.d.   The Census, Social Structure and Objectification in South Asia. Typescript, University of Chicago, Department of Anthropology.

Coleman, William D.
1981   From Bill 22 to Bill 101: The Politics of Language under the Parti Québécois. *Canadian Journal of Political Science* 14:459–85.

1984   *The Independence Movement in Quebec, 1945–1980.* Toronto: University of Toronto Press.

Connor, Walker
1973   The Politics of Ethnonationalism. *Journal of International Affairs* 27:1–21.

Cook, Ramsey
1971   *The Maple Leaf Forever.* Toronto: Macmillan.

CPC (Cultural Properties Commission of Quebec)
1973   *Rapport annuel.* Quebec City: Éditeur officiel du Québec.

1975   *Rapport annuel.* Quebec City: Éditeur officiel du Québec.

1976   *Rapport annuel.* Quebec City: Éditeur officiel du Québec.

Crick, Bernard
1979   On Rereading *The Origins of Totalitarianism.* In *Hannah Arendt: The Recovery of the Public World,* ed. M. A. Hill, pp. 27–47. New York: Saint Martin's.

References

Daoust-Blais, Denise, and André Martin
  1981   La Planification linguistique au Québec: aménagement du corpus linguistique et promotion du statut de français. In *L'État et la planification linguistique,* ed. André Martin, vol. 2, pp. 43–69. Quebec City: Office de la langue française.
Desbiens, Jean-P.
  1960   *Les insolences du Frère Untel.* Montreal: Éditions de l'homme.
Descoteaux, Bernard
  1978   Les Francophones d'Amérique fêtent le "retour aux sources." *Le Devoir,* 4 July: 1, 6.
Le Devoir
(Montreal)
  1959   Un conseil provincial des arts? 16 December: 7.
  1960a   M. Lapalme suggère un nouveau nom: M. Yves Prévost, "ministre des affaires culturelles"? 1 March: 1.
  1960b   Québec et les arts. 17 March: 4.
  1960c   Notre fête nationale: Le Défilé du 24 juin exaltera la "présence canadienne-française." 26 March: 3.
  1960d   Le Parti libéral: Programme neuf et dynamique. 7 May: 1–2.
  1961a   Talbot: L"UN appuie le principe mais présentera des amendements. 3 March: 1–2.
  1961b   M. Jean Lesage à l'hotel de ville de Paris: Nous ne voulons pas être le satellite culturel des É-U. 7 October: 1.
  1962   Le Conseil provincial des Arts a commencé ses travaux. 30 January: 6.
  1963a   La France vous tend la main en face de l'avenir. 15 October: 4.
  1963b   Cette France qui vous parle aujourd'hui. 18 October: 4.
  1963c   Unsigned articles on André Malraux's visit to Quebec. 12 October: 1, 10.
  1963d   Frégault: "La culture n'est pas un simple objet de luxe." 7 November: 9.
  1977   Du duplessisme, il faut séparer l'ivraie du bon grain (Lévesque). 10 September: 1, 6.
Dion, Leon
  1961   Varieties of Nationalism: Trends in Quebec. In McRae 1961:89–99.
Dorris, Michael
  1981   The Grass Still Grows, the Rivers Still Flow: Contemporary Native Americans. *Daedalus* 110 (2):43–69.
Douglas, Mary
  1966   *Purity and Danger.* London: Routledge and K. Paul.
Doyon, Madeleine
  1950   Folk Dances in Beauce County. *Journal of American Folklore* 63:171–74.
Duhamel, Alain
  1978a   Le Cheval canadien. *Le Devoir,* 2 October: 9.
  1978b   La "Protection préventive" du patrimoine. *Le Devoir,* 20 November: 9.

Dumont, Fernand
- 1974   *The Vigil of Quebec.* Trans. S. Fischman and R. Howard. Toronto: University of Toronto Press.
- 1982a   Parlons américain . . . si nous le sommes devenus! *Le Devoir* 3 September: 17.
- 1982b   Vivre en français: Une mise au point. *Le Devoir,* 7 September: 6.

Dumont, Fernand, Jean Hamelin, and Jean-Paul Montminy, eds.
- 1981   *Idéologies au Canada français 1940–1976. Vol. 1. La Presse, La Littérature.* Quebec City: Presses de l'université Laval.

Dumont, Louis
- 1970   Religion, Politics, and Society in the Individualistic Universe. In *Proceedings* of the Royal Anthropological Institute of Great Britain and Ireland, 31–45.
- 1977   *From Mandeville to Marx: The Genesis and Triumph of Economic Ideology.* Chicago: University of Chicago Press.

Durkheim, Emile
- 1912   *The Elementary Forms of the Religious Life.* Trans. J. W. Swain. Rpt. New York: Free Press, 1965.

Durocher, René, and Michele Jean
- 1971   Duplessis et la Commission Royale d'enquête sur les problèmes constitutionnels, 1953–1956. *Revue d'histoire de l'Amérique française* 25:337–64.

Ellis, John M.
- 1983   *One Fairy Story Too Many: The Brothers Grimm and Their Tales.* Chicago: University of Chicago Press.

Ethier-Blais, Jean
- 1963   Vers l'homme universel. *Le Devoir,* 12 October: 11.

Falardeau, Jean-Charles
- 1960   Notre culture: Un phare ou une lampe de sanctuaire. *Le Devoir,* 29 January: 16, 20, 24.
- 1965   Le Sens de l'oeuvre sociologique de Léon Gérin. *Recherches sociographiques* 6:265–89.

Feldman, Elliot J., ed.
- 1980   *The Quebec Referendum: What Happened and What Next?* Cambridge: Center for International Affairs, Harvard University.

Fenwick, Rudy
- 1981   Social Change and Ethnic Nationalism: An Historical Analysis of the Separatist Movement in Quebec. *Comparative Studies in Society and History* 23:196–216.

Filion, Maurice
- 1984   Religion et langue. In Amyot and Bibeau 1984:107–12.

Finlay, Ian
- 1977   *Priceless Heritage: The Future of Museums.* London: Faber and Faber.

Fitch, James M.
- 1982   *Historic Preservation: Curatorial Management of the Built World.* New York: McGraw-Hill.

References

Fortes, Meyer
1969 *Kinship and the Social Order.* Chicago: Aldine.

Fraser, Blair
1967 *The Search for Identity: Canada, 1945–1967.* New York: Doubleday.

Freedman, Jim, ed.
1976 *The History of Canadian Anthropology. Proceedings* of the Canadian Ethnology Society, no. 3.

Frégault, Guy
1963 Le Ministère des Affaires culturelles et la tradition artistique du Canada français. *Le Devoir,* 20 August: 6.
1976 *Chronique des années perdues.* Ottawa: Leméac.

Gagnon, D.
1978 Terre-Québec. *Ma caisse populaire* 15 (4):18.

Galarneau, Claude
1970 *La France devant l'opinion canadienne, 1760–1815.* Quebec City: Presses de l'université Laval.

Garigue, Philippe
1958 *Études sur le Canada français.* Montreal: Faculté des sciences sociales, économiques et politiques, Université de Montréal.
1964 French Canada: A Case Study in Sociological Analysis. *Canadian Review of Sociology and Anthropology* 1:186–92.

Geertz, Clifford
1964 Ideology as a Cultural System. In Geertz 1973a:193–233,
1973a *The Interpretation of Cultures.* New York: Basic Books.
1973b Thick Description: Toward an Interpretive Theory of Culture. In Geertz 1973a:3–30.

Gélinas, Michel
1980 *Livres blancs et verts du Gouvernement du Québec (1960–1979).* Montreal: École nationale d'administration publique.

Georgeault, Pierre
1984 La Conscience linguistique des jeunes: Mythe ou réalité. In Amyot 1984:397–404.

Gérin, Léon
1898 L'Habitant de Saint-Justin. *Proceedings and Transactions* of the Royal Society of Canada 4 (2d series):139–216.
1938 *Le Type économique et social des Canadiens.* Montreal: Éditions de l'A. C.-F.

Gill, Robert
1980 Quebec and the Politics of Language: Implications for Canadian Unity. In *Encounters with Canada,* ed. W. Reilly, 18–45. Durham, N.C.: Duke University Press.

Glazer, Nathan, and Daniel Patrick Moynihan, eds.
1975 *Ethnicity.* Cambridge: Harvard University Press.

Griffin, Anne
1984 *Quebec: The Challenge of Independence.* Rutherford, N.J.: Fairleigh Dickinson University Press.

References

Groulx, Lionel
1917   Une action intellectuelle. *L'Action française* 1:33–43.
1918   Notre histoire. *L'Action française* 2:338–56.
1919   *La Naissance d'une race.* Montreal: Bibliothèque de l'Action française.
1922   *L'Appel de la race.* Rpt. Montreal: Fides, 1956.
1924   *Notre maître, le passé* (première série). Montreal: Bibliothèque de l'Action française.
1935   *Orientations.* Montreal: Éditions du zodiaque.
1936   *Notre maître, le passé* (deuxième série). Montreal: Granger Frères.
1937   *Directives.* Montreal: Éditions du zodiaque.
1943   *Paroles à des étudiants.* Montreal: Éditions de l'Action nationale.
1952   *Histoire du Canada français depuis la découverte.* 4 vols. Montreal: l'Action nationale.

Guédon, Marie-Francoise
1983   A Case of Mistaken Identity. In *Consciousness and Inquiry: Ethnology and Canadian Realities,* ed. F. Manning, 253–61. Ottawa: Canadian Ethnology Service, Paper no. 89E.

Guindon, Hubert
1960   The Social Evolution of Quebec Reconsidered. *Canadian Journal of Economics and Political Science* 26:533–51.
1964   Social Unrest, Social Class, and Quebec's Bureaucratic Revolution. *Queen's Quarterly* 71–62.

Haan, Norma, et al., eds.
1983   *Social Science as Moral Inquiry.* New York: Columbia University Press.

Hamelin, Jean, and Jean-Paul Montminy
1981   La Mutation de la société québécoise, 1939–1976. Temps, ruptures, continuités. In Dumont et al. 1981:33–70.

Handler, Richard
1981   Review of *Le Musée du Québec en devenir. American Anthropologist* 83:748–49.
1983   The Dainty and the Hungry Man: Literature and Anthropology in the Work of Edward Sapir. In *Observers Observed: Essays on Ethnographic Fieldwork,* ed. G. W. Stocking. *History of Anthropology* 1:208–31.
1984   On Sociocultural Discontinuity: Nationalism and Cultural Objectification in Quebec. *Current Anthropology* 25:55–71.
1985   Review of Coleman 1984. *American Political Science Review* 79:552–53.
1986   Authenticity. *Anthropology Today* 2 (1):2–4.

Handler, Richard, and Jocelyn Linnekin
1984   Tradition, Genuine or Spurious. *Journal of American Folklore* 97:273–90.

Haugen, Einar
1973   The Curse of Babel. *Daedalus* 102 (3):47–57.

References

Heidegger, Martin
1967   *What Is a Thing?* Trans. W. B. Barton, Jr., and Vera Deutsch. Chicago: Henry Regnery.

Herzfeld, Michael
1982   *Ours Once More: Folklore, Ideology, and the Making of Modern Greece.* Austin: University of Texas Press.

HMC (Historic Monuments Commission of Quebec)
1923   *Premier rapport.* Quebec City.
1925   *Deuxième rapport.* Quebec City.
1926   *Troisième rapport.* Quebec City.

Hobsbawm, Eric
1983   Mass-Producing Traditions: Europe, 1870–1914. In Hobsbawm and Ranger 1983:263–307.

Hobsbawn, Eric, and Terence Ranger, eds.
1983   *The Invention of Tradition.* New York: Cambridge University Press.

Hogue-Lebeuf, Jacqueline
1978   Quand le joual galope dans les plates-bandes du Franco-québécois. *Le Devoir,* 17 June: 5.

Hughes, Everett C.
1943   *French Canada in Transition.* Rpt. Chicago: University of Chicago Press, 1963.

Jacknis, Ira
1985   Franz Boas and Exhibits. In *Objects and Others,* ed. G. W. Stocking. *History of Anthropology* 3:75–111.

Kemp, William
1984   Attitudes et politiques linguistiques: Les bénéfices sociaux d'une évaluation plus favorable du français québécois. In Amyot and Bibeau 1984:51–64.

Kloss, Heinz
1969   *Research Possibilities on Group Bilingualism: A Report.* Quebec City: Centre international de recherche sur le bilinguisme, Université Laval.

Köngäs-Maranda, Elli
1979   Ethnologie, folklore et l'indépendance des majorités minorisées. In *Emerging Ethnic Boundaries,* ed. D. Juteau, 185–95. Ottawa: University of Ottawa Press.

Lachance, Lise
1976   Un triomphe pour le nouveau premier ministre. *Le Soleil,* 16 November: A8.

Lacourcière, Luc
1961   The Present State of French-Canadian Folklore Studies. *Journal of American Folklore* 74:373–82.

Lapalme, Georges Emile
1970   *Le Vent de l'oubli. Mémoires,* vol. 2. Ottawa: Leméac.
1973   *Le Paradis du pouvoir. Mémoires,* vol. 3. Ottawa: Leméac.

References

Laporte, Pierre

1960 $340,000 pour les sociétés culturelles et artistiques. *Le Devoir*, 16 March: 1–2.

Latouche, Daniel

1979   *Une société de l'ambiguïté: Libération et recupération dans le Québec actuel.* Montreal: Boréal Express.

1983   Une histoire du Québec lucide et tout d'un bloc. *Le Devoir*, 2 April: 15, 25.

Laurendeau, André

1959a   Appartenir. *Le Devoir*, 5 December: 4.

1959b   Sur la crise du théâtre. *Le Devoir*, 15 December: 4.

1961   Gauchement. *Le Devoir*, 6 March: 4.

Laurin, Camille

1977   Notes pour le discours prononcé par Monsieur Camille Laurin, Ministre d'état au développement culturel, lors du colloque "Frontières ethniques en devenir." Typescript, Quebec City.

Lears, T. J. Jackson

1981   *No Place of Grace.* New York: Pantheon.

1983   From Salvation to Self-Realization. In *The Culture of Consumption*, ed. R. W. Fox and T. J. J. Lears, 1–38. New York: Pantheon.

Lebel, André

1978   L'Indépendance est le seul héritage que nous puissions laisser aux jeunes—Pierre Bourgault. *La Presse*, 9 May: A12.

Leclerc, Jean-Claude

1978   Trop c'est trop. *Le Devoir*, 29 September: 4.

Léger, Jean-Marc

1961   Le Ministère des affaires culturelles: Outil précieux. *Le Devoir*, 4 March: 4.

1965   L'Action culturelle doit être une des priorités. *Le Devoir*, 21 January: 4.

Lesage, Gilles

1985   "Nous sommes un peuple différent." *Le Devoir*, 18 May: 1, 12.

Lesage, Jean

1959   *Lesage s'engage: libéralisme québécois d'aujourd'hui.* Montreal: Éditions politiques du Québec.

1961a   L'Université, l'état, la culture. In Lesage 1961d: document L-61-2.

1961b   Speech at Mount Allison University, 17 August. In Lesage 1961d: document L-61-25.

1961c   Le Ministère des affaires culturelles. In Lesage 1961d: document L-61-6.

1961d   *Discours de Jean Lesage, vol. 1.* Mimeo, Bibliothèque Administrative, Ediface H, Government du Québec. Quebec City.

Levasseur, Roger

1982   *Loisir et culture au Québec.* Montreal: Boréal Express.

References

Lévesque, René
1968   *An Option for Quebec.* Toronto: McClelland and Stewart.
1977   Comment les "Canadiens" de l'Ancien régime et les Canadiens français de naguère sont devenus les Québécois d'aujourd'hui. *Le Devoir,* 3 November: 5.

Levine, Marc V.
1986   Language Policy, Education, and Cultural Survival: Bill 101 and the Transformation of Anglophone Montreal, 1977–1985. *Quebec Studies* 4:3–28.

Linnekin, Jocelyn S.
1983   Defining Tradition: Variations on the Hawaiian Identity. *American Ethnologist* 10:241–52.

Locke. John
1690   *Two Treatises of Government.* Rpt. Cambridge: Cambridge University Press, 1960

Lucas, C., ed.
1912   *Lord Durham's Report on the Affairs of British North America.* 3 vols. Rpt. New York: Augustus M. Kelley, 1970.

Lukacs, Georg
1922   Reification and the Consciousness of the Proletariat. In *History and Class Consciousness,* trans. Rodney Livingstone, pp. 83–222. Rpt. Cambridge: M.I.T. Press, 1971.

MAC (Ministry of Cultural Affairs of Quebec)
1965   *Livre blanc.* Quebec City: Éditeur officiel du Québec.
1976   *Pour l'évolution de la politique culturelle.* Quebec City: Éditeur officiel du Québec.
1979a   *Le Musée du Québec.* Quebec City: Éditeur officiel du Québec.
1979b   *Colloque place Royale: les actes du colloque.* Quebec City: Éditeur officiel du Québec.
1979c   *Le Musée du Québec en devenir.* Quebec City: Éditeur officiel du Québec.
1982   *Rapport de la consultation du ministre des Affaires culturelles du Québec.* Quebec City: Éditeur officiel du Québec.

MAC-AR
1962–82 Ministry of Cultural Affairs of Quebec, Annual Reports. Quebec City: Éditeur officiel du Québec.

MacCannell, Dean
1976   *The Tourist.* New York: Schocken.

Macpherson, C. B.
1962   *The Political Theory of Possessive Individualism: Hobbes to Locke.* Oxford: Oxford University Press.

Malraux, André
1953   *The Voices of Silence.* Trans. Stuart Gilbert. Garden City, N.Y.: Doubleday.

Maranda, Pierre
1984   Une langue qui a les dents longues. In Amyot 1984:24–38.

References

Marcus, George, and Dick Cushman
1982   Ethnographies as texts. *Annual Review of Anthropology* 11:25–69.

Maritain, Jacques
1945   *Religion et culture.* Rio de Janeiro: Atlantica Editora.
1951   *Man and the State.* Chicago: University of Chicago Press.

Marx, Karl
1867   *Capital.* Trans. S. Moore and E. Aveling. Rpt. New York: Modern Library, 1906.

Maynard, Kent
1984   Comment on Handler 1984. *Current Anthropology* 25:66–67.

McRae, C. F., ed.
1961   *French Canada Today.* Sackville, New Brunswick: Mount Allison University Publication no. 6.

McRoberts, Kenneth, and Dale Postgate
1980   *Quebec: Social Change and Political Crisis.* 2d ed. Toronto: McClelland and Stewart.

MCCI (Ministry of Cultural Communities and Immigration of Quebec)
1982   *Quebecers Each and Every One.* Quebec City: Éditeur officiel du Québec.
1983   *Rapport annuel, 1982–1983.* Quebec City: Éditeur officiel du Québec.

Meyer, Karl E.
1973   The Plundered Past: The Flying Façade and the Vanishing Glyphs. *New Yorker,* 24 March: 96–121.

Miller, Neil
1984   Culture Wars. *Chicago Tribune,* 14 August, Section 5: 1–2.

Miner, Horace
1937   Letter to Robert Redfield, January 20. Redfield papers, Regenstein Library, University of Chicago.
1939   *St. Denis.* Rpt. Chicago: University of Chicago Press, 1963.
1963   Postscript. In Miner 1939 (1963):255–69.

Morgan, Prys
1983   From a Death to a View: The Hunt for the Welsh Past in the Romantic Period. In Hobsbawm and Ranger 1983:43–100.

Morin, Rosaire
1984   L'Avenir du Québec réside-t-il dans un accroissement de son immigration? In Amyot and Bibeau 1984: 165–73.

Morissonneau, Christian
1983   Le Peuple dit ingouvernable du pays sans bornes: mobilité et identité québécoise. In *Du continent perdu à l'archipel retrouvé: Le Québec et l'Amérique française,* ed. D. R. Louder and E. Waddell, 11–23. Quebec City: Presses de l'universitè Laval.

MTCP (Ministère du Tourisme, de la Chasse et de la Pêche)
1978   *Prenez l'tour du Québec.* Quebec City: Éditeur officiel du Québec.

References

Murray, Don, and Vera Murray
1978   *De Bourassa à Lévesque.* Montreal: Éditions quinze.
Newsweek
1984   Closing the Door? 25 June: 18–24.
Nisbet, Robert
1965   *Emile Durkheim.* Englewood Cliffs, N.J.: Prentice-Hall.
Paille, Michel
1984   Cinq ans après la Charte de la langue française, les transferts linguistiques favorisent toujours l'anglais. In Amyot and Bibeau 1984:159–64.
Parisé, Robert
1976   *Georges-Henri Lévesque, père de la renaissance québécoise.* Montreal: Alain Stanké.
Parsons, Talcott
1975   Some Theoretical Considerations on the Nature and Trends of Change of Ethnicity. In Glazer and Moynihan 1975:53–83.
Parti Québécois
1971   *Le Citoyen.* Montreal: Éditions du Parti Québécois.
1972   *Quand nous serons vraiment chez nous.* Montreal: Éditions du Parti Québécois.
Petrowski, Nathalie
1978   Jean Carignan, musicien. *Le Devoir,* 3 June: 25.
Plourde, Michel
1984   Bilan de l'application des politiques linguistiques des années 70 au Québec. In Amyot 1984:41–66.
Porter, John
1975   Ethnic Pluralism in Canadian Perspective. In Glazer and Moynihan 1975:267–304.
La Presse (Montreal)
1960   Programme Libéral: 53 articles, nombreuses réformes radicales. 7 May: 1–2.
Preston, Richard
1976   C. Marius Barbeau and the History of Canadian Anthropology. In Freedman 1976:122–35.
Quebec, Government of
1956   *Report of the Royal Commission of Inquiry on Constitutional Problems* (Tremblay Commission). 4 vols. in 5. Quebec City: Queen's Printer.
1977   *Quebec's Policy on the French Language.* Quebec City: Éditeur officiel du Québec.
1978   *A Cultural Development Policy for Quebec.* Quebec City: Éditeur officiel du Québec.
1979   *Quebec-Canada: A New Deal.* Quebec City: Éditeur officiel du Québec.
Quinn, Herbert
1979   *The Union Nationale.* 2d ed. Toronto: University of Toronto Press.

References

Redfield, Robert
- 1939   Introduction to Miner 1939.
- 1947   The Folk Society. *American Journal of Sociology* 52:293–308.
- 1953   *The Primitive World and Its Transformations.* Ithaca, N.Y.: Cornell University Press.
- 1967   *Peasant Society and Culture.* Chicago: University of Chicago Press.

Reid, Malcolm
- 1972   *The Shouting Signpainters.* New York: Monthly Review Press.

Reid, Philippe
- 1974   Francois-Xavier Garneau et l'infériorité numérique des Canadiens français. *Recherches sociographiques* 15:31–39.

Reighard, John
- 1984   Les Recherches et les caractéristiques du français québécois. In Amyot and Bibeau 1984:179–87.

Remillard, Gil
- 1984   Les Québécois au lendemain du repatriement. In Amyot and Bibeau 1984:35–43.

Rioux, Marcel
- 1950   Folk and Folklore. *Journal of American Folklore* 63:192–98.
- 1955   Idéologie et crise de conscience du Canada français.*Cité Libre* 14:1–29.
- 1961   *Belle Anse.* Ottawa: Queen's Printer.
- 1964   Remarks on the Socio-Cultural Development of French-Canadian Society. In *French-Canadian Society,* ed. M. Rioux and Y. Martin, 162–78. Toronto: McClelland and Stewart.
- 1971   *Quebec in Question.* Trans. James Boake. Toronto: James Lewis & Samuel.
- 1974   *Les Québécois.* Paris: Éditions du seuil.

Rocher, Guy
- 1973   *Le Québec en mutation.* Montreal: Hurtubise HMH.
- 1984   Le Statut culturel du français au Québec: État de la question. In Amyot and Bibeau 1984:15–27.

Roy, Jean-Louis
- 1971   *Les Programmes électoraux du Québec. Vol. 2, 1931–1966.* Ottawa: Leméac.

Roy, Pierre Georges
- 1927   *Old Manors, Old Houses.* Quebec City: Historic Monuments Commission.

Royer, Jean
- 1978   Aux origines de la parenté. *Le Devoir,* 11 March: 33.

Rumilly, Robert
- 1952   *Histoire de la Province de Québec, vol. 25.* Montreal: Chantecler.
- 1953   *Histoire de la Province de Quebéc, vol. 26.* Montreal: Chantecler.

Ryan, Claude
- 1961   The Church and the New Look in Quebec. In McRae 1961:50–59.
- 1964   Brisé par la politique. *Le Devoir,* 5 September: 4.

References

Sahlins, Marshall

1976   *Culture and Practical Reason.* Chicago: University of Chicago Press.

Sales, Arnaud, Noël Bélanger, and Benoit-Guy Allaire

1984   Langue, groupes linguistiques et positions d'encadrement et de direction dans les secteurs privé et public au Québec. In Amyot 1984:348–58.

Sapir, Edward

1917   Do We Need a "Superorganic"? *American Anthropologist* 19:441–47.

1932   Cultural Anthropology and Psychiatry. In Sapir 1949:509–21.

1938   Why Cultural Anthropology Needs the Psychiatrist. In Sapir 1949:569–77.

1939   The Emergence of the Concept of Personality in a Study of Cultures. In Sapir 1949:590–97.

1949   *Selected Writings.* Ed. David Mandelbaum. Berkeley: University of California Press.

Schafer, D. Paul

1976   *Aspects of Canadian Cultural Policy.* Paris: UNESCO.

Schneider, David M.

1968   *American Kinship: A Cultural Account.* Englewood Cliffs, N.J.: Prentice-Hall.

Sénécal, André

1983   The Growing Role of the Quebec State in Language Corpus Planning. *American Review of Canadian Studies* 13 (2):52–63.

1984   Article 23 of the New Canadian Constitution and the Quebec Language Issue. *Quebec Studies* 2:70–81.

Shea, Albert, ed.

1952   *Culture in Canada.* Toronto: Canadian Association for Adult Education.

Sister Marie-Ursule

1951   *Civilisation traditionelle des Lavalois.* Quebec City: Presses de l'université Laval.

Smith, M. Estellie

1982   The Process of Sociocultural Continuity. *Current Anthropology* 23:127–42.

Sorensen, Arthur P.

1967   Multilingualism in the Northwest Amazon. *American Anthropologist* 69:670–84.

1985   An Emerging Tukanoan Linguistic Regionality: Policy Pressures. In *South American Indian Languages: Retrospect and Prospect,* ed. Harriet Klein and Louisa Stark, 140–56. Austin: University of Texas Press.

Stocking, George W., Jr.

1974   *The Shaping of American Anthropology, 1883–1911. A Franz Boas Reader.* New York: Basic Books.

Sullivan, William M.

1983　Beyond Policy Science: The Social Sciences as Moral Sciences. In Haan 1983:297–319.

Thellier, Marie-Agnes

1978　L'opération OSE a injecté $67 millions en cinq mois. *Le Devoir,* 20 May: 13.

Tocqueville, Alexis de

1835　*Democracy in America.* Trans. Henry Reeve. 2 vols. Rpt. New York: Knopf, 1954.

1959　*Journey to America.* Trans. George Lawrence. New Haven: Yale University Press.

Tour Fondue-Smith, Geneviève de la

1963　Le Ministère des affaires culturelles du Québec. *Le Devoir,* 10 May: 1, 11.

Tousignant, Claude, and Luc Ostiguy

1978　Tentative de definition du joual et du franco-québécois. *Le Devoir,* 10 June: 5.

Tremblay, Marc-Adélard, and Gerald Gold

1976　L'Anthropologie dans les universités du Québec: L'Emergence d'une discipline. In Freedman 1976:9–49.

Tremblay, Maurice, and Albert Faucher

1951　L'Enseignement des sciences sociales au Canada de langue française. In *Royal Commission Studies: A Selection of Essays Prepared for the Royal Commission on National Development in the Arts, Letters and Sciences,* 191–203. Ottawa: King's Printer.

Trevor-Roper, Hugh

1983　The Invention of Tradition: The Highland Tradition of Scotland. In Hobsbawm and Ranger 1983:15–42.

Tribunal de la Culture

1975　Rapport. *Liberté* 17 (5):2–85.

Trofimenkoff, Susan Mann

1982　*The Dream of Nation: A Social and Intellectual History of Quebec.* Toronto: Macmillan.

Trudeau, Pierre Elliott

1956　The Province of Quebec at the Time of the Strike. In *The Asbestos Strike,* ed. P. E. Trudeau, trans. James Boake, 1–81. Rpt. Toronto: James Lewis & Samuel, 1974.

1957　Federal Grants to Universities. In Trudeau 1968:79–102.

1962　New Treason of the Intellectuals. In Trudeau 1968: 151–81.

1964　Federalism, Nationalism, and Reason. In Trudeau 1968: 182–203.

1965　Quebec and the Constitutional Problem. In Trudeau 1968:3–51.

1968　*Federalism and the French Canadians.* Toronto: Macmillan.

Trudel, Clément

1982　La grogne des "intervenants culturels." *Le Devoir,* 24 December: 9, 14.

References

Utley, Francis Lee

1961   Folk Literature: An Operational Definition. *Journal of American Folklore* 74:193–206.

Van Gennep, Arnold

1922   *Traité comparatif des nationalités.* Paris: Payot.

Vigeant, Pierre

1960   La Ville-musée de Québec. *Le Devoir,* 28 January: 4.

Waddell, Eric

1981   Post-Referendum Quebec: A Geographer's Reflections. In *Aspects of the Constitutional Debate,* ed. J. Clarke and S. F. Wise, 139–55. Ottawa: Carleton University, Institute of Canadian Studies, Occasional Paper no. 1.

Wade, Mason

1955   *The French Canadians.* London: Macmillan.

Wagner, Roy

1975   *The Invention of Culture.* Englewood Cliffs, N.J.: Prentice-Hall.

Whisnant, David

1983   *All That Is Native and Fine.* Chapel Hill: University of North Carolina Press.

Whorf, Benjamin Lee

1940   Science and Linguistics. In Whorf 1956:207–19.

1941   The Relation of Habitual Thought and Behavior to Language. In Whorf 1956:134–59

1942   Language, Mind, and Reality. In Whorf 1956:246–70.

1956   *Language, Thought, and Reality.* Ed. John Carroll. Cambridge: M.I.T. Press.

Wilson, William A.

1976   *Folklore and Nationalism in Modern Finland.* Bloomington: Indiana University Press.

Wolfe, Tom

1979   *The Right Stuff.* New York: Farrar, Straus and Giroux.

Woolfson, Peter

1983   Language in Quebec: Legal and Societal Issues. *American Review of Canadian Studies 13 (2):42–51.*

1984   Language Policy in Quebec: *La Survivance,* 1967–1982. *Quebec Studies* 2:56–69.

INDEX

Act to promote the French language in Quebec, 169–73
American Folklore Society, 72
Americanization, 105
Anglicization, 106, 162, 165, 167, 175
Applebaum-Hébert Commission. *See* Federal Cultural Policy Review Committee
Arts Council of Great Britain, 87*n*
Authenticity, 50, 63, 76, 131, 146, 189

Barbeau, Charles Marius, 67–68, 71–74, 151
Benedict, Ruth, 107
Bilingualism, 167, 168
Bill 22. *See* Official Language Act of 1974
Bill 63. *See* Act to promote the French language in Quebec
Bill 101. *See* Charter of the French language
Boas, Franz, 72
Bourassa, Henri, 160–61
British North America Act, 113, 171–72
Bruchési, Jean, 100

Canada Council, 87, 88
Canadian Broadcasting Corporation, 11, 81
Catholicism, 26, 65, 89, 96–97, 100*n*, 104, 107, 130
Catholic social thought, 84–86
Centralization, governmental, 86, 97, 99, 193
Charter of the French language, 5, 42, 116, 169–75, 178, 183
Commission des biens culturels, 141, 147
Conquest of New France by England, 42, 66, 100*n*, 130, 149
Conseil provincial des arts, 103, 105, 111–12, 118
Constitution Act of 1982, 170, 172, 183, 184
Cultural development, 81, 87–88, 101, 105, 119, 131
Cultural Development Policy for Quebec, A, 116, 127, 141, 159, 176–78, 186

Cultural property: legislative definitions of, 145–47; disputes over, 154–57; mentioned, 141–42, 144, 167, 181, 192
Cultural Property Commission. *See Commission des biens culturels*
Culture, American, 49, 125
Culture, Canadian, 127
Culture, objectification of, 11, 13–16, 27, 56, 61, 63, 70, 74–77, 96, 141, 151, 194–95
Culture, Québécois: and French culture, 35, 36, 74, 98, 100–101, 119; and French language, 36, 38, 128, 141; content of, 36, 91–92, 100, 104, 107–8, 118–9, 120, 127–31; and history, 36–37

David, Athanase, 82
de Gaulle, Charles, 101
Département du Canada français d'outre-frontières, 103, 105–6, 111–12
Department of Cultural Affairs. *See Ministère des Affaires culturelles*
Duplessis, Maurice, 17, 86–89, 99, 100, 102, 187
Durkheim, Emile, 4–5, 152

Elections, Quebec: 1976, 3, 5, 9–10; 1970, 9; 1973, 9; 1981, 24; 1952, 99; 1956, 99; 1960, 102–4; 1966, 113
Extra-territorial French Canada Branch. *See Département du Canada français d'outre-frontières*

Family life, changes in, 58–63
Federal Cultural Policy Review Committee, 156
Folk dancing, 13, 16, 54–59, 62, 68–69, 77–79
Folklore: performance of, 12–13; and tourism, 53–54; and folk society, 63–67
Frégault, Guy, 35, 111, 120
French Language Bureau. *See Office de la langue française*
Frère Untel, 163–64

Index

Front de libération du Québec, 9

Gagnon, Ernest, 71
Garneau, François-Xavier, 71, 72
Gérin, Léon, 68
Gérin-Lajoie, Paul, 102
Godbout, Jacques, 114
Green Paper of 1976. *See Pour
l'évolution de la politique culturelle*
Grimm brothers, 78, 157n
Groulx, Lionel, 5, 17, 33–34, 36, 38,
40–48, 67, 71–72, 90n, 140, 161, 166,
169, 186

Hardy, Denis, 124
Hazelius, Artur, 74
Historic Monuments Commission, 82,
103, 105, 111, 142–46, 148, 158
Historic preservation legislation,
142–46
H. M. C. *See* Historic Monuments
Commission

Ile d'Orléans, 142
Immigration to Quebec, 110, 120, 123,
124, 175, 178, 184
*Institut québécois de recherche sur la
culture,* 111

Joual, 163–66

L'Allier, Jean-Paul, 115–16, 124
Language legislation, 169–75
Lapalme, Georges-Émile: and founding
of M. A. C., 98–102; resignation from
M. A. C., 112; mentioned, 39, 88, 104,
108, 111, 118–20, 124, 151
Laporte, Pierre, 39, 112, 119
L'appel de la race, 38, 45, 48, 166
LaRue, Hubert, 71
Laurendeau, Andre, 88, 107
Laurin, Dr. Camille, 4, 116, 127, 174,
176–77, 179
Leclerc, Félix, 22
Léger, Jean-Marc, 107
Lesage, Jean, 99, 102, 104–6, 118–19, 124,
161
Lévesque, Père Georges-Henri, 87n
Lévesque, René, 4, 9, 16, 17, 21–23, 31,
38, 42, 46, 102, 164, 184, 188

Liberal Party of Quebec: in the 1976
elections, 9–10; in the 1960 elections,
102–4; mentioned 93, 99, 108, 113–15,
124
Livre Blanc, 112–13, 115, 120–25, 175, 177
Locke, John, 153, 174

M. A. C. *See Ministère des Affaires
culturelles*
Malraux, André, 98, 101, 119, 120
Marett, R. R., 72, 73
Maritain, Jacques, 85, 89–90, 94
Massey Commission. *See* Royal Commission on National Development in
the Arts, Letters, and Sciences
Ministère de l'Éducation, 110, 112, 113, 171
Ministère de l'Immigration, 110, 178
Ministère des Affaires culturelles: found-
ing of, 102–7; marginality of, 110, 113,
116, 196; organization of, 111–14, 117;
criticism of, 114–15, 117–18; and cul-
tural property legislation, 143–44;
and Place Royale, 148
*Ministère des Affaires intergouvernemen-
tales,* 110
*Ministère des Communautés culturelles et
de l'Immigration,* 178, 179
Minville, Esdras, 90n
Mouvement souveraineté-association, 9
Multiculturalism, Canadian, 125–26,
179n, 195

National Film Board of Canada, 88
National Museum of Man, 156
Nationalist ideology: negative vision of,
5–6, 47, 92, 120, 121, 130, 131, 184;
positive vision of, 5–6, 121, 131; basic
elements of, 6–9, 50–51; and history,
17–20, 42, 66, 70; and social class,
24–26; and individualism, 32, 191–92;
and territory, 33–35; and cultural
property, 154; and religion, 159–60

Objectification of culture. *See* Culture,
objectification of
Office de la langue française, 103, 105–6,
110, 113, 118, 169–70
Official Language Act of 1974, 169–73
Official Languages Act of 1969, 170, 172
O. L. F. *See Office de la langue française*

Parti Québécois: electoral strategies, 9–10; cultural policies, 116; and cultural minorities, 176–81; mentioned, 3, 23–24, 41–43, 102, 111, 128, 184, 188
Patrimoine: definition of, 140–42; and possessive individualism, 153–54
Pearson, Lester, 125
Pius XI, Pope, 85
Place Royale restoration, 113, 148–51
Possessive individualism, 6, 51, 153, 179, 189–91
Pour l'évolution de la politique culturelle, 115, 124–27, 178
Provincial Arts Council. See Conseil provincial des arts
Purism, linguistic, 162–63, 166, 170

Quiet Revolution, 83–85, 93, 100, 108, 110, 123, 129, 146, 163, 164, 175

Radio Canada, 11, 88
Referendum on independence, 9–10, 20–24, 41, 49, 188
Royal Commission of Inquiry on Constitutional Problems, 89–94, 97, 100, 102, 104, 120, 123, 124, 129, 130, 131
Royal Commission on Biculturalism and Bilingualism, 125
Royal Commission on National Development in the Arts, Letters and Sciences, 81–83, 87, 94

St-Jean-Baptiste day, 16, 23, 107

St-Laurent, Louis, 99
Sapir, Edward, 72
Semaine du patrimoine, 16
Skansen, 74
Société québécoise de développement des industries culturelles, 111

Tiersot, Julien, 71, 73
Tocqueville, Alexis de, 25, 159, 162, 192–94
Tremblay Commission. See Royal Commission of Inquiry on Constitutional Problems
Tribunal de la culture, 115
Trudeau, Pierre Elliott: critique of nationalism, 94–97; constitutional ideas, 94–98; and multiculturalism, 125; mentioned, 21, 23, 32, 100, 107–8, 172, 188

Union Nationale, 86, 88, 99, 102, 107, 113

Vigneault, Gilles, 22

White Paper of 1965. See Livre Blanc
White Paper of 1978. See Cultural Development Policy for Quebec, A
Whorf hypothesis, 160
Winter Carnival, 12
Wyman, Loraine, 73

DESIGNED BY WENDY SIMONS
COMPOSED BY CONNELL TYPESETTING COMPANY, KANSAS CITY, MISSOURI
MANUFACTURED BY BRAUN-BRUMFIELD, INC., ANN ARBOR, MICHIGAN
TEST AND DISPLAY LINES ARE SET IN GARTH GRAPHIC

Library of Congress Cataloging-in-Publication Data
Handler, Richard, 1950–
Nationalism and the politics of culture in Quebec.
Bibliography: pp. 199–214.
Includes index.
1. Nationalism—Québec (Province) 2. Québec
(Province)—Cultural policy. 3. Culture—Political
aspects—Québec (Province) I. Title.
F1053.2.H36   1988   306.4′09714   87-40362
ISBN 0-299-11510-0
ISBN 0-299-11514-3 (pbk.)